English Pape
Bretish Rul

KT-145-921

B Disvelie york and importance
(congess of Berlin) / 1846 - 80

(forright Polic

European Paper =
The second empir Nap 3rd 1851-
Stays after unification 18(7) 19.14

November's

English
Disrelie

failure of chartism in and 1848

What were the terms of the 2nd reform act 1867
and explain why it was brought in by the
liberals and passed by the Torys. →161-

4) (Why Dizzy lost the general election in 188

5) account for the rise of home rule party in
Pliment under Parnell, why did Gladstone
feel in nescenary to adopt home rule
plan

) Reasons for and results of British in
forcement of Suzeránty over the bur
republics

) Explain the constitutional crisis of 190
and the passing of the Paliment act

3) Efforts made by Paliment and other
bodys to improve housing

7) career and importance of To Cha
and "Bloody" Balfour.

o) Account for Palmerstones long term

) Why the labour representation comt
was formed and its part in politics
in 1900-1914

AN ILLUSTRATED HISTORY
OF MODERN EUROPE
1789—1945

62

) → ✳ PTO

<u>Europe</u>

1) Napoleons the 3rds Plans for Italy
2) What reforms did Alex 2nd make in
   Russia and why was he assass—
3) Frances recovery from defeat in
   1870
4a) Why Congress of Berlin held in
   1878 How Sucessfully did it settle
   the Balkan Question
b) Explain the Growth of the German
   Social democratic party
5) By what stages did European
   powers divide into rival armed groups
   at the of the century 1890 - 1913
6) How far did Austro-Hungarian gov—
   in the Balkans provoke the 1914 war

AN ILLUSTRATED HISTORY OF
MODERN BRITAIN

by

Denis Richards, M.A.

and

J. W. Hunt, M.A.

A HISTORY OF BRITAIN

General Editor

Denis Richards, M.A.

Vol. I. Britain and the Ancient World

JAMES A. BOLTON, M.A. AND DENIS RICHARDS, M.A.

Vol. II. Medieval Britain

DENIS RICHARDS, M.A. AND A. D. ELLIS, M.A.

In preparation

Vol. III. Britain under the Tudors and Stuarts

DENIS RICHARDS, M.A.

Vol. IV. Britain 1714–1851

DENIS RICHARDS, M.A. AND ANTHONY QUICK, M.A.

Vol. V. Britain 1851–1945

DENIS RICHARDS, M.A. AND ANTHONY QUICK, M.A.

Vol. VI. Twentieth Century Britain

DENIS RICHARDS, M.A. AND ANTHONY QUICK, M.A.

AN ILLUSTRATED HISTORY
OF MODERN EUROPE
1789–1945

BY

D E N I S   R I C H A R D S,   M.A.

Formerly Principal of Morley College and Longman Fellow,
University of Sussex

LONGMAN

LONGMAN GROUP LIMITED
London

*Associated companies, branches and representatives
throughout the world*

First Published   1938
Second Edition   *August* 1939
Third Edition   *May* 1940
New Impressions   *February* 1941
January 1942, *June* 1942
Fourth Edition   *May* 1943
New Impressions   *January* 1944
October 1944, *May* 1945
September 1946, *April* 1948
January 1949
Fifth Edition   1950
New Impressions   1951, 1952, 1954,
1955, 1956, 1957 (*Twice*), 1959,
1960, 1962, 1963, 1964, 1965,
1967, 1969

SBN 582 31485 2

*Printed in Great Britain by
William Clowes and Sons Ltd, London and Beccles*

PREFACE TO FIFTH EDITION

'HISTORY' nowadays is created at a speed which leaves us all breathless. In this latest edition I have attempted to catch up a little with events by including a brief survey of the Second World War. My most fervent hope is that no comparable additions will be needed in the future.

D. R.

PREFACE

In writing this book I have tried to observe certain principles and to incorporate certain features. In the belief that an explanation of these may be of service to teachers using the book in class, I should like to draw attention to the following points :

1. *Illustrations*. These have been included partly with the idea of making pupils feel more 'friendly' towards their text-book, and partly with the idea of aiding the memory. The cartoons (all of which are contemporary with the events on which they comment) may help both to clarify an issue and to implant it more firmly in the reader's mind. The picture-charts are summaries of movements or causes of great importance, presented in this way to assist the memory of the many students best approached through their visual sense.

2. The *Running-Summaries* at the side of the page should enable easy reference to any point and again assist the memory. They should prove valuable for purposes of revision.

3. The *Glossary of Political Terms* may save the conscientious the trouble of consulting a dictionary, or help to eliminate woolliness of definition in those who would never dream of doing such a thing. Some trouble has been taken to avoid conventional historical phraseology, but at times such terms are unavoidable, and those which have proved inescapable are collected in the glossary. Although, in general, the limitations of the youthful vocabulary have been kept in mind throughout the book, there has been no attempt to write in monosyllables for the illiterate—a course which would have been bound to destroy all style, and with it, all interest.

4. The *Bibliography* is purely for the reader with some love for the subject of history. It may safely be stated that there are no first-class works of history completely suited to the taste and powers of any one under sixteen years of age. The

works recommended are simply less technical than most others.

5. The *proportions* of this book have been framed with the definite idea of reducing the excessive space customarily devoted to the French Revolution and Napoleon. Russia, on the other hand, is given greater attention than usual, for the reason that while the Revolutionary period is customarily treated in form with great thoroughness, Russia often receives barely a mention from the teacher harassed by the pressure of a too too solid syllabus. The text-book may thus be used to fill in that particular gap. In general the story has been kept fairly strictly to the internal history and interplay of the Great Powers, and those seeking comprehensive information on Spain, Switzerland, Scandinavia, and the Netherlands will, I regret, have to consult other works. Such compression is, I think, unavoidable in a work of this length if the main points are to emerge clearly. For the same reason, the pursuit of clarity, all military and diplomatic detail except the most essential has been omitted. In substitution I have included biographical detail, which, I hope, is more picturesque. Many such details, it is true, may not be of great importance, but they may serve to arouse interest in their subject. The alternative is Fisher-like generalization, which, however brilliant, means very little to the non-adult mind. Finally, the story has been kept to the path of politics and economics, apart from the excursions into personality. It is perhaps the fashion to include a few pages on the painting, music, literature, drama, architecture, costume, transport, science, and religion of the period, but I have avoided following it, in the belief that in a work of this size such a review cannot be more than the merest catalogue of meaningless names.

I should like to record my very deep gratitude to a number of friends who have helped me in some way during the writing of this book. Mr. G. Auty, Mr. J. W. Hunt, and Mr. I. Tenen all read the manuscript and offered me the most valuable criticisms. To Mr. R. F. I. Bunn, too, I am indebted for many excellent suggestions and for a most helpful interest. Miss Margaret Hunt showed woman's intuition at its most brilliant in divining what I was aiming at from the rough (almost brutal) sketches I sent her : and, finally, I cannot be sufficiently grateful to my sister, Mrs. Dora Whittle, who performed a labour of love in preparing a none too legible manuscript for the press.

D. R.

INTRODUCTORY

The French Revolution is probably the most important event in Modern European History. The ideas of 'liberty' and 'equality' which inspired the Revolution affected not only France and the generation of 1789 but the whole of Europe and the whole of the 19th century. As time went on, state after state rose to overthrow the greatest obstacles to 'liberty'— foreign rule or autocratic kingship. A climax was reached in the World War of 1914–1918, when the Allies, fighting 'to safeguard the rights of small nations' (among other things), helped to free the despotically ruled districts of Central Europe and set them up as new, independent, democratic states—such as Poland and Czecho-Slovakia. The ideas of the French Revolution had at last been fully worked out. But history never stands still—other problems, other sets of ideas presented themselves in the years immediately after 1918 ; these in turn contributed to a fresh world conflict ; and the history of the 20th century now looks like being that of the clash of the ideas of the Russian Revolution of 1917 against our existing system, just as the history of the 19th century was that of the clash of the ideas of the French Revolution of 1789 against the system of those days.

CONTENTS

xiii

MAPS

Charts and Maps drawn by
MARGARET HUNT

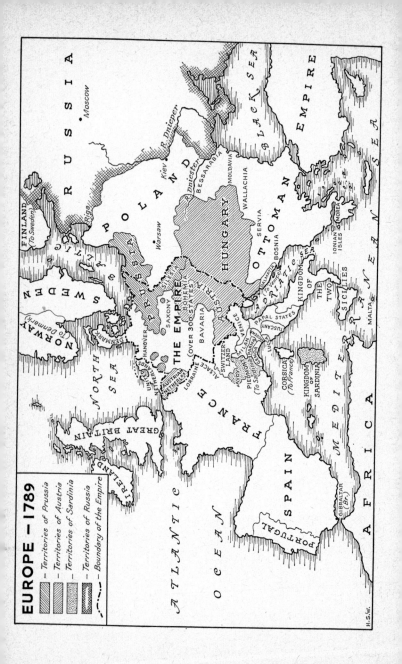

EUROPE – 1789

Territories of Prussia
Territories of Austria
Territories of Sardinia
Territories of Russia
Boundary of the Empire

FINLAND
(To Sweden)

RUSSIA
Moscow

PRUSSIA

R. Dnieper
Kiev

POLAND
Warsaw

R. Dniester
BESSARABIA

MOLDAVIA

WALLACHIA

BLACK SEA

OTTOMAN EMPIRE

SERVIA

BOSNIA

HUNGARY

AUSTRIA

BOHEMIA

SILESIA

SAXONY

THE EMPIRE
(OVER 300 STATES)

BAVARIA

HANOVER

DENMARK

SWEDEN

NORWAY
(To Denmark)

BALTIC SEA

Riga

NORTH SEA

GREAT BRITAIN

IRELAND

ATLANTIC OCEAN

UNITED NETHERLANDS

AUSTRIAN NETHERLANDS

SWITZER-LAND

FRANCE

LORRAINE

ALSACE

PIEDMONT

SAVOY
(To Sardinia)

MILAN

PARMA

GENOA

TUSCANY

PAPAL STATES

VENICE

DALMATIA

ADRIATIC SEA

KINGDOM OF THE TWO SICILIES

IONIAN ISLES

MOREA

CORSICA
(To France)

KINGDOM OF SARDINIA

MEDITERRANEAN SEA

MALTA

SPAIN

PORTUGAL

GIBRALTAR
(Br.)

AFRICA

H.S.W.

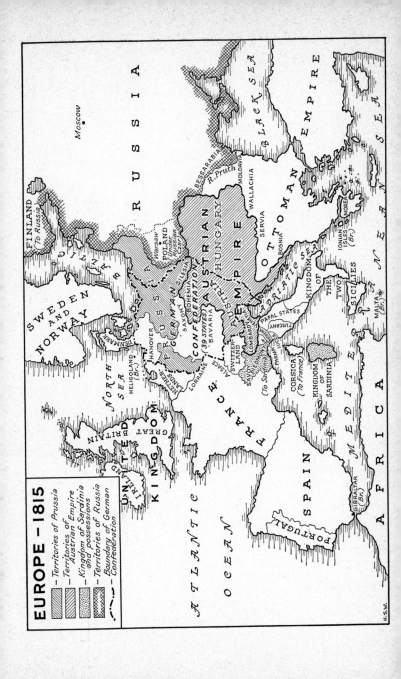

EUROPE — 1815

- Territories of Prussia
- Territories of Austrian Empire
- Kingdom of Sardinia and possessions
- Territories of Russia
- Boundary of German Confederation

FINLAND (To Russia)

SWEDEN AND NORWAY

R U S S I A

Moscow

BALTIC SEA

BLACK SEA

OTTOMAN EMPIRE

BESSARABIA

R. Pruth

MOLDAVIA

WALLACHIA

SERVIA

BOSNIA

Warsaw

POLAND (Under Russian Czar)

PRUSSIA

SILESIA

SAXONY

BOHEMIA

GERMAN CONFEDERATION (39 STATES)

BAVARIA

AUSTRIA-HUNGARY

AUSTRIAN EMPIRE

ADRIATIC SEA

MOREA

IONIAN ISLES (Br.)

MALTA (Br.)

KINGDOM OF THE TWO SICILIES

PAPAL STATES

TUSCANY

LOMBARDY

VENETIA

PARMA

MODENA

SARDINIA (To Sardinia)

SWITZERLAND

LORRAINE

ALSACE

HANOVER

DENMARK

HELIGOLAND (Br.)

NORTH SEA

GREAT BRITAIN

UNITED KINGDOM

F R A N C E

CORSICA (To France)

KINGDOM OF SARDINIA

SPAIN

PORTUGAL

GIBRALTAR (Br.)

A T L A N T I C   O C E A N

M E D I T E R R A N E A N   S E A

A F R I C A

H.S.W.

CHAPTER I

The Causes of the French Revolution.

The Revolution was not the event of a single month or year. In its most novel, violent, or revolutionary aspects, it lasted from 1789 to the rise of Napoleon ; but just as its effects carried forward to the 20th century, so its causes stretched back into the 17th and 18th centuries.

The prime cause was the existing system of government— the methods of the *Ancien Régime*. Indeed, it is charitable to dignify this with the name of system, for in general it came nearer to chaos. So chaotic, in fact, was the organization of government that there still existed 360 different feudal codes of law applying to different parts of France. In one town alone there were 29 feudal courts ! In matters of taxation the chaos is shown by the fact that when a geographer in 1739 tried to prepare a map showing the customs dues of the various districts, he had to give it up as being too complicated for human endeavour—for example, a boat bearing wine from the South of France to Paris paid over 40 tolls and lost a fortnight in the process. In the sphere of administration, an overworked central government tried to regulate affairs in over 40,000 townships and struggled hopelessly against overwhelming arrears of business—one parish, for instance, which petitioned the government for a loan to repair its leaking church roof, waited over ten years for an answer. But in spite of all this utter confusion two principles stand out—that all power was concentrated in the hands of the King and his personal advisers, and that all the burdens of taxation were borne by the classes least able to support them.

In the magnificent palace of Versailles (a glance at which will explain the French Revolution better than a dozen textbooks), remote from contact with any but the nobility and the clergy, Louis XVI controlled the destinies of France. There were royal Councils, a royal Controller of Finances,

1

royal deputies in the Provinces known as Intendants, royal officials everywhere through whom the King governed—but the system rested primarily and throughout on Louis himself, for his word was law. "The State," Louis XIV had said, with vanity but with accuracy, "is—myself." Louis XVI was later on to remark, concerning a disputed issue, "The thing is legal because I wish it." Such a statement sums up the whole nature of the government of the *Ancien Régime*. There was no vestige of popular or middle-class influence in government, for though there remained a few of the old mediæval institutions, these had lost all effective power of opposing the King. The last time the States General, or French Parliament, had met was in 1614. In fact, the will of the sovereign was so completely the law that any critic of the government or opponent of some powerful noble was liable to find himself arrested quite arbitrarily by means of a writ known as a *lettre de cachet*, and lodged in prison without a trial or even an accusation of having committed any particular crime.

(b) Privileg-
ed position
of nobles
and clergy

As allies and buttresses in this system of royal power, the Crown had the clergy and the nobility—the First and Second 'Estates'—all the rest, from lawyers down to peasants, being the Third Estate. Together the first two Estates numbered some 300,000 out of a population of 25,000,000. Yet the whole system of the *Ancien Régime* in France was directed to their profit. They owned nearly all the land ; the nobility were gathered round Louis at Versailles in useless attendance, and did no work ; the higher clergy drew princely rents and shared the general characteristics of the nobility. (Here it is important to note that the lower clergy, such as the parish priests, were poorly paid and had plenty to do. Whereas bishops drew some 60,000 livres (£2500) a year, parish priests all too often received only 500 livres (£20)—consequently we find the latter all in sympathy not with their superiors but with the Third Estate.) Extraordinary privileges were possessed by these two classes in return for no services whatever—the most outstanding being exemption from nearly all taxation. The full extent of these privileges can best be seen by examining the corresponding burdens of the peasant.

(c) Un-
privileged
position of
peasant

The financial burden of the peasant was crushing. Not only did he pay the poll-tax and the twentieth of his income which most nobles paid, but in addition he paid a tithe of the produce of his land to the Church, another large land-tax to the King, a *gabelle* (or salt-tax—and everyone over seven years of age had to buy 7 lb. of salt a year), a customs-duty if he took his goods through a village, and a money-due to the local lord when his grapes went to the lord's wine-press or his corn to the lord's mill (and they had to go). By a system of game-laws he had to be the powerless witness of game or its hunters destroying his crops ; he alone of all classes was not exempt from militia service ; and, as if these burdens were insufficient, he was liable to forced labour on the roads or public buildings (*corvée*). It is little wonder that the peasantry, taxed more and more heavily as the expenses of the French government mounted in the 18th century, and seeing their superiors living in the greatest luxury, were on the verge of revolt. Some 10,000 of them were annually imprisoned, 2000 condemned to the galleys, and several hundred executed for offences against the salt laws alone.

And yet it was not so much from the peasantry as from the more prosperous members of the Third Estate—the educated section of lawyers and doctors especially—that the impulse towards revolution came. The reason for this is that, though not suffering the economic burdens of the peasant, they resented their exclusion from official positions at the head of the army, the navy, and the diplomatic service. They resented their inability to offer open criticism of a ridiculous system of government. They resented the lack of religious freedom— if a Protestant service was discovered, the pastor might be hanged and the congregation all sent to the galleys. They resented the liability of the Third Estate to suffer torture, breaking on the wheel, and forms of mutilation which were spared nobles and clergy. Above all, they felt themselves unfairly excluded from all share in government. "What is the Third Estate ?" said one of their leaders. "Everything. What has it been hitherto in our form of government ? Nothing. What does it want ? To become Something." It is not surprising that almost all of the revolutionary leaders came from this class. *(d)* Grievances of educated bourgeoisie

Naturally there was a further reason, apart from their actual grievances, to account for the leadership of the reform CAUSE II: THE INFLUENCE

The Burden of the Third Estate. [*Photo, Hachette.*

The peasant shoulders the whole burden, while the noble presses on it to increase the weight and the priest supports it merely with one finger.

movement by the bourgeoisie. It was, of course, they, rather than the peasants, who enjoyed the possessions and self-confidence necessary to direct a revolution ; but, above all, it was they who had the requisite political education. This political education they had found in the works of certain French philosophers of the 18th century, whose influence in causing the revolution was extremely important. In the first place there was Voltaire. Famous all over Europe as a historian, a popularizer of science, a tragic dramatist, and a poet, he was also an unsparing critic of existing institutions, and especially of the Church. In matchless satire he poured scorn on the pretensions of the Church, the folly of governments, and the credulity of those who are taken in by both. He himself had known the inside of the Bastille, the great prison of Paris, and what a *lettre de cachet* could mean. Over some flagrant miscarriages of justice he fought for years to secure the reversal of a verdict and the rehabilitation of the honour of a wronged man. Too often death or hideous mutilation had done their irrevocable work, but what human effort could achieve, Voltaire's did. He became at once the most admired and the most feared man of Europe—while the very classes he criticized, nobility and royalty, competed for the honour of entertaining so great a literary man and political force. Only his great enemy, the Church, could never forgive him for his criticism—and his deism. The friend of the two most completely unscrupulous monarchs of the 18th century, Frederick the Great of Prussia and Catherine of Russia, he was equally willing to hold up a monarch to admiration for 'enlightened' intentions and to ridicule for unenlightened achievements. With four estates on the borders of France and Switzerland he could speed from one to the other according as intelligence reached him that French or Swiss officials were on his track. Only at the end of his life was he secure in France—in his final days, indeed, he came to Paris to see his last play produced : the populace went mad with hero-worship as it thronged to welcome the man who had fought injustice so long and so bravely. But Voltaire knew humanity. "Ah," he said, "they'd come in just the same crowds to see me executed." Yet with all his devastating satire and his wit, and for all his campaigns against religious persecution, antiquated and unfair taxation, and torture, this fiercer, crueller Bernard Shaw of the 18th century had nothing positive to suggest to take the place of monarchy. He was no democrat. "I had rather," he remarked, "be ruled by one lion than by a hundred rats." His contribution, great though it was, was negative, not positive.

(b) The Encyclopædists (1751-1772)   Together with Voltaire may be mentioned the work of the group known as the Encyclopædists, led by Diderot. They set out to write an encyclopædia which should be an account of all existing knowledge. As it went on it became more and more a criticism of the *Ancien Régime*—indeed, it was obvious that no account of contemporary knowledge could be given which did not demonstrate at the same time the folly and injustice of existing claims and practices in Church and State. A group known as the Economists advocated the abolition of all taxation except that on land (which would be paid principally by the clergy and the nobility) ; but for a general scheme of government, they too, like Voltaire and Diderot, had no other solution than enlightened despotism.

(c) Montesquieu (1689-1755)   A more positive contribution was made by a far less sensational figure than Voltaire—Montesquieu. A deep student of politics, he saw the importance of geographical conditions. After conducting an experiment by freezing a tongue, and observing that the little taste-papillæ were smaller and less sensitive in the cold than in the heat, he came to the conclusion that people in hot climates would feel both physical and mental matters more passionately than dwellers in cold or temperate regions, hence that they would be less able to keep themselves calm and under control, hence that a strict despotism was best suited for them ; Northern Europeans, however, might be trusted with the introduction of a democratic element. In England he found the model he sought, and accordingly, in his chief book *De l' Esprit des Lois* (which ran through twenty-two editions in eighteen months), he held up the English constitution, with its parliament, its independent judges, and its constitutional king as worthy of imitation by France. He was especially keen on the idea of the various parts of the government—parliament, king, judges, for example—working quite separately, and acting as checks on the power of each other, thus helping to preserve the liberty of the individual. Incidentally he imagined far more of this than there actually was in the English constitution, but his influence, both on the French and American revolutionary leaders, was profound.

But the 'philosopher,' who, more than all others, provided a positive creed was Rousseau. His stormy and unconventional life, in the course of which he was driven out first from his native city of Geneva and then from his adopted France, typifies the spirit of revolt which was to flare up in the Revolution. A poet and a musician who had written a successful opera, he turned his attention to politics and preached the equality of men—a doctrine which naturally brought on his head the wrath of the French government. His greatest political work, *Du Contrat Social*, sketches his ideas of the basis of government—he seeks a justification for the fact that man, though 'born free, is everywhere in chains'(i.e. is everywhere subject to government). This justification he can find only if the ideas and desires of the people are really carried out by the government—or, as he puts it, if the General Will is sovereign. Only thus is liberty retained, and equality realized. Obviously, however, the General Will is much less likely to be carried out in a monarchy than in a democracy, where the people govern themselves. It is true Rousseau did not think a democracy was workable in a large state, because he wanted a direct democracy, where all men actually decide great issues, not a representative democracy, like ours, where we elect other people to decide them for us. "The English people," he wrote, "is free only during the election of its M.Ps. As soon as they are elected, it is a slave, it is nothing." His solution was the division of a large state into a number of small direct democracies, and the binding of these into a kind of federation. But it was the spirit of democracy, rather than the practical details, which affected the Revolutionary leaders. Catching from Rousseau also a certain amount of his strong vein of sentiment and emotion and love of nature (new developments in 18th-century France, which had concentrated rather on reason and self-control), they developed the passion and violence without which the Revolution could not have been made. Rousseau thus supplied not only the main doctrine—the Sovereignty of the People, the Supremacy of

(d) Rousseau (1712-1778)

the General Will—but the emotional spirit which made people ready to rebel.

CAUSE III:
THE
EXAMPLE OF
THE
AMERICAN
REVOLU-
TION

The philosophers, then, supplied the theory ; it was left to America to furnish the practical example. In 1776 the thirteen English Colonies revolted, issued their Declaration of Independence, and by 1783 had secured their freedom as the United States of America. France, anxious to obtain revenge for her loss of Canada and India in the Seven Years War (1756–1763), willingly helped the Americans against England, and enjoyed her most successful war of the century. She little thought what consequences were to follow. French soldiers who had served in America poured back to France full of American democratic ideas : they had helped to free a nation whose only real grievance was not that the English *did* tax them, but that they *might* tax them. An extra tea-duty of threepence, the sole tax payable by Americans to England in 1776, broke up the British Empire. When the French compared this with the overwhelming burdens of the peasantry at home, it rapidly became apparent that if the Americans were justified in revolting against the English, the French were far more justified in revolting against the French. The Americans rebelled not against misgovernment but simply for the sake of self-government ; the French, with the additional spur of misgovernment, were not slow to learn the lesson. It is no accident that one of the earliest leaders of the French Revolution was the Marquis de Lafayette, returned six years before from the War of Independence.

CAUSE IV:
THE BANK-
RUPTCY OF
THE FRENCH
CROWN

But the influence of the American Revolution did not end there : perhaps even more important, the cost of the war to France meant the last straw on the already cracking back of her finances. All the century the situation had been getting worse. The enormous luxury of the French court under Louis XIV and XV (and under Louis XVI, too, although he was by comparison very economical, and had only 2000 horses and 200 carriages in the royal stables, while his Queen, Marie Antoinette, managed with only 500 servants and four pairs of shoes a week) alone accounted for one-twelfth of the whole revenue of the government. The ridiculously inefficient system of taxation (by which the nobles, clergy, and crown, who owned three-fifths of the land, escaped extremely

The Meeting of the States General.

[Photo, Mansell.

lightly, while the peasantry, owning the remaining two-fifths, paid practically everything) had nothing to commend it. By 1785 even the nobles and clergy were beginning to see that the situation was impossible. Further, the cost of tax-collection, sometimes done by selling the right of collection to the highest bidder, who made what he could, swallowed a ludicrous proportion of the taxes. Thus the salt-tax, for example, brought in 60,000,000 livres but cost 20,000,000 to collect, and necessitated the employment of about 50,000 troops and agents to suppress smuggling. Above all, the constant wars for over a century and the ruinous loss of the French Empire in the Seven Years War had entailed continuous borrowing, and had piled up an enormous amount of debt. Each year, of above 472 million livres income, 236 million livres, or one-half, had to be set aside to pay interest on debts—and even then the monarchy had five times defaulted by reduction of interest or repudiation of debt in the 18th century. When on top of this chaotic and dangerous situation the government of Louis XVI joined in the War of American Independence and expended an unnecessary 1,200,000,000 livres on purchasing the defeat of England, it purchased also its own bankruptcy. The situation could no longer go on. Controllers-General in rapid succession tried to grapple with the problem, and whether they started with reforming ideas like Turgot and Necker, or spendthrift ideas like Calonne, or just conservative ideas like Brienne, all rapidly came to the same conclusion—that nothing could be done until the exemption of the nobles and clergy from the bulk of taxation was given up. It was primarily in the hope of destroying the immunity of nobles and clergy, equalizing taxation, and thus filling the royal treasuries, and secondarily in the expectation of granting in addition a few much needed reforms such as the abolition of *lettres de cachet*, that Necker in 1788 advised the King to call the States-General, the representatives of the three Estates, for the first time in 175 years. Minister and Monarch little thought that their device for ending bankruptcy would begin revolution.

CAUSE V:
THE
CHARACTERS
OF LOUIS
XVI AND It was natural, of course, though it surprised the government, that the calling of the States-General, and the official request for lists (*cahiers*) of grievances which preceded it,

should open the flood-gates of criticism. But the issue of it MARIE
ANTOI-
NETTE all depended on how the demands of the Third Estate were to be handled by the King—and unfortunately for France, Louis XVI was a King in name and in power, but not in character. Full of the best intentions—had he not rapidly appointed as Controller-General first one outstanding reformer, Turgot, then another, Necker ?—he could never be relied on to carry out those intentions consistently—had he not dismissed Turgot and Necker with equal promptitude ? As we shall see, at every stage in the Revolution he was to encourage reform and then to draw back. Such inconsistency was to bring its inevitable reward : it is not the strong, brutal ones of this earth who most frequently lose their thrones— not men like William the Conqueror and Henry VIII— but the inconsistent, well-intentioned ones like Henry VI and Charles I. "When you can keep together a number of oiled ivory balls," one of his relatives said of Louis, "you may do something with the King." Mildly interested in reform, more interested in his kingship, but most interested in hunting, Louis XVI was to hesitate, to temporize, to yield and to deny, till the forces which he had released caught him up in their torrential current and swept him and the monarchy to destruction. Nor was he more fortunate in his advisers. Necker lacked firmness, and the one great man who was later to try and save the King, Mirabeau, died at a critical moment. For the most part, in fact, Louis was under the fatal influence of his wife, Marie Antoinette. Extremely unpopular among the French as the representative of the hated Austrian alliance which had led to the Seven Years War and lost the Empire, they could find no greater term of abuse for her than 'l'Autrichienne'—the Austrian woman. Ignorant of the need for reform, unsympathetic to her people's needs and incapable of grasping the political situation, she poisoned Louis' mind first against Turgot and then against Necker, and everywhere advised a fatal firmness at precisely the wrong moments. She indeed knew her own mind—"The King," said Mirabeau, "has only one man about him, his wife "—but unfortunately her mind was not worth knowing. France's destiny rested in the hands of a King who was too weak-minded to be stable and a Queen who was too strong-minded to be sensible.

CAUSE VI:
FAMINE,
COLD AND
MOBS

Finally, as a last factor in leading to the Revolution, we may mention the extraordinary climatic conditions of 1788, which ruined the harvest, raised corn to a famine price, and caused widespread starvation : only to be followed by the desperately severe winter of early 1789, when all the great rivers of France were frozen and even the port of Marseilles in the extreme south was blocked with ice. The consequence was even greater distress than usual. A free-trade treaty with England admitting our cheap goods had already caused much industrial suffering. Now there gathered in Paris hordes of people from the surrounding countryside, hoping to find food and shelter in urban conditions. Thus came into being the Paris mob—idle, desperate, ready to cheer on the most extreme measure, and destined to control the fortunes of events on more than one vital occasion.

So there was all the material for a great combustion. An outworn, inefficient, unfair, and bankrupt system of government ; a strong body of opinion created by the philosophers ; the successful example of the American revolution ; a weak king ; widespread economic distress ; and a mob in Paris. It needed only one spark to set it all alight. On May 5th, 1789, the States-General met.

The System of the Ancien Régime

L'ETAT C'EST MOI

ALMOST TAX FREE

TERRIBLY TAXED

The Work of the Philosophers

CANDIDE PAR VOLTAIRE

ESPRIT DES LOIS PAR MONTESQUIEU

DU CONTRAT SOCIAL PAR ROUSSEAU

L'ENCYCLOPÉDIE

PAR DIDEROT ETC. 26 VOLS.

The Example of the U.S.A.

1776
DECLARATION
OF
INDEPENDENCE

The Bankruptcy of the Crown

DEBTS LOANS DEFICIT BILLS DEBTS LOANS DEBTS DEFICIT

M.H.

THE CAUSES OF THE FRENCH REVOLUTION.

CHAPTER II

The Progress of the Revolution, 1789-1795.

1. *From the Meeting of the States-General to the War, 1789–1792*

The cahiers

The government of Louis XVI, preparatory to calling the States-General, had asked for *cahiers* of grievances. It got them—over 60,000 of them. From every part of the country the Third Estate sent up the same demands : reform of taxation (with abolition of the privileges of the First and Second Estates as the first step), a settled constitution with a regular parliament and no *lettres de cachet*, and the abolition of all feudal rights and dues. The remark of the men of one district, "How happy we should be if the feudal system were destroyed !" expresses perfectly the main trend of the peasants' requests.

The meeting of the States, May, 1789

It might have been thought that Louis and Necker would examine these grievances, draw up a programme of reforms, and present it to the assembly which was meeting after so great an interval. But that was not Louis' way. Instead of placing himself at the head of the reform movement, he immediately made reform more difficult by expecting the three Estates to deliberate separately, as they had done in the mediæval past. The effect of this would be that reform measures, voted on by Estates as Estates, would be defeated by two Estates to one (First and Second *v.* Third Estate). On the other hand, if all met in one assembly, the fact that the Third Estate had twice as many representatives as either of the others would mean that reform measures could be carried. It would require only a very few individuals from the poorer clergy to support the Third Estate, and they would have a clear majority. It was thus essential to the cause of reform that the Estates should meet as one, and not three, assemblies. Louis had seemed to recognize this by granting the Third Estate double representation, and now, typically, he nullified the whole effect by insisting on separate meeting. Thwarted in this way and irritated by the absence of any positive lead in Necker's opening speech, the Third Estate soon lost its first fine careless rapture. Refusing to admit the policy of separation, under the leadership of Mirabeau, it called itself 'The National Assembly' and left the other Estates to join it if they would. Soon the parish priests began to trickle over, and within four days the rest of the clergy followed. Finding that Louis had ordered the hall where the National Assembly was meeting to be closed for repairs, the Third Estate took the worst possible interpretation of the action. Straightway they adjourned to a local tennis-court, and there solemnly swore the famous 'Tennis-Court Oath' that they would never separate until a constitution was firmly established. When called to a special royal session to hear Louis' firm command to meet separately, the Third Estate refused to follow the nobles and clergy in obeying the royal order to retire. Mirabeau put it precisely to a nobleman who acted as messenger for the King : "Tell your master that nothing but bayonets will drive us from here." ("If they come we buzz-off quick," he is reported to have added in an undertone to a friend.) But they did not come. The vacillating Louis left the Third Estate undisturbed ; soon the clergy came back again, and on June 27th, 1789, the three Estates amalgamated officially by the King's command. The joy was universal and there were cries of 'the Revolution is over'—somewhat prematurely, as it subsequently proved. *The Tennis-Court Oath*

The Estates amalgamate to form the National Assembly, June 1789

Meanwhile events were moving rapidly outside the Assembly. The increasing hunger of the Paris mobs and the massing of troops by Louis led to a state of uneasiness. Crimes of violence became frequent. The government could keep no order. As a measure of self-defence the Parisian electors set up a committee in the Hôtel de Ville and a voluntary militia later known as the National Guard. From the press, now entirely neglecting the feeble orders of the government, there poured a flood of revolutionary pamphlets, while in open spaces such as the gardens of the Palais Royal young orators and journalists like Camille Desmoulins (who was soon to start a brilliant political newspaper) fired the mob by their intoxicating eloquence. Then came the dismissal of Necker from his post of Controller. It seemed that Louis had followed his *The Commune and the National Guard*

Queen's advice and got rid of the only reforming element in his court.

The result of it all was a mob explosion, for which Desmoulins gave the signal. First stealing arms from the depot at the Invalides, they moved to storm the Bastille, which summed up, as it were, the whole idea of royal despotism. There political prisoners often lingered and there the unfortunate victims of *lettres de cachet* learnt to loathe the system of arbitrary despotism. After several hours assault and 200 killed and wounded, the mob managed to induce the Governor to surrender on the promise of safety for himself and his men. Pouring into the great fortress it found—seven prisoners : four forgers, two madmen, and a notorious rake. Typically, it also massacred both governor and garrison, tearing out their hearts and bowels —Paris was soon to see that the friends of liberty could be tyrants too. The deed was hailed throughout the land and through Europe as heroic ; the Bastille, the symbol of despotism, had fallen, and July 14th was to become the national holiday. The rebels were now in command of Paris. The committee at the Hôtel de Ville became a regular town government, or Commune, with a mayor at its head. Lafayette, who had learned his politics in America, was installed as commander of the National Guard. Accepting these measures, the mob was soon quieted, and those who were anxious for more disorder were suppressed by Lafayette and the Guard. It remained to secure Louis' approval of accomplished facts. He had little alternative. Three days later he came to Paris and had to recognize the new government of Paris and the National Guard, and wear in his hat the cockade of the Parisian *tricolore*—the emblem of the

Revolution. Nor was all the activity confined to Paris. In the provinces there was a universal move to storm the 'forty thousand Bastilles'—the feudal castles—and everywhere towns organized committees of electors into Communes and gave themselves self-government on the Parisian model.

The Aboli-
tion of
feudal
privileges,
August
1789
Soon in the Assembly, on August 4th, occurred one of the most remarkable nights in history. A nobleman suddenly rose to propose the abolition of all feudal rights and dues. Others followed. An emotional atmosphere was created, akin to that of a Salvationist meeting. Noble after noble rose,

The Taking of the Bastille.

amid scenes of weeping and embracing, to announce his agreement in the surrender of his own privileges. An orgy of self-sacrifice set in (and naturally others got sacrificed in the process), and by eight o'clock next morning thirty decrees had been passed and the whole fabric of French law altered. One effect of this should never be forgotten. The night of August 4th gave the peasants practically all they wanted from the Revolution ; as time went on and extremism and violence grew, the peasants turned naturally to anybody who could promise them security in their newly won rights. They were not democrats, and they happily accepted Napoleon later because he seemed to make secure for them their principal gains from the Revolution.

The Declaration

The Assembly next concentrated on the production of a preface to the new constitution—'The Declaration of the Rights of Man.' It was in vain that a realist like Mirabeau urged that in such a time of anarchy people needed to be reminded not of their rights but of their duties. Most of the members of the Assembly, in their idealistic, inexperienced, philosophic, and phrase-drunk sort of way, imagined that the mere statement of the general principles guiding the Revolution would be almost sufficient to free mankind from the whole load of past oppression. So they produced a document designed not for the France of 1789 alone but for all times and all peoples. Men were by nature equal ; the people were sovereign, and must participate in the making of law, which was the expression of the General Will ; liberty of person and speech were sacred rights ; rebellion against injustice a holy duty. A statement of democratic principles so complete naturally led to great expectations—which in the nature of facts at the time it was simply impossible to fulfil. As one sensible person remarked : ' It was not wise to lead men up to the top of a mountain and show them a promised land which was afterwards to be refused them.'

The March of the Women, October 1789

It was time for the mob to take a hand again. When the Assembly accepted the idea of Louis' being able to hold up proposed laws for a six-year period, feeling ran high : and the additional facts that he refused to accept the Declaration and the nobles' and clergy's sacrifices of August 4th inflamed matters. When, added to this, there was the ever-increasing famine and the news of royal negotiations with the loyal Flanders Regiment coupled with a lavish military banquet at Versailles, affairs came to a head. Paris decided to stage a 'March of the Women' to Versailles to air its grievances. Women were chosen as their hunger cries would be shriller—though, in fact, many men, some appropriately painted and petticoated, swelled the throng. Hearing of the March, Lafayette set off after them with the National Guard to prevent disorder. In response to popular requests he persuaded the King that it would be more acceptable to the people if he and the National Guard, not the Flanders Regiment, were entrusted with the defence of the palace. Unfortunately while Lafayette was asleep the mob attacked and penetrated the palace, and eventually he was able to calm them down only by promising that the King would come to Paris. So the whole royal family—'the baker, the baker's wife, and the baker's son'—were brought to Paris and lodged practically as prisoners in the palace of the Tuileries. Ten days later the Assembly decreed that it would follow. The importance of these two moves can hardly be overestimated. Mob action had again been decisive : Lafayette was obviously unable to control the forces he had helped to set in motion, and both King and Assembly were virtually at the dictation of the most extreme elements of Paris. The transactions of the Assembly were public ; it became the mob fashion to attend its debates, to cheer the most revolutionary speakers and boo and hiss and jeer at the rest—even to waylay them afterwards ; and the whole effect was to make moderate deputies stay away and leave affairs to be regulated more and more by the extremists.

King and Assembly move to Paris

Soon another decisive step in the Revolution was taken by the Assembly. Desperate for money, it turned its eyes to the vast property of the Church. Mirabeau helped to secure the passage of the measure, which was put into effect by the issue of *assignats*, or paper currency, based not on gold but on the forfeited Church land. Unfortunately the standing temptation of paper money with embarrassed governments is to print off far more than the nature of its backing, whether gold or land, warrants—and an *assignat* which started by being worth a hundred francs by a successive process of inflations degenerated in seven years to the value of about a halfpenny.

The Nationalization of Church Property

The measure, too, offended most of the clergy, who had soon, however, to witness anti-clerical decrees much more extreme.

The Civil Constitution of the Clergy, July 1790

In July 1790 the radical Civil Constitution of the Clergy was passed. By this the State, not the Pope, undertook responsibility for paying the clergy, who were thus turned into state officials, with leaders appointed by a form of election. Rome was allowed no power at all in the scheme. Louis, a good Catholic, heart-brokenly agreed ; but when, as he had feared, the Pope in April 1791 solemnly condemned the whole measure, his remorse knew no bounds. From this point must be dated his determination to seek foreign aid in checking the ever-increasing momentum of the Revolution.

The flight to Varennes, June 1791

At last he resolved to flee whither he could either find loyal French troops in Eastern France or accept the help of his brother-in-law, the Emperor Leopold, and whence, at the head of an army of foreigners and *émigré* French nobles, he could return to dictate terms to the Assembly. It was a fatal plan even had he succeeded in escaping, and one from which Mirabeau, who had at last come to better terms with the court and who was doing his best to keep the Revolution within reasonable bounds, would certainly have dissuaded him. But Mirabeau had died in April 1791, with the full and despairing realization that the monarchy was doomed. "I carry with me," he said, "the last rags of the monarchy." Removed from his wise advice, Louis proceeded on his rash course. At night, disguised as a valet, he escaped in a coach with Marie Antoinette and his family ; but news outstripped his slow rate of progress, and at Varennes, a little town near the frontier, a butcher's cart across the road finished his hopes. At the Hôtel de Ville, Lafayette, who had taken charge, issued orders for the return of the captives. It was a terrible journey for them. Exposed to every form of insult, they were brought back, humiliated by ruffians who poked their heads through the coach windows to spit in the Queen's face and by the alternate jeers and stony silence of the crowd. In twenty-four hours Marie Antoinette's hair turned completely white. It was the end of the last remnant of the royal prestige—the complete extinction of the blaze of popularity which had at first surrounded the good-natured, 'reforming' King. 'At

The Press.

"Patience, my lord, your turn is coming."

Varennes the monarchy had died. All that Paris had to do, a year later, was to bury it.'

The Clubs   The net result was the growth of a deliberately republican movement. Mirabeau was dead, Lafayette rapidly lost his great popularity by ordering the Guard to fire on a rioting mob in the Champ de Mars, the King was disgraced—the leadership of affairs drifted into the hands of the politicians who were making their name by their eloquence in the political clubs. The most important of these clubs was the Jacobin Club (so-called since its parent branch met in the disused convent of St. Jacques), which within two or three years of its formation rapidly affiliated over four hundred branch organizations in the provinces. The history of the control of the Jacobins till 1794 is the history of the Revolution. Originally embracing all shades of reforming opinion, it gradually became confined to extremists as they succeeded in getting their policy approved. Already now on the question of republic or monarchy one group of monarchical supporters was driven out. Another Club, the Cordelier Club, limited to Paris and composed of working-men rather than the professional classes, was extremely democratic from the very beginning.

The new Constitution and the end of the National Assembly, September 1791   Meanwhile the Assembly, weary of its activities, was anxious to complete the new constitution and dissolve itself. At last, in September 1791, the Constitution was duly accepted by the hapless King and Paris again celebrated the 'end of the Revolution.' Unfortunately the Constitution was far from perfect. On paper the King was allowed a considerable amount of power, which was quite unacceptable to the new republicans (though he could be baulked from using it by the financial hold of the Assembly). Voters were to have a fairly high property qualification—a measure which annoyed the extremists. But the really vital defect was that the Communes in the provinces were allowed to be almost entirely self-governing—the central government had practically no control over them. As the U.S. Ambassador remarked, "The Almighty Himself could not have made it work unless He created a new species of man." [1] To increase the difficulty the members of the Assembly unselfishly declared themselves ineligible for re-election in the new Legislative Assembly—

[1] See note on page 23.

thus cutting off from the conduct of affairs the only body of men who had begun to accumulate any experience in them.

NOTE.—The constitution confirmed a new administrative division of French territory recently voted by the Assembly. By this the old boundaries and units of the royal administration (including the historic Provinces of Normandy, Brittany and the rest) and the old royal officials (including the powerful Intendants) were swept away, and France was laid out anew in a series of 83 Départements. Each of these was sub-divided into six or seven Districts, and each District into eight or nine Cantons; and in every Département and District there were locally elected councils and executive officers. In none of the new divisions, however, was any place given to a representative of the central government. The whole idea, in fact, was to have only a minimum of control from above; and to this end very large powers, including command of the local contingents of the National Guard, were left with the lowest units in the scale—the Communes, or munici-palities, which also had elected officers. Of these Communes, which varied in size from villages to large towns, there were some 40,000 within the various Cantons.

2. *From the War to the Establishment of the Directory, 1792–1795*

It was the war which conditioned the rest of the Revolution. *The approach of war* Many of the members of the Assembly were idealistic pacifists, who had earlier passed a motion renouncing all wars of acquisition. The threatening attitude of the *émigré* nobles on the border, however (by now about 150,000 in all and led by Louis' brother), and the danger of Louis' suddenly receiving help from Austria and Prussia led to the atmosphere of fear which produces war. At the same time a group of politicians known as the Girondins (from the Gironde in the south-west *The Girondins* of France) began to desire war from motives of their own. Though still members of the Jacobins and thus extremists of a kind, they were by no means the most extreme element there, since although they ardently desired to preserve the work of the Revolution and even to advance to a republic, they were opposed to the terrorist views of the most Left-wing section. Under the leadership of Vergniaud and Roland, though still more under that of Roland's wife, Madame Roland, whose salon was the centre of the group, they forced themselves into the ministry. Now they became filled with the idea that war would both unite the country and place it behind its leaders, and at the same time reveal Louis' sympathies with the country's enemies—and thus provide an excuse for getting rid of him. In April 1792 the Council decided on war against *War declared, April 1792* Austria, and the Assembly agreed on the basis of 'war against

Paix aux Peuples, Guerre aux Tyrans.

The fighting basis of the Revolution.   Note the combination of olive branch, cap of liberty, and sword.

Kings, peace with all peoples.'   It was a challenge against the rulers of the world—one which they were not slow to accept. The immediate consequences were disastrous.   The entirely unprepared French army was routed in the Austrian Nether-lands, and the King took the opportunity of vetoing two decrees and dismissing some of his Girondin ministers, including Roland.   The mob in anger invaded the Tuileries and Louis was compelled to fraternize with them, to drink their health and to wear the red cap of liberty.   Lafayette made a last effort to save the monarchy by leading the Guard against the Jacobins, but he came up against the invincible folly of Marie Antoinette, who, distrusting Lafayette as an erstwhile leader of the Revolution, declared she would "sooner perish than be saved by M. Lafayette" and actually warned the Jacobins of Lafayette's intention.

As the suspicion that the King had betrayed the army's plan in the Austrian Netherlands grew into a certainty, the movement for his deposition developed apace. Orators on the Left pointed out the danger of a stab in the back, and at the Cordelier Club Danton, a patriot and democrat of extreme violence in spite of his innate good nature, began to prepare the next decisive step in the Revolution. The Girondins, republicans as they were, offered to save the throne if Louis would recall Roland to the ministry, but he refused their help as he had done Lafayette's. When in August Paris learnt of the foolhardy Manifesto of the Duke of Brunswick (commander of the enemy forces), threatening the most terrible punishments to Paris if it dared to touch the royal family and treating all resistance to Brunswick as rebellion, deposition was loudly demanded. The initiative was taken by Danton. At a given signal (the bell of the Cordeliers) the forces controlled by the Clubs seized power at the Hôtel de Ville, replacing the moderate rulers of the Commune by men of the extreme Left. Then came the attack on the Tuileries. Though Louis' Swiss Guard resisted this to a man, their lives were spent in vain by a monarch who generously but foolishly ordered them to retire at the wrong moment. The King hurriedly took refuge in the Assembly, but this was now powerless before the armed forces of the Commune. The Assembly had perforce to suspend the King, who was lodged with his family in the Temple Prison. Robespierre, a Jacobin of the extreme Left, now led a movement to dissolve the Assembly and call a Convention which should draft a new and more democratic constitution, in which the King would have no place. Danton's revolution had succeeded, and had left him in charge of affairs. But it had set a fatal precedent. In the attack on the Tuileries some 2000 had perished and subsequently 800 royalist sympathisers had been massacred. Thenceforward it was simply a question of one gang of revolutionaries replacing another, and disposing of them by the simple process of wholesale butchery.

The deposition of Louis XVI

The
September
Massacres,
September
1792

The deposition of the King was the first step in the reorganization of the defences. France was indeed in a parlous condition. In the Vendée district insurrection against the government had broken out, prompted by Catholic horror of the measures against the Church. Now, on August 19th, the Prussians (who had joined with the Austrians, annoyed by the confiscation of the lands of German nobles in Alsace) crossed the frontier, and captured Longwy and Verdun. The resulting fear led to further extreme measures against royalist supporters in Paris, and on the night of September 2nd Marat (another leading spirit of the Cordeliers, who ran a virulently democratic paper *L'Ami du Peuple*) organized a vast massacre of priests and royalists who were being held in prison. Over 2000 perished in this foul way. The Reign of Terror had begun with a vengeance.

Valmy,
September
1792

Suddenly the face of the war altered. On September 20th, at Valmy, the Prussians were repulsed. It was a mere cannonade ; and the Prussian retirement was due rather more to their suspicion of Austrian preoccupation with the Netherlands, Russian designs on Poland, and Danton's bribing activities than to French reorganization. But it made all the difference to the spirit of the French. The invasion was checked—the revolution might be preserved. "Here and now," said the great German poet Goethe, "begins a new era in the history of the world." Within a few weeks the French occupied the Austrian Netherlands, conquered by the battle of Jemappes, and proceeded to advance to the Rhine and the Austrian dominions in Italy. The Convention (in which the Jacobins were even stronger than in the old Assembly) intoxicatedly voted that France would give her help to all peoples desiring to recover their liberty, and thus hurled a further challenge at the world.

The execu-
tion of
Louis,
January
1793

The trial of the King followed. He had no chance, although technically by the 1791 constitution his ministers were responsible for all his actions. But as Robespierre said, "You are not judges—you are statesmen," and the King was unanimously declared guilty. When it came to a question of the punishment, the Girondins and Danton, who really wished to save him, hesitated thus to lay themselves open to a charge of monarchism, and it was Robespierre's policy of execution which triumphed. The consequence was further terror, dictatorship, and war with most of Europe.

Within a month England and Spain had been forced into the conflict. Both objected on principle to the doctrines of the Revolution and the execution of the King, and both were naturally conscious of the danger to their national security arising from the French advance to the Pyrenees, the occupation of the Austrian Netherlands, and the violations of the Treaty of Utrecht of 1713. Immediately the French armies suffered reverses again, and the consequences were seen in the institution of a Revolutionary Tribunal and a Committee of Public Safety for dealing speedily with opposition. And indeed there was opposition to deal with, for with the introduction of conscription there was a further rebellion in the west. By April the last Girondins had been excluded from the Committee, and the stage was set for another act in the sanguinary drama. The tension increased when the leader of the French armies, Dumouriez, tried to induce his men to march on Paris and suppress the Clubs, failed, and deserted to the Austrians. At once the Mountain (the extremist section of the Convention, so called from their raised seats) worked hand in glove with the Commune to destroy the last advocates of moderation, the Girondins, whose leaders were guillotined in a batch—the perpetual fate of moderates who start revolutions. Roland, who had escaped, wandered, hunted and miserable, in the country till he heard of the death of his wife, and then committed suicide. A further rebellion broke out in the Girondins' support, but it was soon defeated. Its only permanent result was that one Norman girl, Charlotte Corday, burning with hatred of the brutal and irreligious policy of the Jacobin leaders, sought an interview with Marat, was admitted to him as he sat in his bath, and murdered him with one sure thrust of her knife.

War v. England and Spain, January 1793

The end of the Girondins, June 1793

Meantime the Convention had drawn up the new constitution, which was extremely republican, including votes for all men and plebiscites on important questions. But it was never applied. Government rested in the hands of the Committee of Public Safety, and the Convention merely agreed automatically, since they knew what resistance meant, to whatever it proposed. Altogether the Convention sanc-

Reorganization

tioned 11,250 decrees in three years, without even so much as giving a single one of them a second reading. All over the country the Committee used the local Jacobin societies to enforce its policy. Agents were sent down to enforce obedience, the work of organizing the conscript armies being brilliantly achieved by Carnot, 'The Organizer of Victory.' Resistance was met ruthlessly, and blood flowed riotously in Paris.

Robespierre and the Terror, 1793-1794
The terrible Robespierre was now in the ascendant—honest in money matters, no lover of women, and believing in his democratic, Rousseauite creed far more sincerely than any other of the revolutionary leaders—but vain and fanatical and determined to enforce his own ideas of virtue at all costs. Believing that terror was necessary to inspire virtue, he *organized*—there is no other word for it—the Reign of Terror. Others helped him, either from pure criminality, or more often because they realized that the choice was between being a guillotiner or a guillotined. Fouquier-Tinville, the ruthless Public Prosecutor, claimed nearly 3000 victims in a few months —from Marie Antoinette down to nobles, priests, Girondins, and even harmless women like Madame du Barry, whose days of glory in the court of Louis XV were long since over. A dreadful bloodlust grew, developing into a kind of worship of Madame Guillotine. Tremendous crowds attended the 'Red Mass,' and it is possible that the government deliberately ordered executions with the object of providing entertainment for the populace and distracting their minds from the war. At Nantes over 4000 were butchered in four months, some by being sent out in a boat which was then deliberately sunk ; and at Lyons 2000 perished in mass executions conducted by volleys of gunfire. No one was safe. The Commune, more extreme than anyone, offended Robespierre by tentative efforts to introduce socialist measures and by trying to destroy all Christian worship. It succeeded in establishing 'The Worship of Reason' as the religion of France, in getting the Convention to pass a 'law of the Maximum,' limiting the price of bread and corn, and in introducing a revolutionary calendar which eliminated saints-days and Sundays. Then Robespierre struck, aided by Danton. The leaders of the Commune went the way of the rest, and Robespierre appointed creatures suitable to himself.

By now, however, the French armies, ragged but full of revolutionary fervour, were triumphant again, and Danton conceived that the Terror had worked its purpose. Sickening of the bloodshed and happy in the love of a young girl he had just married, he tried to call a halt to the whole ghastly business. It was fatal; Robespierre immediately accused him of counter-revolutionary sentiments, and Danton and Desmoulins, his great friend, followed whither they had sent so many others. Robespierre, now under practically no restraint, established the worship of the Supreme Being (his own particular form of religion), and proceeded with the Terror. By one ruthless law, known as the Law of Prairial, suspects were deprived of the help of counsel and could be condemned to the one possible punishment, death, on the reputation of a 'bad moral character' alone—which might be made to mean anything. After this in fifty days nearly 1500 heads fell. But opposition grew—too many leaders, far less honest men than Robespierre, feared that their turn was coming next. A momentary alliance among them lost him his hold of the Committee of Public Safety and his control of the Jacobin Clubs. He was shouted down in the Convention, lodged with his closest followers in prison, and though he was released by the Commune, which still favoured him, he was recaptured in the Hôtel de Ville as he was about to sign an illegal appeal to the troops. The next day he and his followers had their turn. Strangely enough, though those who overthrew Robespierre were far worse men than he, the fall of Robespierre meant the end of the Terror. The country now was so obviously tired of the bloodshed that the new rulers, from the sole motive of gaining popularity, destroyed the organization which had made the Terror possible—the Revolutionary Tribunal, the Committee of Public Safety, and the Jacobin Clubs, and repealed the Law of Prairial. Yet another new constitution was voted by the Convention, in which the electorate was restricted to tax-payers (a reaction against extreme democracy), and power was split between a two-housed Assembly and a Directory of five men. Aided by the prolongation of the war and by public feeling aroused against England's unsuccessful attempts to promote a rising in La Vendée and a landing on the west coast,

The end of Danton, April 1794

The end of Robespierre, July 1794

The Directory, 1795

the men who had ousted Robespierre kept their hold on affairs, and their leader, Barras, soon secured one of the Directors' positions. When there was a royalist rising in Paris they ordered out the troops, and a 'whiff of grape-shot' dispersed the mob. The officer in command was a sallow-skinned Corsican named Napoleon Bonaparte, who thus began by being the Directory's servant and was soon to prove its master.

How are we to explain this almost incredible French Revolution—this astounding mixture of highest idealism and deepest villainy, resolute courage and contemptible cowardice, breathless reform and starkest tyranny ? Chiefly by bearing this fact in mind—that France, a country in dissolution, undergoing a radical reshaping of her organs of government, at the critical moment was plunged into war, both national and civil. War—we have seen the same process going on under our eyes quite recently—by generating fear, which in turn produces reckless violence, strips off our all too thin veneer of civilization and tolerates the most outrageous bestiality at the same time as it calls to the fore bravery and patriotism. It thus has the elements of fantastic contradiction in itself. Further, the particularly democratic creed of the French Revolutionaries, based on philosophy and sentiment rather than practicability or experience, encouraged a pathetic belief that the mob is always right, and robbed leader after leader of the will or courage to call a halt to mob violence when it was manifestly wrong. By the system of open debates in Assembly, Convention, and Clubs, the advocate of modera-tion was always liable to be shouted down and accused of the unforgivable offence of counter-revolutionary sentiments. At critical moments, too, the undue importance of the Municipal Government of Paris, or Commune, which was early captured by the extreme Left, told to disastrous effect against the more moderate Convention. Thus partly because of the war, internal and external, partly because of the genuine difficulty of keeping a hold on a country freed from the shackles of centuries, partly because of the unrealistic theories of the revolutionaries and the practice of open debating, partly because of the independence of the Commune, the conduct of affairs inevitably drifted to the extremists, and the Revolution

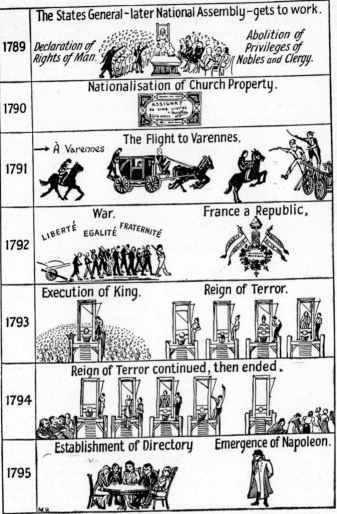

1789	The States General – later National Assembly – gets to work. *Declaration of Rights of Man.* *Abolition of Privileges of Nobles and Clergy.*
1790	Nationalisation of Church Property.
1791	À Varennes → The Flight to Varennes.
1792	War. LIBERTÉ EGALITÉ FRATERNITÉ France a Republic.
1793	Execution of King. Reign of Terror.
1794	Reign of Terror continued, then ended.
1795	Establishment of Directory Emergence of Napoleon.

THE PROGRESS OF THE FRENCH REVOLUTION.

developed from a movement for peaceful reform to an orgy of blood-letting. Yet it must never be forgotten that when the frenzy of violence died, the permanent benefits of reform remained—not democracy, because France had shown herself incapable of it, but equality before the law, administrative reform, fairer taxation, liberated industry and commerce, the foundation of schools, colleges, museums, libraries and the metric system, the abolition of feudalism and the distribution of feudal land among the peasantry, the transference of the major share in the State from nobles and clergy to the bourgeoisie. It was the greatest achievement of Napoleon not to destroy the Revolution but to preserve many of its essentials.

APPENDIX TO CHAPTER II

Some Characters of the Revolution

MIRABEAU (died 1791)

A rather terrible, brilliant, dissolute noble, who had among other misdemeanours run off with another man's wife and embezzled great sums of money, Mirabeau was to find that his unsavoury reputation was to baulk him of his greatest ambition. Rejected by his own Estate, he was elected by the Third Estate and immediately became their leader. "A mad dog, am I ?" he said at his election. "But elect me, and despotism and privilege will die of my bite." He led the opposition to the Crown till the Third Estate became the National Assembly, and advocated the nationalization of Church land. Knowing he was big enough to direct the movement he tried desperately to strike an alliance with the court, for he could see himself in the rôle of a Richelieu. But it took too long to break down Marie Antoinette's distrust ; and when at length his advice was accepted he allowed Louis to pay his debts for him and thus gave room for suspicion of his fidelity to the Revolution. To rob him of his ambition the rather frightened Assembly passed a law that members of it were not eligible to become royal ministers. Mirabeau, beaten, with graceful but desperate humour moved an amendment "to except the name of M. de Mirabeau." Had he lived beyond April 1791 he *might* have saved the monarchy—but it is only a 'might.' His powerful face was fearfully pock-marked, and this, combined with his violence of expression and burning eyes, made his oratory frequently irresistible in the Assembly—though it has since been proved that he got other people to write his speeches for him.

LAFAYETTE (died 1834)

Essentially the man who started events he did not understand. A volunteer for the Americans in 1776, he returned to France filled with ideas of liberty, and took a prominent part in framing the Declaration of the Rights of Man, for which theoretic business he was admirably suited. Wildly popular at first, he seemed to personify the whole Revolution, and was installed as Commander of the newly created bourgeois National Guard. Unfortunately he rejected a proposed alliance with Mirabeau, being deeply suspicious of that turbulent genius, and soon found himself outpaced by the course of the Revolution. Hated by the Court, however, he could do little. When the King was attacked after he had accepted the 1791 Constitution, Lafayette was very indignant, and his order to fire at the mob demanding Louis' deposition made him loathed by those who a year before had been kissing his horse and his boots. When the mob stormed the Tuileries in August 1792 he left his army, appeared before the Assembly, and denounced the trend of events—but he would have had more influence had he brought the army with him. Danton's policy triumphed, his arrest was ordered, and he had to flee into the territory of the Austrians, who promptly imprisoned him for five years. Later he helped to upset Napoleon's Government in 1815 without knowing what was going to take its place, and again in 1830 he took part in the Revolution against Charles X. Under Louis Philippe he expressed himself as willing to help the countries of Europe to loose their bonds, and only his death at the age of seventy-four prevented his cheerfully starting a dozen or more further revolutions. He was brave, honest, chivalrous, sentimental, and not very clever. Napoleon called him the 'Simpleton' and Mirabeau termed him the 'King of Clowns.'

MADAME ROLAND (executed 1793)

The centre of the Girondin group, of which M. Roland was one of the leaders. Fed on classical literature, the Girondins imagined they were creating a Roman Republic when they were only paving the way for the triumph of the extremists. They helped in the deposition of the King and led the demand for war, but succumbed to the plotting of Robespierre. Throughout they displayed a fatal facility for violent eloquence and an equal incapacity for resolute action. They met their death with the Roman fortitude they so much admired. Madame Roland summarized not only her opponents' but her own party's record when, regarding the statue of Liberty erected near the guillotine, she exclaimed, "Ah, Liberty, what crimes are committed in thy name !"

MARAT (murdered 1793)

A doctor and scientific inventor and an extreme Cordelier from the start. To us one of the most unattractive figures of the Revolution, which he helped to direct on the course of bloodshed by his violent journal *L'Ami du Peuple*, and by his organization of the September Massacres. A painful skin-disease may have helped to produce the nervous violence which satisfied itself by causing others to be executed. Warm baths gave his skin-trouble relief, and it was in one of them that he met his death by Charlotte Corday's knife. His creed was simple —'270,000 heads to cut off and mankind will be happy.' 270,000 was the estimated number of the First and Second Estates.

DANTON (executed 1794)

The most deserving of the name of statesman of the revolutionary figures. A lawyer, universally regarded as a goodnatured fellow, he aided the extreme democratic section by his foundation of the Cordelier Club. An ardent patriot, he resented 'the treason of the Tuileries' and led the movement for the deposition of the King by planning a *coup d'état* at the Hôtel de Ville on August 10th, 1792, and the consequent attack on the King's palace. He accepted responsibility for the September Massacres, and made the Terror possible by the creation of the Revolutionary Tribunal and Committee of Public Safety, on which he had a prominent place. But he kept the end in view as well as the means, and when he had helped to place the armies on a victorious footing he had no desire to prolong the Terror, and lost his life for advocating its abolition. He would have saved the Girondins, too, had they accepted his proposed alliance. Unfortunately for him his recklessness and unscrupulousness in money matters gave a weapon to his opponents. His broad, powerful head expressed the *bigness* which was his essential characteristic (Robespierre was a thoroughly *small* man in both features and mind). He died bitterly regretting his share in creating the machinery of the Terror. As he passed Robespierre's house on the way to the guillotine he shouted, "Infamous Robespierre, you will follow me !" And then on the scaffold itself his superb courage was responsible for one of the most famous remarks of history : "Shew my head to the people : it is worth the trouble."

ROBESPIERRE (executed 1794)

The most puzzling figure of the Revolution. A narrow, bigoted provincial lawyer of no great eloquence, intelligence, or decision, he gained a gradual ascendancy at the Jacobins by his unswerving and fanatical devotion to the ideas of Rousseau (whose *Contrat Social* lay always on his desk) and by that honesty in money matters which earned him the title of the 'Incorruptible.' 'Virtue' and 'terror' were his two key-words—'virtue' consisting of chaste morals, democratic opinions, and belief in the Supreme Being, and 'terror' being that which was meted out to all who held other views. He came into his own after he had hounded first the Girondins then Danton to death as being 'too indulgent,' and instigated the Terror in its fullest form until, frightening all by indiscriminate threats, he caused his next prospective victims to combine against him. On Thermidor 9th,

Robespierre.

[*Photo, Bulloz*

year II (July 27th, 1794) he was arrested in the Hôtel de Ville, where the Commune still supported him, and together with his closest associates, who were devoted to him, was guillotined the following day. His feline features and spiteful green eyes (blinking behind blue-tinted spectacles), together with his invariably neat appearance and the high heels worn to increase his height, give some indication of that jealousy and pride which made him so fatally certain of his own wisdom and virtue. He provides one of the supreme examples in history of the truth that the honest fanatic may be infinitely more terrible than the worst scoundrel.

CHAPTER III

The Revolutionary Wars and the Career of Napoleon, 1793–1815.

1. *From the First Coalition to the Peace of Amiens, 1793–1802*

We have now to follow the career of the genius who is per- The First Coalition, 1793 haps the most fascinating and the most repellent personality of modern times. We have seen how, partly because of her doctrines and partly because of her occupation of the Austrian Netherlands, revolutionary France had been driven to face a European coalition in 1793, and how the price of her pre- liminary failure against it was the Terror and a move towards dictatorship. By 1795, however, the genius of Carnot (who not only planned campaigns and organized armies, but turned Carnot, the "Organizer of victory" up in person in civilian dress to lead the advance which recaptured the Austrian Netherlands at Fleurus !) and the enthusiasm of the ragged French troops had eliminated Prussia and Spain from the attack. Holland, too, had not only been defeated on land and had her fleet captured by a Collapse of Holland and Spain cavalry charge over the ice, but had been compelled to sign a peace treaty which put her military forces at the disposal of France. Thus, of the First Coalition, besides Austria, only the originator and paymaster, Pitt's government in England, remained.

England's record in the war so far had been uninspiring— an unsuccessful landing in Brittany, her troops defeated in the Netherlands, Toulon captured only to be lost soon after, and an unimportant 'Lord Howe' victory (as Nelson called it) outside Brest on the 'Glorious First of June.' The ambition of the Directory in France was thus to knock out first her more dangerous land opponent, Austria, and then concentrate on her commercial and naval rival, England. It will be noticed that though the French conscript soldier still maintained— indeed, it was one of the secrets of his success—an astounding

faith in 'liberty' and 'equality,' the actual government of
France, the Directory, was moving far from the original 1792
position of enthusiasts who would remodel the world for a new
faith, and was considering the war along the classic Louis XIV
tradition of foreign conquest, glory, and 'natural frontiers.'
The French, indeed, still offered the new liberty to all peoples
—but its particular quality only too often turned out to savour
of the old tyranny.

The Italian
Campaign,
1796–1797

The attack on Austria was planned in two directions. Not
only was Austria to be directly attacked along the Rhine–
Danube route by two armies, but a third was to enter Italy,
capture the Austrian possessions there, and then join in the
attack on Austria itself by a passage through the Tyrol.

Napoleon
Bonaparte

The soldier appointed by the Directory, on the motion of
Carnot, to command the Italian expedition was the Napoleon
Bonaparte who had already proved his worth in ousting the
English from Toulon in 1793 and the royalists from the streets
of Paris in 1795. A penniless, friendless, one-meal-a-day
young artillery officer in 1789, he had welcomed the Revolution as a keen disciple of Rousseau, and had maintained
sufficiently close relations with Robespierre to be thrown into
prison on his fall. But he had learnt to despise the mob and
to loathe mob violence in the scenes he witnessed in Paris,
and gradually his strong sense of order triumphed over his early
revolutionary principles. Still partly in disgrace, he had been
on the spot in the difficult situation of 1795, and his prompt
order to fetch cannons and fire on the mob had saved the
Directory. His rewards were the command of the Italian
Expedition and the hand of a mistress of the Director Barras,
by name Josephine Beauharnais, with whom he was passionately in love and whose aristocratic connections would help
his social progress to equal his military advancement.

On March 11th, 1796, after a two-day honeymoon, Bonaparte departed for Italy. Within a month he had pulled his
lax, ill-equipped, and disorganized troops together, and was
ready for action. His words to them on the opening of the
campaign are famous : "You are badly fed and nearly naked
—I am going to lead you to the most fertile plains in the world.
You will find there great cities and rich provinces. You will
find there honour, glory, and wealth." Four days after he

entered Italy he had succeeded in his first object of separating the Austrian and Sardinian armies, and the King of Sardinia was demanding peace from a general whose troops had practically "no artillery, no cavalry, and no boots." The rest of the campaign continued on the same lines. By brilliant strategy and marching he contrived to manœuvre numerically superior opponents into positions where they could engage only a small proportion of their forces against the entire strength of the French Army. He had, too, a most powerful moral weapon— the appeal of the doctrine of 'liberty' to the enslaved Italians. A month after setting foot on Italian soil he had forced the Lodi bridge at Lodi and entered Milan, capital of Lombardy and the Austrian headquarters, amid the rejoicing of its Italian population. A temporary check came when for some months the enemy held out in Mantua, but finally by the battle of Rivoli, in early 1797, resistance was crushed, the Austrians Rivoli became demoralized, and the victorious Bonaparte was pulled up from chasing them out of Italy right into Vienna itself only by the Austrian acceptance of the severe treaty of Campo-Formio.

By this treaty Austria was compelled to recognize not only Treaty of France's conquest of the Austrian Netherlands and her newly Campo-Formio, won Rhine frontier, but also the loss of Lombardy and its 1797 incorporation into a new state, the Cisalpine Republic, which, nominally independent, in fact was entirely under French control. In return Bonaparte threw Austria a shameful bribe —Venice, which had no quarrel with France and which had preserved her existence as an independent republic for 1100 years. The Italians, who had helped the French, were thus soon to find that 'liberty' was not everywhere applied, and that even where it was, it was expensive. From Venice and the Cisalpine Republic and the Papal States (which were equally at his mercy) Napoleon poured back tribute over the Alps in the form of cash and masterpieces of art—the Papacy alone, for instance, had to pay 300,000,000 francs compensation for the murder of a French envoy by the Roman people. Thus within a year Austria had been beaten out of the Coalition, North Italy completely reorganized, France enriched and glorified, and the name of Napoleon Bonaparte sent ringing throughout Europe.

The war against England   There remained to France one stubborn opponent, England, who would never rest while a major sea-power occupied the coast of the Low Countries and constituted a permanent threat to her security.   Accordingly 1797 witnessed a determined effort to crush her.   It was, indeed, a critical year for England, with no allies, an imminent revolt in Ireland, mutinies in the fleet, corn shortage, a financial crisis, and our hold on India threatened by the French-inspired Tippoo Sahib.   But the schemes of France went astray, in spite of the fact that Holland and Spain had now to move their fleets at her dictation.   At the end of 1796 an attempted invasion of Ireland had been scattered by storms, nor were the efforts of 1797 and 1798 in the same direction to advance the cause of Wolfe Tone and his United Irishmen much more successful.   The graver danger at the moment, however, came from France's compulsory allies rather than her own disorganized navies—till Jarvis (in name) and Nelson (in fact) defeated the Spanish at Cape St. Vincent and Duncan disposed of the Dutch at Camperdown.   England for the moment was safe.

England's critical year, 1797

The Egyptian Campaign, 1798–1799   It was left to the conqueror of Italy to devise a more brilliant, if fundamentally impracticable, scheme of attacking the obstinate island.   His method was characteristically clever and comprehensive.   Knowing that England in fact was far more than an island, that she was a world power to whom commerce was the life-blood, Bonaparte planned to capture Egypt (which belonged to Turkey), ruin England's trade in the Mediterranean, and possibly even advance overland and wrest India from our grasp.   The fascination which the East had exercised over his mind from boyhood urged him to adopt the scheme, as well as that vaulting ambition which could say : "My glory is already threadbare.   This little Europe is too small a field.   Great celebrity can be won only in the East."   The Directory readily approved the proposal—Bonaparte was becoming too powerful to be acceptable to them in Europe.   So with an army of 38,000, a host of scientists and antiquarians, 400 boats by way of transport, and with the whole expedition financed by plunder from two new French vassal-republics (the Helvetic and the Roman), Bonaparte sailed for Egypt.   He took Malta from the Knights of St. John *en route*, cleverly gave Nelson the slip, and arrived safely off Alexandria in July 1798. Before the month was out he had massacred the famous Turkish force, the Mamelukes, at the Battle of the Pyramids ("Forty centuries look down on you," he had said to his troops before the battle), and Egypt lay at his feet. Within a week, however, Nelson came on the French fleet at anchor in Aboukir Bay and utterly destroyed it, thereby cutting off French communications with Europe. Without sufficient reinforcements Bonaparte could not advance to India, and he was thus forced to an alternative plan, almost equally ambitious, of invading Syria, forcing his way through Asia Minor, capturing Constantinople, and completely smashing the Ottoman Empire. Syria proved an easy victim (he again posed as the 'deliverer' from Turkish rulers), till he was held up at Acre by Sir Sydney Smith, and had eventually to retire hastily to Egypt to crush a Turkish attempt to recapture it. {.margin: Battle of the Pyramids}

At this stage—August 1799—master of Egypt but a prisoner there because of the loss of his fleet, Bonaparte learnt some astonishing news from English newspapers thoughtfully sent him by the eccentric Sir Sydney Smith. In Europe France was on the run. A second Coalition had been formed, this time between England, Turkey, Austria, and Russia. Austria was alarmed at the fresh French aggression in Italy, which had driven the Pope from Rome, set up another republic in Naples, and captured Piedmont, while the new ally, Russia, joined because her half-mad Czar Paul was sentimentally attached to the Order of St. John and resented Bonaparte's move towards the East. From Italy, Bonaparte learnt, the French troops were being expelled by the fierce Cossack General Suvoroff, while the other French armies were hanging on with difficulty to their conquests on the Rhine, in the Netherlands, and in Switzerland. There were, too, rumours of royalist plots and treachery among French generals. In France a wave of unpopularity was almost submerging the Directory. The moment was ripe. Bonaparte and a few followers stole away from Egypt in two small ships, leaving his deserted expedition to its favourite sports of measuring ruins, trying to find a substitute for hops, and fishing in the Nile with bent bayonets for dead Mamelukes, and leaving it also to the later

Margin notes:
Battle of the Nile
Acre
The Second Coalition, 1799
French losses
Napoleon returns to France and overthrows the Directory

prospect of a certain surrender to the enemy. By luck and skill in hugging the coast of Africa, he again eluded the English fleet, landed in France and received a delirious welcome as the conqueror of Egypt and the man who could recapture Italy. Within a few weeks he had carried out a *coup d'état* by an alliance with one of the Directors, and dismissed the Assembly. For once his nerve here failed him, for he nearly fainted, and was saved only by his brother Lucien, the President, who was in the plot and who ordered in the troops in the nick of time. He now established a new government of three Consuls, of whom he was the first and the only one who counted. A show of democratic government was still preserved, but no one was taken in by appearances. The new dictatorship was approved by an overwhelming plebiscite—a political weapon used with great effect by the Bonaparte family long before Hitler and Mussolini imitated the procedure.

The Consulate

Secure in his new power, Bonaparte marched to restore the situation in Europe. In actual fact the tide had already begun to turn in France's favour, but Bonaparte monopolized the credit. By 1800 his military genius and a good slice of luck had recaptured Italy at the battle of Marengo, while in Germany the Austrians were badly defeated by Moreau at Hohenlinden. Russia had already quarrelled with Austria and England and retired, and by the Treaty of Lunéville of 1801 Austria had again to recognize the French republics in Italy, Switzerland, and Holland.

Treaty of Lunéville, 1801

The full weight of France could thus be brought to bear once more against England, and a particularly difficult situation developed in the form of the "Armed Neutrality of the North"—a league of the Baltic powers (Prussia, Sweden, Denmark, and Russia) opposed to the very extensive 'right of search' claimed by the British admiralty over neutral powers. This was a claim which had caused wars with Holland in the past, was to cause a war with the U.S.A. from 1812 to 1814, and might have brought the Americans in against England in 1915 had not Germany adopted the even more drastic policy of sinking American vessels by her submarine campaign. Russia, too, was prompted by Paul's passion for Malta, which had now been seized by the English. The British Government dealt with the situation partly by relaxing some

The Armed Neutrality

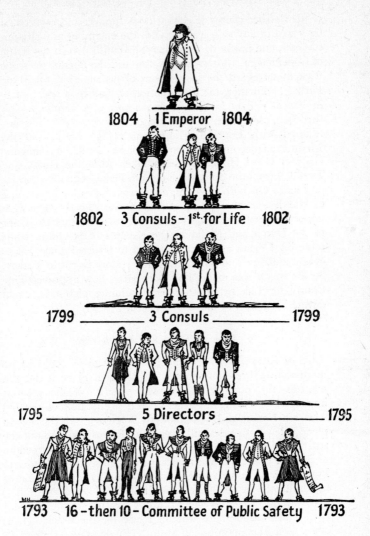

1804   1 Emperor   1804

1802   3 Consuls – 1st for Life   1802

1799 ———— 3 Consuls ———— 1799

1795 ———— 5 Directors ———— 1795

1793   16 – then 10 – Committee of Public Safety   1793

THE DRIFT TO DICTATORSHIP.

of the harsher claims (e.g. that iron, timber, and corn could be seized in any ship trading with the enemy in any circumstances), and partly by smashing the Danish fleet at the Battle of Copenhagen, 1801 (where Nelson did the famous telescope trick to disregard the instructions of his superior, Sir Hyde Parker). Further, the assassination of Paul by a court party in Russia tired of his insane freaks was very helpful, as his successor, Alexander I, was opposed to France. So 1801 finished with England triumphant in the Baltic and the Mediterranean, and even farther afield—for Ceylon and the Cape of Good Hope had been taken from the Dutch and Trinidad from the Spanish—but with France equally supreme on land. On both sides there were overtures for peace, and in March 1802 the Treaty of Amiens was signed. The most important terms were that England was to restore the Cape to the Dutch and Malta to the Knights of St. John, while retaining Ceylon and Trinidad, and in return France was to evacuate Rome and South Italy and restore Egypt to Turkey. So the treaty was made, and Bonaparte, now approved First Consul for Life by another overwhelming plebiscite, could devote his genius to the arts of peace.

Copenhagen, 1801 {.marginnote}

Treaty of Amiens, 1802 {.marginnote}

2. *From the Renewal of War to 1810*

Reasons for renewal of war {.marginnote}

Of its nature, however, the Peace of Amiens could be no more than a breathing space. In the first place it did not mention the question which was possibly of the greatest importance to England—the French occupation of the old Austrian Netherlands (the modern Belgium). In the second place it left both sides still deeply suspicious and without the real will to peace. France refused to give any greater freedom to English trade : English caricaturists refused to be kinder to Bonaparte. France was obviously planning an extension of her influence in the Near East, India, and the West Indies, and equally England would brook no important colonial rival. The atmosphere was all ready for the break, which came over the question of Malta. England determined to violate the treaty by holding on to Malta till Bonaparte stopped investigating the possibilities of reviving his power in Egypt ; Bonaparte determined to violate the treaty by holding on to

South Italy till England terminated her occupation of Malta. By 1803 the two rivals were at grips again, France being aided by Spain after the English seizure of some Spanish treasure ships destined as subsidy for France. The struggle, too, had become a more personal one with the more and more open dictatorship of Bonaparte in France ; by 1804, when he had become the Emperor Napoleon, the spirit of Revolution was becoming less and less prominent, and the ambition of one man rather than the burning zeal of a nation was to determine the remaining ten years of the conflict.

With the idea of a direct attack on England, Napoleon now marshalled an enormous force in camp at Boulogne. "The Channel," he said, "is a ditch which it needs but a little courage to cross." So an army of 100,000 men was held ready for the adventure, and some 1500 flat-bottomed ferry-boats constructed. But the scheme depended entirely on the absence of the British Fleet, for Napoleon's first idea of slipping across one dark or foggy night was obviously absurd when it was realized that, even after the harbour had been enlarged, five or six tides would be required to embark so great a body of men. Accordingly he directed his fleets to escape blockade, effect a junction with the Spanish, lure the English away from the Channel by a feint attack on the West Indies, race back across the Atlantic before the English realized the scheme, and secure an overwhelming predominance off Boulogne for the necessary period. Villeneuve, the French Admiral, was successful in the first part of the scheme—he escaped, according to plan, with the Spanish to the West Indies, drew Nelson there, duly gave him the slip, and set off back to Europe. But within three days Nelson had realized the manœuvre, had sent off a fast ship to race Villeneuve and warn the Admiralty, and had begun to follow in person with the Fleet. The British Admiralty, in fact, learnt of Villeneuve's return twelve days before Napoleon did—and he only got it once more from the English newspapers ! Moreover, the French fleet at Brest had not escaped blockade at all. Villeneuve, seeing his schemes tottering, obeyed his alternative orders and eventually put in to Cadiz, deeply pessimistic at the state of his fleet—"bad masts, bad sails, bad officers, and bad seamen —obsolete naval tactics : we only know one manœuvre, to

The projected invasion of England

form line, and that is just what the enemy wants us to do."
In a rage, Napoleon broke camp at Boulogne and prepared
to march instead against Austria. From the refuge at Cadiz,
where Collingwood had the nerve to begin blockading the
thirty-five French and Spanish ships with a total force of
three vessels, Villeneuve was moved to emerge by the taunts
of Napoleon. In October 1805 his thirty-three sail faced the

twenty-seven of Nelson and Collingwood off Cape Trafalgar,
and when the day finished 'the Nelson touch' (breaking the
enemy line in two and concentrating an overwhelming force
on one half of it at a time) had won its last and greatest
triumph. The French Navy was broken, and for the rest of
the war English sea power, supreme from the beginning of
hostilities, was to be quite unchallenged. England was safe
from invasion. The hapless Villeneuve committed suicide.

Meanwhile a Third Coalition, consisting of Russia, Austria,
and England, had been formed to combat the ever-increasing
designs of Napoleon. Speedily the men from the Boulogne
camp were marching to Central Europe as only the French
armies could march—Napoleon 'wore his long boots,' as they
put it. Before the year was out the great success of Trafalgar
had been offset by the surrender of a hopelessly outmanœuvred
Austrian army at Ulm, and by a crushing defeat of both

Austrians and Russians at Austerlitz. The news of this came
as a death-blow to Pitt, old and worn-out at forty-seven from
the strain of over ten years' warfare. Napoleon promptly
proceeded to take more territory from Austria, including
Venice and the Tyrol, abolish the Holy Roman Empire (which
had endured at least in name for a thousand years), and set
up a union of west German states known as the Confederation
of the Rhine, whose princes were sworn to carry out his orders
in matters of foreign policy.

The turn of Prussia came next. Prussia had delayed
joining the coalition until late, and her armies had not been
present at Austerlitz. A separate engagement was reserved

for their honour, and in 1806 the battlefield of Jena witnessed
the most crushing defeat ever inflicted on Prussian arms.
Then, in 1807, advancing to the East with the help of the

Poles, to whom again he appeared as 'the liberator,' Napoleon
encountered the Russians at Friedland and beat them so

severely that Alexander decided to reverse his whole policy and make peace. The Treaty of Tilsit, first broached by the two Emperors on a raft on the River Niemen, represents the height of Napoleon's power. By its terms Alexander recognized Napoleon's conquests on the Continent, in return for the promise of a free hand in Eastern Europe and a share in the Turkish Empire when it was to be annexed. More important still, he agreed, if England should refuse to give up her colonial conquests or her right of search, to join Napoleon's Continental System.

The Continental System is the basis of Napoleon's career from this point. After Trafalgar Napoleon had been driven to see that England could not be conquered by sea, and he therefore sought to use against her not a military or naval but an economic weapon—in other words, to strike a death-blow to her trade and wealth. It was a policy which the earlier Revolutionary governments had initiated, but which he was to systematize. For this purpose he issued from Berlin in 1806, after the Battle of Jena, and later from Milan a series of orders known as the Berlin and Milan Decrees, the effect of which was to forbid France or any of her allies or subject territory to accept British goods, which were to be confiscated whenever found. British ships were to be excluded from all ports, and by thus cutting off our means of export, while still allowing us to import certain French goods (i.e. allowing us to buy but not to sell), Napoleon hoped to rob us of our gold reserve, start a financial crisis, and bring England to bankruptcy. It followed that, if the scheme were to be successful, it would have to be applied practically all over Europe—hence his effort to make it really a 'Continental' System, applying as widely as possible. The importance of this move cannot be overestimated, as it meant that the whole of Europe must be controlled in order to beat England—Napoleon, in other words, was beginning to bite off rather a dangerous amount. Yet his capacity for chewing seemed unlimited ; by 1807 he had crowned himself King of Italy in the old Austrian dominions in the north ; made his brother Joseph King of Naples in the south ; made another brother, Louis, King of Holland, and a third, Jerome, King of Westphalia (formed from the Western lands of Prussia) ; while

Treaty of Tilsit, 1807

The Continental System

The Berlin and Milan Decrees 1806

from Eastern Prussian territory he had formed the Grand Duchy of Warsaw. Master of the Continent and secure in the new Russian alliance, he hoped that the exclusion of English goods would soon settle his last outstanding problem.

The Orders in Council, 1807

England's retaliation was swift and effective. By a series of Orders in Council of 1807 and later, all countries which accepted Napoleon's orders were declared to be in a state of blockade, and any port excluding British vessels was to be deprived of the opportunity of welcoming those of other nations. England thus aimed at starving the Continent of alternative sources of supply, causing rising prices and hardship in each country, and therefore discontent against Napoleon, who had started the whole business. The absence of any French navy worth mentioning made the English blockade practicable ; and when the British Government heard that Napoleon was planning to seize the Danish navy, it took prompt if lawless action, ordered the Danes to hand over their fleet to English keeping till the end of the war, and

Capture of Danish fleet, 1807

on their refusal bombarded Copenhagen till the vessels were duly surrendered. The last naval competitor being thus removed, England could carry out her Orders in Council effectively, and the grim trade war began to stifle the commerce of Europe.

The Peninsular War

The first country to revolt against the system was Portugal, which had long carried on a very profitable trade with England. Napoleon used the occasion typically, collecting five French armies on Spanish soil for the advance on Portugal, then, when this was conquered, bullying the Spanish royal family into resigning their throne to his brother Joseph. But the move was fatal. His doctrines of liberty made no impression on the extremely backward and intensely Catholic Spaniards. Encouraged by their priests, they firmly resolved not to accept the rule of the man who, by 1809, had caused the Pope to be kidnapped and the Papal States to be incorporated in France. Moreover, the hostility of the Peninsula to Napoleon supplied England with the base for her army she was looking for—a highly important development. With the battle of Vimiero in 1808 fortune began to desert the French in the Peninsula. For the moment Napoleon restored matters by coming from Central Europe to take charge himself, but the English under Sir John Moore staged a desperate hit-and-run attack, ending in a hurried embarkation at Corunna, and this diverted the Emperor from overrunning the whole country. As soon as he was gone the tide turned again. At Torres Vedras the future Duke of Wellington, after devastating the country in front to rob it of supplies and cover, constructed an elaborate series of defensive earthworks, which were so strong that even Marshal Ney, 'the bravest of the brave,' refused to attack them. From these defences Wellington could emerge and support the peasantry in their ceaseless guerilla warfare against the French—a warfare so intense and so savagely cruel on both sides that prisoners who were merely shot or blinded thought themselves lucky. One captured French general was thrown into a vat of scalding water. Like previous invaders the French found the eternal difficulty of fighting in mountainous, communicationless Spain—where 'a small army is beaten and a large army starves.' Nowhere else had they operated in a barren country and amid a fanatically hostile population. French commanders in different parts of Spain learnt of each other's movements only from Napoleon in Austria, who got it as usual from the English newspapers, while a force of two hundred cavalrymen was necessary to get a message from one village to another, as a lesser number would be murdered by peasants. Slowly Wellington grew stronger and prepared to advance. The first cracks were appearing in Napoleon's great edifice.

Elsewhere, however, the system as yet remained intact. In 1809 England despatched an expedition to Walcheren to free Holland, but it did not even succeed in fighting, let alone winning, a battle. Lingering under inefficient commanders it fell a victim to the swamps and fevers of the island, and perished miserably. Austria, too, tempted to try conclusions once more by French failures in Spain, found Napoleon still far too strong at the battle of Wagram, lost even more territory, and had to promise to adhere to the Continental System. Moreover, she was forced to supply Napoleon with an alliance and a new wife, the Princess Marie Louise, for Josephine had proved incapable of providing the Emperor with an heir and was therefore conveniently divorced. So by 1810, with opposition again crushed in Europe, with

Retreat to Corunna

Torres Vedras

Europe in 1810

The Walcheren expedition

Wagram

The Austrian Alliance

Sweden compelled to adhere to the Continental System and Holland now completely incorporated in the French Empire following Louis Bonaparte's unwillingness to apply the System rigorously, Napoleon might hope that his mastery of Europe was secure and that the last remaining problems of England and the Peninsula would soon be cleared up.

3. From 1810 to Waterloo

The Moscow campaign, 1812

Napoleon's hopes of 1810 were not to be realized. The Continental System rapidly made him more and more unpopular as trade stagnated, as tea and coffee and sugar and tobacco became unobtainable or enormously expensive, as ships were laid up and firms closed down. The conscription and taxes he applied to his dependent allies or conquests made matters worse, and completely failed to compensate for all the improvements in other directions that his Government had made. In 1811 came the revolt which was to prove the beginning of the end. The Czar, tired of doing without English and overseas goods, annoyed at the annexation of a relative's territory (Oldenberg), slighted by Napoleon's marriage with an Austrian rather than a Russian princess, and dissatisfied at Napoleon's failure to help him in his Eastern ambitions, broke away from the Continental System. The result was the most tremendous military disaster in history —the Moscow campaign. In 1812, with an overwhelming army of 610,000 men, forced from almost every country in Europe, Napoleon crossed the river Niemen into Russia to teach Alexander his lesson. Before such a force the Russians could only retreat, and as they retreated they devastated the country of supplies and shelter. The vast army could not be fed ; death and desertion carried off thousands, so that long before the cold set in two-thirds had disappeared. Napoleon struggled on to Moscow, hoping that its capture would end not only the war but all the difficulties of supply. Outside the capital was fought the greatest battle of the campaign— Borodino—which the French won at the cost of 30,000 horses and 50,000 men, with the dead left seven or eight deep on the field of conflict. Moscow was in their grasp—only for them to find their longed-for haven turned into a raging inferno when

Alexander breaks from Continental System

Borodino

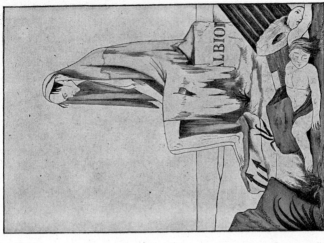

Before.

[*Photo, Bulloz.*]

After.

Historically, England, though severely troubled, was not as worried as all this by the Continental System.

the Russians fired the city rather than let it fall a prey to their opponents.   There was nothing for the French to do but turn back—and, since Russian armies blocked other routes, to retreat over the desolate line of the advance.   The dreadful sight—and sounds—of Borodino had to be encountered again, but one man at least was not sickened : "the most beautiful battlefield I have ever seen in my life," remarked Napoleon. By November the cold had come to complete the catastrophe. As they struggled on, with Ney in the rear heroically fighting a battle a day against the ever-harassing Russian forces, the Emperor realized that his presence was essential in Paris if he was to rebuild the shattered military strength of his Empire. As before in Egypt, he left his forces to escape as best they could and hastened ahead back to Europe.   By December there were 60 degrees of frost.   Finally, of the 610,000 who started on the great campaign, a tattered, starving, disorganized, delirious, and shell-shocked remnant of 20,000 recrossed the Niemen. Not more than a thousand were of any further military use. The largest army in history had been completely wiped out.

The retreat from Moscow

The tide of disaster did not stop at that point.   Encouraged by the shattering blow to the French in Russia, Prussia and soon Austria were again at grips with the old enemy, thus forming with England and Russia the Fourth Coalition. Prussia since Jena had witnessed a remarkable revival of national spirit and efficiency.   Although allowed by Napoleon to have an army of only 42,000 men, the Prussians had adopted a system of short service, and thus had a reserve of about 120,000 strong within three years.   The Prussian War Minister, Scharnhorst, had also revised methods of arms, training, and tactics, had secured the introduction of universal liability to serve and the abolition of degrading punishments, such as flogging, and had thus completely reorganized the Prussian military forces.   Moreover, Prussia had been fortunate in two statesmen, Stein and Hardenberg, who transformed in five years a practically mediæval into a modern state.   Stein had secured the emancipation of the serfs, thus allowing them liberty to leave their ancestral soil and work for wages anywhere they pleased ; had broken down restrictions by which certain land was only for nobles, certain trades only for

The Fourth Coalition, 1813, and the Revival of Prussia

Scharnhorst, Stein, and Hardenberg

burgesses ; had abolished the monopolies of the old gilds ; had given a measure of municipal self-government by allowing the craftsmen and landowners in each town to elect a council ; and had set up a new Ministry of State which had been lacking before, competent to deal with not one but all the various provinces combined in the Kingdom of Prussia. Hardenberg's most famous land law had given the peasants two-thirds of their former land as freehold, the other one-third going to their lords in place of services owed. New patriotic literature had appeared, education was being reformed, universities had been founded at Berlin and Breslau. Prussia at last felt itself not only united in desiring to overthrow Napoleon but competent to do it. So began 'The War of Liberation.'

By a miracle of organization Napoleon within three months of the Russian campaign had a new army of a quarter of a million in the field. But he had enormous odds to face, including yet another powerful opponent, Sweden, whose ruler, Bernadotte, though one of Napoleon's marshals, declared he was "not going to be one of the Emperor's customs officials." Bernadotte, having thus refused to apply the Continental System, was tempted to join the Allies by the promise of being given Norway. Against the Prussian forces Napoleon won three battles, including the big victory of Dresden, but he was becoming less superhumanly active and he missed an opportunity of following up the retreat. Finally numbers triumphed after the Prussians, Austrians, Russians, and Swedes had managed to join up their armies, and at the battle of Leipzig, 1813 (sometimes known as the 'Battle of the Nations'), the French forces were overwhelmed. Rapidly they retreated across Germany with the Allied forces in pursuit. Rejecting a very generous peace offer which would have given France her 'natural frontiers' and thus left her with the Rhineland and Belgium, Napoleon laid himself open to the inevitable—an invasion of France. At the same time in Spain Wellington had at last succeeded in capturing Madrid and expelling Joseph after the battle of Vittoria, and was pushing the French forces back towards the Pyrenees, so that the English were invading France from the south while the Allies operated from the east.

The War of Liberation

Leipzig, 1813

Vittoria

3*

The invasion of France

On the sacred soil of France itself, in spite of the fact that the army, the marshals, and the country were longing for peace, Napoleon put up a brilliant fight against overwhelming odds. With armies which included youngsters ignorant even of the way to load a rifle, he actually won four victories before Blücher, the Prussian commander, wisely decided to give up chasing such a military genius and marched straight on Paris. With the capital at the mercy of the Allies, the marshals compelled him first to accept terms and then to abdicate.

Treaty of Fontaine-bleau, 1814

By the treaty of Fontainebleau he gave up the throne, but was allowed the title of Emperor, an income of about £200,000, and the little isle of Elba as his kingdom. The Bourbons were restored in the person of the brother of the executed Louis XVI, who took the title of Louis XVIII, and promised

First Treaty of Paris

to rule by the terms of a Charter which guaranteed a Parliament and a constitution. By the First Treaty of Paris France was restored to her 1792 boundaries, which still gave her half a million more inhabitants than in 1790, although she lost all her great conquests, such as Belgium and Holland, Italy and Germany. She had no indemnity to pay and she kept most of her stolen works of art. All other questions were to be referred to a European congress, which soon met at Vienna. From November 1814 to February 1815 the Allies thrashed out the thousand questions that arise at the end of a war, and were just on the point of falling out irretrievably over the division of the spoils when the staggering news was announced that Napoleon had escaped from Elba and landed in South France.

The Hundred Days, 1815

Of all the episodes in the career of Napoleon none is more remarkable than 'The Hundred Days' of his liberty between the exile of Elba and the exile of St. Helena. He landed with only a few hundred soldiers in a country which less than a year before had been heartily glad to see the back of him. Louis XVIII instantly despatched forces to capture him, Marshal Ney vowing that he ought to be "brought back in a cage." But the magnetism of his personality, the memory of campaigns shared in common, the shabby treatment of the army by the restored Bourbon government, the fear of the peasants that the government was about to confiscate the lands they had secured at the beginning of the Revolution, all led to a very different result. The tactics of Napoleon helped too, for he promised peace and a parliament ; he also exhibited his considerable talent for falsehood when he informed the first troops sent to capture him that he had been summoned to Paris by the Allies. So the soldiers, including Ney, simply fell in behind him and helped him to continue his march to Paris. Ere long Louis XVIII was in flight, while the French newspapers underwent a rapid change of tone— 'the scoundrel Bonaparte' becoming first 'Napoleon,' then finally 'our great and beloved Emperor.' Three weeks sufficed for him to establish himself again as master of France. Sure of the hostility of the Allies, he determined to take the offensive, and marched into Belgium to strike at the English and Dutch under Wellington and the Prussians under Blücher, before they could be joined by the Austrians and the Russians. Supreme again in France

The campaign of Waterloo consisted of three main battles. As Napoleon had only half the forces of his opponents he sought to engage them separately. On June 16th he defeated the Prussians at Ligny, but fatally neglected to follow up the victory. The same day he challenged Wellington at Quatre Bras, imagining the Prussians to be in flight. On June 18th at Waterloo Wellington knew that the Prussians had retired in good order and would probably succeed in joining him during the day. He therefore stood his ground, while Napoleon confident that his opponent was 'a bad general' commanding 'bad troops,' flung his men recklessly against Wellington's. But the attacks of the French columns, for all their dash, could not penetrate the thin British lines whose rifle fire was so deadly, and when Blücher appeared in the late afternoon Napoleon's fate was sealed. In France the parliament demanded his abdication on his return from the campaign, and resisting the temptation to start a civil war for his own throne, he gave in, and surrendered to the English as the "most generous of his enemies." The compliment, however, cut no ice, and he was banished to the inaccessible island of St. Helena, in the South Atlantic. Six years later he died, after interminably discussing and arranging the history of his career to present it to the best advantage. Europe would never Waterloo, 1815 The end again be troubled by his brilliant talents, his restless energy, his inflexible will, and his complete lack of moral sense. With an eye, as ever, to the best effect on public opinion, he directed in his will that his ashes should rest "by the banks of the Seine, in the midst of the French people, whom I have loved so much." And this was the man, who, in 1814, had remarked that he "cared little for the lives of a million men" !

Reasons for Napoleon's success and failure

It is instructive to consider the causes of the extraordinary success and of the equally tremendous failure of Napoleon. In the first place it must be realized that he was a general of unparalleled brilliance. Wellington said that "his presence in the field was worth a difference of 40,000 men." But as the years went on a certain decline showed itself, not in his talents, but rather in his energy—still tremendous enough, but not quite so superhuman as before. At Ligny, for example, the neglected pursuit of the Prussians made a vital difference. Even more important is the fact that as the scale of the war grew, as hundreds of thousands instead of tens of thousands became involved, so it inevitably followed that his marshals rather than himself must direct a greater proportion of the army. And though the marshals were mostly young and talented and brave, they had not Napoleon's genius, and they quarrelled among themselves—in Spain, for example, they refused to help each other's armies, and in Russia one even tried to murder another. When ex-Marshal Bernadotte, King of Sweden, deserted Napoleon in 1813 the simple advice he gave to his new allies was "When you face the marshals, attack ; when you face Napoleon, retreat." But while military reasons were, of course, vital in causing both Napoleon's rise and his downfall, another set of reasons is equally important. It must never be forgotten that in his early days Napoleon was practically carrying the French Revolution to downtrodden populations eager to welcome it. To Italians ruled by Austrians, to Poles ruled by Russians, to Germans longing for some larger state than the hundreds of petty princedoms in Germany, to all dissatisfied with the absolute rule of their monarch, Napoleon appeared as a kind of saviour. Even in England Napoleon always relied on being supported by a popular uprising should he land. In other words, his rise was inspired by the two enormously

Military talents

Increasing scope of war

National and demo-cratic feel-ing—at first with Napoleon, later against him

[Photo, Mansell. Philippoteaux Pinxit.

Napoleon as a young artillery officer in 1792.

Degeneration

[Photo, Hachette.

Napoleon in exile at St. Helena.

powerful forces whose history is the history of the 19th century
—the forces of democracy and nationalism. Yet, strangely
enough, it was also precisely these two forces which caused
his downfall. While he fought against governments he was
consistently successful ; but when he fought against peoples
he began to fail. The Germans, for example, turned against
him wholeheartedly after 1806, when his rule had proved to
give them little freedom. The Italians, the Swiss, the Dutch
were all over-taxed. In Russia and Spain the French
revolutionary doctrines made no impression at all on very
backward peoples, and here he was faced with disaster right
from the beginning. Further, after his introduction of the
Continental System, the middle and lower classes in every
country felt the effect of his rule in high prices and strict
customs rules and declining trade. Everywhere the tide of
sentiment turned against Napoleon, and he was defeated by
the hostility of those whose good will had enabled him earlier
to triumph. Finally, it is obvious that Napoleon, in his
increasing pride and self-confidence and in his determination
to beat England, simply took on too much. To beat England
he introduced the Continental System : to maintain that
system he had to control the whole of Europe. It was a task
beyond the power of any one man or any one nation, even
when the man was Napoleon and the nation the French.
Even if he had crushed all Europe utterly, he would have gone
on to the Turkish Empire, to India, to the Americas. A
restless demon of energy drove him on—a demon he himself
was aware of when he loved to picture himself as the Man of
Destiny, driven on by Fate. His schemes were all too big ;
he simply could not last. If it had not been Waterloo, it
would have been another battle a little later.

*The
Continental
System*

4. *Napoleon's Achievements in France*

*Local
government*

It remains to consider the work of Napoleon in the domain
of peace, and here at least he achieved something of permanence. As a general his enormous military talents all
came to naught in the end because he took on too much ; as
a statesman he gave to France institutions which in different
forms have endured to this day. His empire, of course,

perished with him, but his plan of local government—a sphere in which the early revolutionaries had failed disastrously—became the basis of the modern French system. He retained the division into Départements, and created a new sub-division, the Arrondissement, to replace the District (which had been abolished by the Convention). The details of the divisions and sub-divisions, however, were unimportant compared with the fact that under Napoleon's scheme the leading official in each of them was appointed, directly or indirectly, by the central government. Local councils continued to be elected, but their powers became largely advisory : the real business of local administration was done by officials who represented, and owed their positions to, the central government—namely, the Prefect in the Département, the sub-Prefect in the Arrondissement, and the Mayor in the Commune. Thus control over the provinces, lost in 1789-91 and successively re-asserted by every government since then in more vigorous form, was now re-established on a permanent footing. From this achievement of Napoleon's, Frenchmen, of course, got very little effective share in the business of governing their own localities ; but they got excellently chosen officials, good order, and the possibility of a strong and unified national policy.

In the realm of education, too, Napoleon's government was responsible for some important reorganization. Elementary education was badly neglected, but secondary education was encouraged by the foundation of secondary schools (to be run by the Communes) and *lycées*, or semi-military secondary schools (to be run by the government). Science and mathematics held important places in these, second only to military training ; at Eton, at the same period, it must be remembered, the main idea was still to flog Greek and Latin into the hapless pupil. A university, too, was founded—not one in any special place, but the University of France—consisting of seventeen Academies in different districts, forming local centres. **Education**

Another innovation of Napoleon's well illustrates his mentality. As a clever man who had himself risen solely by virtue of his abilities, he was determined that the great state positions should be open to all men of talent, irrespective of birth. Accordingly, while he allowed the *émigrés* to return, he no longer permitted them to consider themselves the true **The Legion of Honour** nobility of France ; instead he created a kind of nobility of intellect by means of a new foundation, the Legion of Honour. There were various grades in the Legion, awarded for services in such matters as politics, civil service, local government, art, music, literature : and to this day the little red ribbon in the buttonhole of the Legionary is to the Frenchman a cherished, if cheapened, honour. "Men," Napoleon said, "are led by toys."

The Concordat

In religious affairs, too, Napoleon, for all his irreligious nature, left a mark on the destiny of France. During the Revolution the extremists had severed France from the Catholic Church, and though the worship of the fancy religions then introduced, such as the Goddess of Reason or the Supreme Being, had passed rapidly, France was not yet part of the Catholic system again. Nevertheless the overwhelming majority of her peasants were Catholic at heart, even if the intellectuals were not. Napoleon, anxious to secure his régime by winning the favour of the peasants and at the same time to pacify the religious strife in the west of France, determined to come to an agreement with the Church. Accordingly in 1801 he made a Concordat with the Pope by which Catholicism again became the religion of France, though other religions were not forbidden. But he drove a hard bargain—the State was to choose bishops, control the Church, and pay the clergy, and above all the Church lands lost at the Revolution were to remain in their present hands. Thus the peasants were won over to Napoleon not only because he restored their religion but because he confirmed them in the gains of the Revolution. The Concordat, of course, did not please everyone—one of his marshals, for instance, was overheard to remark : "The only thing lacking at this ceremony is the million dead men who died to get rid of this nonsense." Napoleon, however, knew he was building on firm ground in appealing to the old religious instincts : he saw in religion what he called "the cement of the social order"—something useful in binding men together, in keeping them satisfied and quiet, something that young ladies were to study particularly, to make them meek and obedient wives. Religion was, in other words, for Napoleon a mere instrument. The true depth of his Catholic devoutness may be gauged by the way he later annexed the Papal States and caused violent hands to be laid on the Pope. Nevertheless, in the Concordat he built soundly for France at the time.

Mention must also be made of Napoleon's work for the industry and commerce of France. Commercial exchanges and chambers of commerce were created, and advisory boards set up in connection with many manufactures, arts, and crafts. By a system of high protective tariffs French industries were sheltered from foreign competition ; technical schools, prizes, loans, and exhibitions encouraged new processes ; and France, deprived of certain staple articles by the Continental System, managed to develop effective substitute foodstuffs in the form of chicory for coffee and beet for cane-sugar. New cotton machines were invented and factory acts passed. Further, by maintaining a stable currency based on gold, instead of the old unreliable revolutionary finance, Napoleon won to his support all the business interests. In this direction the creation of the Bank of France was a step of great importance. In fact, by an elaborate series of decrees Napoleon regulated almost the whole of the national life—art, theatre, press, commerce, industry, religion. The defect in it all was that the high tariffs inflicted great hardship on many consumers in the form of increased prices, and that regulation of industry can hinder as well as aid its development. Industry and commerce

Nevertheless, whatever can be said in criticism of his general financial and commercial policy, Napoleon's great schemes of public works have permanently beautified and enriched France. Canals, bridges, and roads gave France an infinitely finer system of communication. Museums were founded and the Louvre was completed and filled with the priceless treasures stolen from Italy. Palaces like Fontainebleau were restored. The planning of a great group of arterial roads radiating from the Arc de Triomphe and the clearing of the Tuileries Gardens gave Paris the start of its modern beauty. Everywhere the Napoleonic influence was felt. It is, in fact, little wonder that he was immensely popular with the French up to about 1808—until, in other words, his plans grew too vast, he began to lose, and he cost France too much in men and money. Public works

The Code Napoléon   Napoleon's greatest achievement in peace, however, was the Civil Code or Code Napoléon—a summary of the laws of France on such topics as rights and duties, marriage, divorce, parentage, and inheritance, and a statement of the general principles which should govern these matters. After the old tangle of Frankish, Roman, Royal, Provincial, and Baronial laws, it was crystal clear. The Code was, of course, not entirely the work of Napoleon ; the decision to compile one had been taken before he came into power, but he attended regularly the meetings of the committee who framed it and exercised a decisive influence on its development. Other codes on commerce and criminal law followed, but the first was recognized to be outstanding in merit and was soon widely adopted by different states in Europe and in South America. Thus Napoleon gave one of the main bulwarks of domestic peace—a great legal system—not only to France but to the world.

In brief and to sum up the whole significance of the career of Napoleon—he gave to France institutions and the social benefits of the Revolution ; to Europe a taste of modern government and such a stir that the vast force of nationality was aroused ; to the world one of the most appalling examples in history of colossal talents unrestrained by religion or morality.

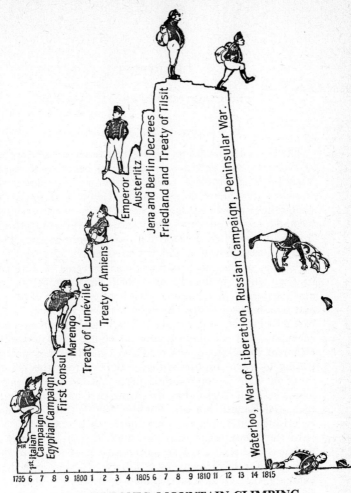

1st. Italian Campaign
Egyptian Campaign
First Consul
Marengo
Treaty of Lunéville
Treaty of Amiens
Emperor
Austerlitz
Jena and Berlin Decrees
Friedland and Treaty of Tilsit
Waterloo, War of Liberation, Russian Campaign, Peninsular War.

1795 6 7 8 9 1800 1 2 3 4 1805 6 7 8 9 1810 11 12 13 14 1815

NAPOLEONIC MOUNTAIN-CLIMBING.

CHAPTER IV

The Congress System, 1815-1830.

1. *The Arrangements at Vienna, 1815*

The European Coalition, having finally disposed of Napoleon at Waterloo, was now free to resume its peace conference at Vienna. The problem which confronted the Allies was twofold : first, how to reward the victors and punish the vanquished without setting all at each other's throats ; and secondly, how to prevent a recurrence of the great catastrophe that had convulsed Europe for over twenty years. These weighty tasks, however, did not prevent the Congress from being one of the most sparkling social events in European history, where brilliantly uniformed kings, emperors, and ambassadors gave attention to the lighter pursuits of dancing and love-making in the intervals between the more serious business of spying and intrigue. The bills for hospitality were enormous, and cost the Emperor a fortune. The only entertainment for which guests paid was provided, it is not surprising to learn, by Sir Sydney Smith. From the political point of view the outstanding personalities of the Congress were the Czar Alexander, the Austrian Chancellor Metternich, the English Foreign Minister Castlereagh, and, more surprisingly, the French representative, Talleyrand.

In the matter of sharing the spoils certain arrangements had already been agreed on by the treaties of 1814, but there was grave disagreement over others. It was agreed, for example, that Louis XVIII should be restored to the French throne, on condition he ruled by a Charter which guaranteed a parliament, and that France should pay an indemnity and suffer an army of occupation for a few years. Prussia, however, wanted Alsace and Lorraine, which were inhabited largely by German-speaking peoples, and which had been absorbed into the French kingdom just over a century before.

To this demand England and Russia opposed a united front, holding that such hard terms would discredit the new French king in the eyes of his people and make his overthrow certain. In this attitude they were, of course, encouraged by Talleyrand, who pleaded that Europe had been fighting Napoleon, not France, and that only Napoleon, and not the country, deserved punishment.   Prussia at last had to give up her claim, though she received certain nearby territories which had been included in Napoleon's Confederation of the Rhine, thereby gaining a Rhine frontier.   This, by making Prussia the guardian of German interests, was to make of France her permanent enemy.

Alexander of Russia, whose unstable mind was at this period in a highly religious and fairly liberal phase, wanted to restore the Kingdom of Poland, which had been annexed in the previous century by Prussia, Russia, and Austria.   He planned to give it a constitution and a parliament, but to retain the kingship himself.   This idea, of course, was impossible if Prussia retained her very important portion, which included the capital, Warsaw.   Therefore Prussia had to be bribed out of some of Poland.   To do this the major powers decided to victimize one of the last two small states to remain faithful to Napoleon—and Prussia was accordingly presented with about half of the Kingdom of Saxony.   Then Russia had conquered Finland from Sweden in an earlier part of the war, and naturally wanted to keep it.   But Sweden had been very useful in the closing stages of the war to the Allies, and therefore must have compensation—where was she to get it ? The solution was the victimization of the second small ally of Napoleon, Denmark, who was made to give up Norway to Sweden.

Or again, what was Austria to get ?   The answer was most of North Italy and large sections of the Illyrian coast, as here there were no powerful European monarchs to speak for themselves : "republics," Alexander remarked when Venice and Genoa protested at the loss of their independence, "are no longer fashionable."   This, too, was to act as compensation to Austria for the surrender of her claim to her old Netherlands, Belgium, which was now forcibly united with Holland to form a larger barrier-state on the boundaries of France.

The incorporation of Belgium in Holland was supposed, too, to compensate the Dutch for the loss of the Cape of Good Hope to the English, who also kept Heligoland, Malta, the Ionian Islands, Ceylon, and part of the West Indies.

In Germany Napoleon's Confederation of the Rhine was of course abolished, but the old Holy Roman Empire was not set up again ; instead, a loose conglomeration of thirty-nine states known as the German Confederation took its place. Everywhere, in fact, Napoleon's changes were cancelled ; and rotting thrones he had pushed down were propped up again in South Italy and Spain. The royal connections of the Spanish Bourbons and the Austrian Hapsburgs reappeared in all their glory—united in their hatred of parliaments, united in their colossal incompetence, divergent only in that the Spanish Bourbons had hearts which were cruelly hard, whereas the Austrian Hapsburgs merely had heads which were painfully soft.

The weak-nesses of the settle-ment   Thus the map of Europe was redrawn, and the weak points in the draughtsmanship are easy enough to see—the Congress took no notice of the very fact which had caused the overthrow of Napoleon, the factor of nationality : nations and peoples were bandied about as though they were goods, to supply 'compensation' here or constitute a 'barrier state' there. Norwegians, Belgians, Boers, Finns, Italians, Serbs, Poles were placed under foreign governments they intensely disliked. Very little was done to satisfy the desires of the Poles and the Germans, awakened by Napoleon's work, for large and power-ful states to represent their nationality. Nothing at all was done for the Italians. Wars were simply bound to occur to upset the treaty ; one by one in the 19th century its provisions were cancelled, and nearly always by force. In this respect the Treaty of Versailles in 1919 after the First World War tried to learn a lesson from the mistakes of Vienna, and gave far greater attention to national demands by setting up a host of new states, such as Czecho-Slovakia, Poland, Jugo-Slavia.

The Quadruple Alliance and the Congress System   The second object of the Congress, the prevention of any such outbreak in future, was thus rendered impossible at the start by bad treaty provisions. But the Congress, of course, did not realize this at the time, and the powers agreed to a system which was a novelty in European politics. By a

Quadruple Alliance Russia, Austria, Prussia, and England agreed not only to ally if necessary in defence of the Vienna Settlement, but to meet in future congresses to discuss problems as occasion arose.   There is thus in this the germs of a League of Nations idea, except that it was confined to the four great powers, and thus gave itself a dictatorial atmosphere at the very beginning.   The idea was particularly Castlereagh's, though he was later to disapprove of the developments the Alliance underwent.

Sometimes confused with this practical attempt to lessen the conflicts of the great powers is another alliance, the Holy Alliance.   This was not a military alliance, but a league of sovereigns who promised to rule on Christian principles, acting as fathers to their peoples and brothers to each other. It was the creation of the religious and well-meaning Alexander, and had no effect worth mentioning.   Castlereagh disapproved of it, terming it a "piece of sublime mysticism and nonsense."   Even Metternich called it "a loud-sounding nothing" and said that "the Czar's mind was quite clearly affected," but, though no one except Alexander took it seriously, every sovereign in Europe signed it, with the exception of the Sultan (who, not being a Christian, had not been invited), the Prince Regent, and the Pope !   It was one of those amiable gestures of good will, like the Kellogg Peace Pact of 1928 'outlawing' war, which people sign because they really sympathize with its objects and because they know that there is no particular provision for carrying them out when they prove inconvenient.   The confusion with the Quadruple Alliance has arisen because Liberals in Europe, finding the adjective 'holy' in connection with Metternich too rich to forget, insisted on referring to the Russia-Austria-Prussia group as the 'Holy' Alliance.

The Holy Alliance

Thus, in intention, both the Quadruple Alliance and the Holy Alliance were instruments to preserve the peace and an atmosphere of brotherhood.   When criticism is directed against the effects of the Congress, it should be remembered that it was, in fact, a quite original attempt to improve the lot of mankind.   Unfortunately, however, the problem of peace is a thorny one.   In the absence of international government, peace implies keeping territories and governments

Defects of the Alliance

arranged as they are, except in the rare cases when both parties to a dispute can agree on a peaceful alteration. But when one side feels genuine injustice and the other refuses to remedy the grievance ? The Italians in Lombardy, for instance, might have appealed peacefully for a century to the Austrians to clear out and nothing come of it. In that case it is possible that keeping the peace will perpetuate what one side passionately feels to be a wrong. This was the problem with the Vienna settlements ; everywhere there were outraged nationalities longing either to throw off their rulers or else to claim a constitution and a parliament. But everywhere the Quadruple Alliance was anxious to keep the peace. Thus it is not difficult to see what the Alliance, so good in intention, developed into. Directed by men who had spent their whole lives in fighting the French Revolution and its heir, Napoleon, it was inevitable that the Alliance should regard extreme nationalism and democracy of the French kind as wicked delusions which had plunged Europe into untold bloodshed. So the Alliance became, in effect, a kind of trade union of Kings in Possession to stop the possibility of Peoples in Possession. As this aspect of it came more to the fore it incurred the hatred of Liberals all over Europe, and the English support of it grew more and more lukewarm. The guiding spirit became, not Castlereagh, with his practical common sense, nor Alexander, with his religious enthusiasm, but the supreme anti-Liberal, Metternich. Metternich knew—or thought he knew—that the first breath of democracy and nationalism would blow the ramshackle Austrian Empire to the ground, for in it lived Germans, Poles, Czechs, Croats, Slovaks, Ruthenes, Magyars, Serbs, and Italians, all more or less restrained by Vienna. And it was Metternich who had declared that democracy could only "change daylight into darkest night," and who had attacked the ideas of the French Revolution as "the disease which must be cured, the volcano which must be extinguished, the gangrene which must be burned out with the hot iron, the hydra with jaws open to swallow up the social order."

2. *The Later Congresses*

As yet, however, in 1815, this side of the Quadruple Congress of Aix-la-Chapelle, 1818 Alliance was not uppermost. The first problem which the Allies had to tackle was the position of France. France was proving punctual in the discharge of her obligations, but was naturally resenting the army of occupation. Accordingly in 1818 a Congress of the four powers met at Aix-la-Chapelle, and there it was unanimously agreed to withdraw the army of occupation and to invite France to co-operate in future congresses. The Alliance thus wisely prevented France becoming a permanent enemy of Europe ; it can hardly be claimed that the Allies of 1918 treated Germany in so statesmanlike a fashion. In other respects, too, the Congress was a great success. Agreement was reached on the protection of Jews in Europe, on Swedish debts to Denmark, on the treatment of Bonaparte on St. Helena, on the old matter of the English claim to a Channel salute. Significantly, however, the powers could not agree on a joint expedition to punish the notorious Barbary pirates, because of fear of Russian vessels in the Mediterranean. Above all, in one highly important matter there was considerable disagreement before Russia and Prussia gave way. These two powers wanted the Quadruple Alliance to guarantee not only all the frontiers established at Vienna, but all the *governments*—in other words, it would be the Alliance's duty to intervene whenever there was a successful revolution in any country in Europe. Prussia even wanted an international army under Wellington to be kept at Brussels for this purpose. Castlereagh, however, managed to secure an agreement limiting promised intervention to the case of France, if she should again undergo a revolution which obviously threatened the peace of Europe. His argument was masterly — "nothing would be more immoral . . . than the idea that . . . force was collectively to be prostituted to the support of established power without any consideration of the extent to which it was abused." Till there was a system of perfect justice everywhere, he maintained, it would be wrong to guarantee all existing governments.

In opposing the Russian and Prussian plan he was doubly

spurred on by his government at home, now coming under the influence of Canning, and anxious to limit Britain's promises and commitments on the Continent as much as possible, for fear of being involved in future wars which were not our concern.   So Castlereagh's view of the limited Alliance triumphed—for the moment.   The Congress broke up, after having agreed to meet again whenever circumstances demanded.   It is worth remembering that the Congress of Aix-la-Chapelle was the first conference of the European powers ever to be held except to make a peace treaty at the end of a war.   The Congress system in 1818 thus, as Castlereagh said, appeared to be "a new discovery in the European government, at once extinguishing the cobwebs with which diplomacy obscures the horizon, bringing the whole bearing of the system into its true light, and giving to the counsels of the Great Powers the efficiency and almost the simplicity of a single State."

Unrest in Europe

Unfortunately any hopes that Europe had suddenly discovered the way to govern itself peaceably were soon dashed to the ground.   By 1820 there was a rising tide of protest against established governments and the spirit and arrangements of Vienna.   In Spain a revolution against the restored Bourbons forced the king to grant a very democratic constitution drawn up in a previous revolt of 1812.   A similar revolution followed in Portugal ; while on the other side of the Atlantic the Spanish colonies, which had thrown off the rule of Spain during the war, still refused to acknowledge the rights of their mother country over them.   In Italy there was restlessness everywhere, fomented by the Carbonari, a secret society aiming at democracy and the expulsion of foreign rulers.   1820 saw two revolutions on Italian soil—the Spanish King of Naples being also compelled to adopt the 1812 constitution and the King of Piedmont having to grant a measure of democracy.   In Germany university students agitated for German union and a constitution, and a leader of the opposition to these ideas, Kotzebue, an anti-Liberal writer and a secret Russian spy, was assassinated.   In England there were riots at Spa Fields, brutal acts of repression like the Peterloo Massacre, and even a plot to murder the whole Cabinet.   Accordingly Metternich and with him the Czar, now alarmed at the spread of such movements and won over from his earlier Liberalism, demanded a new Congress where measures might be concerted against such violence.

The Congress of Troppau thus met in 1820 to consider these and kindred problems. Castlereagh knew from the start that the objects of Metternich and the Czar were to use the Alliance to interfere to put down the revolutions in Naples, Piedmont, and Spain, and perhaps even restore to the latter country her revolted South American colonies. But while he too detested revolutionary movements, he was not prepared to see England associated with the other two powers in such wholesale revolution-breaking. His reasons were threefold— partly that there had existed genuine grievances in Naples and Spain ; partly that the Opposition in Parliament would be very embarrassing on the matter ; but principally that internal affairs of other countries were no business of England's where they did not directly interfere with her interests. England thus refused to join in the declarations of the other three powers concerning their right to interfere to suppress revolutions—indeed, Castlereagh even declined to participate in the Congress, sending instead of a participating repre- sentative only an 'observer.' The direct result of this Con- gress, and of its sequel at Laibach in 1821, was thus not only the suppression of the Naples and Piedmont constitu- tions by the use of Austrian troops, but the beginning of a split in the Alliance which was to widen fatally in the next few years.

The Congress of Troppau, 1820

Interven- tion in Italy

By 1821 the situation had been still further complicated by a revolt of the Greeks against their Turkish rulers. The Greeks undoubtedly relied on the aid of their co-religionists, the Russians, who anyway were notoriously anxious to break up the Turkish Empire and extend their influence south to the Mediterranean. England and Austria, on the other hand, were equally anxious to uphold Turkey as a bulwark against Russian expansion. The Czar himself was faced with a difficult problem—should he help fellow-Christians and extend Russian influence, or should he show his usual disapproval of revolutions ? For the moment Castlereagh and Metternich were able, by playing on Alexander's fondness for the Alliance, to hold Russia off Turkey. A new Congress to consider this

The Greek Revolt

and the Spanish question, however, was called to meet at Verona in 1822.

Canning

Before it met, Castlereagh, worn out by incessant labours and saddened by his unpopularity among the English lower classes, had lost his reason and, with typical efficiency, though left unguarded for only two or three minutes, had succeeded in cutting his throat. His position as English Foreign Secretary was filled by Canning, who was determined to break up the European Alliance which had become the tool of reaction. We have seen that Castlereagh himself, by refusing to associate England in suppressing the revolutions in Spain, the Spanish colonies, Naples, and Piedmont, was already drifting apart from Russia, Prussia, and Austria. Canning, who, unlike Castlereagh, was not one of the original framers of the Alliance, had no parent's fondness for it, and therefore determined to speed up the process of destroying the Congress System. He did this the more readily in that his sympathies were more liberal than Castlereagh's, and he marked an innovation in the conduct of foreign affairs by appealing for popular approval through brilliant speeches aimed at English public opinion.

The Congress of Verona, 1822

At the Congress of Verona in 1822, then, Canning took a firm stand against Allied intervention in Spain. France, however, decided to intervene on her own responsibility, backed by the other three powers, and within a year the

Intervention in Spain

Spanish king had been restored by French troops to complete power, in which position he was free to conduct a magnificent revenge on the late rebels, setting up the Inquisition once more and imprisoning and executing so many hundreds that France and the Alliance grew ashamed of the man they had helped. And, now that absolute monarchy was restored in Spain, came the crux of the matter—would the king, backed by

The South American States.

France, go on to reclaim his revolted South American colonies ? On this point Canning was absolutely decisive. South

Canning's firm line

America offered the prospect of valuable trade for England : Spain refused to promise open trading conditions for England with her colonies if she should recapture them ; therefore— quite simply—Spain must not be allowed to recover her lost possessions. The Alliance was distinctly warned off interfering in South America by a double stroke. In the first place

Canning warned Polignac, the French minister, in an out-spoken Memorandum that England would fight France if she attempted to intervene in South America. Secondly, the United States, fearful of Russian operations in America and the claims she might develop through her ownership of Alaska, and seeing the drift of Canning's policy, not only granted official recognition to the South American Republics, but warned Europe, in the famous 'Monroe Doctrine,' that any interference by European powers on the American Continent would be regarded "as the manifestation of an unfriendly disposition to the United States." Canning, seeing his cue taken up, promptly welcomed the Monroe Doctrine and recognized the South American republics. Faced with the prospect of fighting both England and the United States if the Alliance persisted in interference, Austria, Russia, Prussia, and France drew back and let revolution triumph in South America. Thus the principle of interference was defeated by England, who had, in so doing, split up the Alliance. The Congress System was on its last legs. It remained to give it the death-blow—soon to be administered over the question of Greek independence.

The Greek revolt, which will be described more fully in a later chapter, had now reached a critical stage. The Sultan's powerful vassal, Ibrahim Pasha of Egypt, had been called in and was suppressing the rebels with a systematic brutality which threatened to leave the Sultan with no Greek subjects at all. In 1825, too, Alexander had died and been succeeded by his brother Nicholas I, a man of more stable and deter-mined character, who was resolved to help his co-religionists in Greece. Seeing that Nicholas meant to help the Greeks, anyway, Canning decided it would be better to include Eng-land in the enterprise to give her a voice in the subsequent peace treaty and stop Russia monopolizing the benefits of intervention. He therefore acted with Russia—to control her —and by 1827, at the Treaty of London, England, Russia, and France had agreed to enforce independence in all but name for Greece. Against this policy Prussia and Austria protested strongly, being anxious not to encourage rebellion and to reserve the Balkans for their own influence. It all ended, as we shall see, by the English, French, and Russian fleets

The Greek revolt again. The Powers disagree

destroying the Turkish and Egyptian navy almost accidentally at Navarino Bay, and thereby making certain of independence for the Greeks.   But there was another effect, too—the powers of Europe were hopelessly divided over the matter : England, if only for a moment, was ranged with Russia and France against Prussia and Austria.   It could no longer be pretended that there was any effective Quadruple or Quintuple Alliance. The Congress System was dead.

The end of the Congress System

So, on the questions of intervention in Italy, Spain, the Spanish colonies, and Greece, England had gradually drawn away from her Continental allies.   By 1828 Castlereagh and Canning had smashed the system the former had helped to create, because both could see that the Alliance was being turned to uses of which England could not approve.   Canning, indeed, revelled in the work of destroying the first experiment in international co-operation—as he said not long before his death—"Things are getting back to a wholesome state again. Every nation for itself, and God for us all."   He did not add "and Devil take the hindmost," but that would have completed the description more faithfully.

Reasons for its failure

The Congress System thus broke down in the first place because vital issues arose, such as the matter of the Spanish colonies, on which England could not possibly agree with the other powers.   In the second place it never really captured the sympathy of European public opinion, even in the way that the League of Nations did.   This was partly because it did not represent the small powers, and partly because the views and characters of men like Metternich and Alexander made the Alliance appear something like a league of tyrants for the suppression of liberty, constantly urging intervention to put down popular movements.   Thirdly, England, as usual soon after the end of a war, began to object to the policy of Continental obligations which the war had rendered necessary. There came the inevitable desire to have our 'hands free' again, to be without alliances and commitments which would certainly bring us into war if another European conflict developed. This was, indeed, one of the chief motives in leading Canning to smash the Congress System.   Actually, however, in causing the break-up of the Alliance, he claimed to be " resisting the spirit of foreign domination," and it is in this light, as the

Exclusion of Small Powers.

Intervention Against Liberal Movements.

NEAPOLITAN LIBERAL

SPANISH LIBERAL

PIEDMONTESE LIBERAL

CAPTAIN METTERNICH

Canning's Anti-Congress Policy.

ISOLATION

TRADE TREATIES WITH SOUTH AMERICA

Divisions Among Powers.

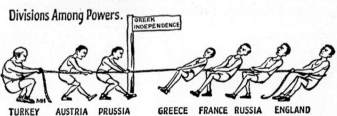

GREEK INDEPENDENCE

TURKEY   AUSTRIA   PRUSSIA   GREECE   FRANCE   RUSSIA   ENGLAND

REASONS FOR BREAKDOWN OF CONGRESS SYSTEM.

champion of freedom, that one tends to see Canning's and England's opposition to the Alliance. But though English historians love to picture Canning, in breaking up the Congress System, as a sort of George the Giant Killer tackling the wicked Russian and Austrian ogres, we must remember that what he was really doing was simply getting back to the ordinary post-war British policy of isolation. We can easily exaggerate England's liberalism if we lose sight of the fact that Castlereagh, for example, was the leading spirit in the Tory Government which approved the Peterloo massacre and ruthlessly opposed all working-class political movements at home. (Canning's 'resistance to foreign domination' did not go so deep, either, as to make him propose to abolish the British Empire, which was founded on it.) England thus destroyed the System a little out of love of 'liberty,' but much more from the typical English desire to avoid Continental obligations and because the Alliance threatened our interests in important and pocket-touching matters, such as trade with the Spanish colonies.

CHAPTER V

France under the Bourbon and Orleans Monarchies, 1815–1848

1. *The Restored Bourbons, 1815–1830*

The final defeat of Napoleon at Waterloo in 1815 meant for France the second return of the Bourbon line in the shape of Louis XVIII. Already previously restored by the Allies in 1814, he had left Paris, when the news of Napoleon's landing from Elba was announced, with a speed remarkable in view of his advancing age and figure. Now in 1815 he was back again, to exhibit in his fat, gouty, and unromantic personage the Divine Right of Kings. This fact, however, did *not* mean that the whole gains of the Revolutionary and Napoleonic periods were lost and that France simply went back to the position before 1789. Louis, a sensible old gentleman, retained most of Napoleon's great institutions, such as the Code, the Legion of Honour, the system of local government, and at the same time had promised to rule constitutionally by the terms of a Charter.

Louis XVIII, 1815–1824

This Charter—a suggestion of the Allies in 1814 to make his return less unpopular, and bribe the French people over from Napoleon—is of extreme importance. Its main effects were to provide France with a parliament and to secure her from the possibility of absolute government such as the Bourbons had exercised before 1789. All Frenchmen were to be subject to the same system of law, all were to be free from the possibility of arbitrary imprisonment by *lettres de cachet*, and all were to be equally eligible for important civil and military positions. Furthermore, liberty was guaranteed in the form of a free press and complete religious toleration. The middle classes' fears were quietened by a provision that those who had purchased confiscated property during the Revolution were to enjoy it undisturbed. All these were valuable concessions

The Charter

to Liberalism ; but to Frenchmen who had known the extreme theories and practices of 1791 the new parliament appeared extremely undemocratic. To possess a vote one had to be over thirty years of age and pay 300 francs in direct taxation ; while to be a Member, it was necessary to be over forty and to pay 1000 francs. This meant that of a population of 29,000,000 only 100,000 people had the right to vote—and here was a sure source of future trouble and agitation.

"The White Terror"

Louis XVIII in 1815 found himself in some ways in a very similar position to Charles II of England in 1660—a sensible and easy-going monarch, willing to let bygones be bygones, and chiefly anxious "not to go on his travels again." But like Charles II, too, he found himself surrounded by groups of returned nobles who were fiercely keen to recover their positions and revenge themselves on their late enemies. Of these nobles the relentless leader was Charles of Artois, the King's younger brother. So, just as the English Royalists of 1660 savagely persecuted the Cromwellians against all the wishes of Charles, so the French Royalists of 1815 (returned in full strength by the upper middle classes to the Parliament) savagely persecuted the Bonapartists against all the advice of Louis. A 'White Terror' was organized in 1816 in the course of which 7000 supporters of Napoleon were imprisoned or executed, and Marshal Ney, 'bravest of the brave,' was shot. Fortunately this excess in turn produced the opposite reaction, and by 1817, when the upper middle classes had lost their panic-struck fear of Bonapartism, the more moderate counsels of Louis began to have effect.

Artois

The Murder of the Duc de Berri

Till 1820 Parliament and Louis then proceeded along fairly liberal lines, when all at once the extreme Royalists (or Ultras, as they were called) were presented with a magnificent opportunity in the murder of the Duc de Berri, a son of Artois, by a Bonapartist. They were not slow to see the value of the crime to their cause, and just as Hitler in 1933 used the Reichstag fire to persuade the German people that Communism must be crushed, so the Ultras used the murder of the Duc de Berri to persuade King and Parliament that Liberalism and Bonapartism must be stamped out. So by 1821, when a severe law limiting the freedom of the press was passed, the short Liberal phase of Bourbon rule was ending. Louis XVIII,

too, racked by a terrible disease, was literally breaking up—
his horrified valet even discovered pieces of his toes in pulling
off his stockings. He thus lacked the physical strength to
resist Artois and the Ultras. In Spain, for instance, as we
have seen, the French intervened to restore the absolute rule
of the unsavoury Ferdinand. All the same, by the time
Louis' reign closed in 1824, a great deal had been done for
France by his government—a heavy war indemnity paid off,
the country rid of the foreign occupying troops, the army
reorganized, and France readmitted to the ranks, councils,
and alliance of the Great Powers.

The reign of Artois, now ascending the throne as Charles X <sup>Charles X,
1824–1830</sup> was almost bound to come to grief before long. If Louis XVIII
was the Charles II of French history, Charles X was the
James II. He longed to restore the French monarchy to all
its ancient power, and despised constitutional kingship. "I
had rather chop wood than reign after the fashion of the King
of England," he said. Further, he had as passionate a conviction as Robespierre that his enemies were not only mistaken
but sinful. The first acts of his reign were typical. At his
coronation ceremony, while he lay prostrate on cushions, he
was pierced in seven sections of his anatomy, via seven
apertures in his clothes, with a golden needle dipped in holy
oil said to have been miraculously preserved from the 5th
century. He then visited hospitals to heal the diseased with
his holy touch. Before long acts were passed making sacrilege
punishable by death and, above all, granting 1,000,000,000
francs compensation to the nobles for losses suffered during the
Revolution. The religious orders were encouraged to return,
while by 1827 a censorship was applied to all books and
journals, and the National Guard, the middle-class citizen-
militia, had been disbanded lest it should prove unfavourable
to such royalist schemes. But even this pace was too slow for
Charles ; in face of the growing protests of the Liberals and
Bonapartists he resolved on sterner measures, dismissed the
last of his moderate Royalist councillors, and appointed as his
chief minister the Prince de Polignac, an Ultra of the Ultras.

Events now moved fast towards their conclusion. Polignac's ^{Polignac}
aims were simple—"to reorganize society, to give back to the
clergy their weight in state affairs, to create a powerful

aristocracy, and to surround it with privileges"—a programme which would have completely cancelled out the Revolution. To carry it out, he had, so he claimed, the assistance of visions from the Virgin Mary. These, however, proved of doubtful value. Opposition to him boiled up even in Parliament, which reproached Charles with choosing a minister who did not represent them. Charles's answer was the one which might have been expected of him—to dissolve Parliament. The new elections, however, showed an ever greater majority against Polignac. Charles, therefore, to deal with this situation, issued in July 1830 a series of drastic proclamations, known as the Ordinances of St. Cloud. By the terms of these ordinances even stricter laws were passed to control the press, the newly elected Parliament was declared dissolved before it met, and three-quarters of the electors were deprived of their right to vote. The whole effect would have been to destroy completely the Charter. "At last you are ruling," said Charles's daughter-in-law, with more enthusiasm than accuracy.

The
Ordinances
of St.
Cloud, 1830

The 1830
Revolution

Thiers

The opposition was instantaneous, foremost in it being the very printers who were supposed to set up the Ordinances and the journalists whose livelihood was threatened by the enslavement of the press. Their leader in the preliminary agitation was a writer, Thiers, whose name is to recur many times in the history of the next forty years. It was not he, however, whose action was decisive. While the Liberal deputies and the upper middle classes were still wondering what to do, the working classes had taken action. The revolutionary tradition was strong in Paris, and it did not take long for a mob, under Republican leaders, to seize the Hôtel de Ville, Notre-Dame, some important guard-houses and arsenals, and crown their captures with the fluttering 'tricolore.' The troops, who anyway had no great enthusiasm for the Bourbons, were unable to make headway against the barricades of the populace, constructed by cutting down the trees of the boulevards and tearing up the paving-stones. The disheartened soldiers had no food, owing to the fact that the rebels had captured the military bakeries. Yet even at this stage of the revolt Charles and Polignac did not realize the gravity of the situation. The latter, comforted by a fresh vision from the

"The Swing" by Fragonard.   [*Photo, Mansell.*

Note the light-hearted frivolity of this typical painting of the Ancien Régime.
The gentleman who commissioned it even wanted Fragonard to draw a bishop
pushing the swing. Fragonard went completely out of fashion with the Revolution, being regarded as insufficiently serious for such heroic days.

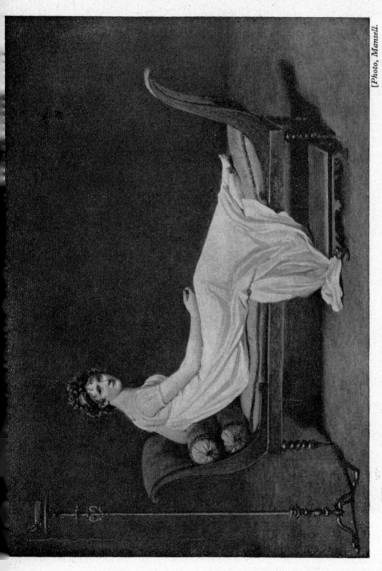

History through Painting (2). "Madame Récamier" by J. L. David.

Now see the previous effect in the

[*Photo, Mansell*]

History through Painting (3). "The Barricade" by Delacroix.

This famous picture, mixture of realism and symbolism, illustrates the struggle of 1830. In its vigour and violence, typical of the romantic movement, it parallels in paint the revolutionary spirit which was so strong in 19th Century France.

History through Painting (4).

"A Funeral at Ornans" by Courbet.

[*Photo, Mansell.*]

This realistic presentment of a village funeral shows the democratic spirit at work in art, though conservative circles regarded Courbet with horror for painting anything so near the life of the people. Exhibited in 1850, it drew on Courbet the epithet "socialist". Courbet, incidentally, later became one of the leaders of the 1871 Commune.

Virgin Mary, declared that a couple of hours, four men, and a corporal would settle the whole business. But the next day the mob proceeded to rout the troops who were guarding the Tuileries. Seeing the evident success of the popular insurrection the middle-class deputies realized that they had better take advantage of it, and Thiers returned from the day he had been spending tactfully in the country.

Charles now in haste offered to dismiss Polignac and restore the Charter, but the time was past for such concessions. Events were fast moving towards the establishment of a republic when Thiers, on July 30th, had the walls of Paris posted with placards in favour of Louis Philippe, Duke of Orleans, head of a younger branch of the Bourbon line. He was a prince who might be calculated to appeal to the middle and lower classes, since he was the son of the Philippe Egalité who had voted for his cousin Louis XVI's death, and since he had fought on the revolutionary side at Jemappes. But he was not well known, and when, a day later, he appeared at the Hôtel de Ville to receive the 'call of the people,' his reception was distinctly lukewarm until he embraced the veteran republican Lafayette and received from his hands the sacred tricolore. The main fact, however, was that at the critical moment Thiers had produced a candidate when all was confusion—and so the claims of Charles X, and the grandson in whose favour he soon abdicated, and the Republic for which the revolutionaries had been fighting were pushed into the background. Charles X and his family were soon on ship for England, and Louis Philippe of Orleans, the 'Citizen-King,' was King of the French—on condition he ruled as a constitutional monarch.

Louis Philippe

2. *The Orleans Monarchy, 1830–1848*

The reign of Louis Philippe proved to be eighteen years of disappointment. Clever, sensible, kindly, and well-intentioned, he yet came to grief in an even more undignified way than his predecessor. Apparently with much to attract the people to him—his revolutionary parentage and past, his years of poverty, during which he had earnt his living by giving lessons in drawing and mathematics, his simple and unaffected

Unpopularity of Louis Philippe

4*

ways—he nevertheless failed to capture the loyalty of anyone beyond the wealthier middle classes. The old Royalists despised his democratic habits of lighting his own study fire, shaving himself, living principally on soup, and strolling round the shops with no greater protection than an eternal umbrella. They thought nothing of his proudest accomplishment—that he had learnt in exile, from a waiter with whom he shared lodgings, how to cut ham in beautifully thin slices. The working classes equally disliked his government for the simple reason that, though it was their blood which had established it, it did nothing at all to improve their lot. The consequence was that almost every year of his reign there were plots and attempts to assassinate him, which Louis Philippe for his part met with cheerful and unfailing courage. He had some amazing escapes : once an infernal machine consisting of an arrangement of twenty-four muskets to be fired simultaneously mowed down the front of his bodyguard in a procession, one of the bullets grazing his chin. Another time a bullet lodged in his hair, but he was imperturbable—"it is only in hunting me that there is no close season," he remarked humorously.

His peaceful policy

The problems which faced his government were enormous. In the first place he had to secure recognition of his accession in Europe, which, frightened of French revolutions, might have been tempted to intervene to restore Charles X. Nicholas I of Russia, indeed, nearly did, only he was soon too busy suppressing a Polish rebellion against himself. But by an inflexible policy of peace—much as this was distasteful to certain elements in France—Louis Philippe calmed down the fears of the powers, and first of all winning over the new Whig Foreign Secretary in England, Palmerston, he soon secured general recognition. To do this, however, he had to sacrifice certain opportunities of action which would have appealed strongly to a large section of the French.

The Belgian Revolt, 1830

The first such occasion was the Belgian revolt of 1830. The Belgians, forcibly joined with the Dutch by the Vienna Treaties of 1815, had resented the union ever since. Their main grievances were the use of the Dutch language as official, the religious difference between Catholic Belgium and Protestant Holland, and the fact that the Dutch practically monopolized all official positions. At one time, for example, six cabinet ministers out of seven were Dutch, thirty out of the thirty-nine ambassadors, and all the nine generals. The Belgians, it is true, were allowed half of the number of M.P.s, but as there were three and a half million Belgians to two million Dutch in the country, even this seemed unrepresentative and unfair to them. Further, as some of the Belgian M.P.s were government officials who depended for their livelihood on not offending the Dutch king, these men constantly voted with the Dutch against their own com-

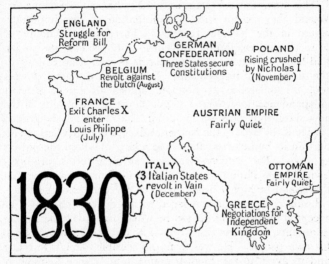

ENGLAND
Struggle for
Reform Bill

GERMAN
CONFEDERATION
Three States secure
Constitutions

POLAND
Rising crushed
by Nicholas I
(November)

BELGIUM
Revolt against
the Dutch (August)

FRANCE
Exit Charles X
enter
Louis Philippe
(July)

AUSTRIAN EMPIRE
Fairly Quiet

ITALY
3 Italian States
revolt in Vain
(December)

OTTOMAN
EMPIRE
Fairly Quiet

GREECE
Negotiations for
Independent
Kingdom

1830

patriots. This, by giving the Dutch a majority, led to all laws passed being more or less against the Belgian interest. Bread, for example, the main article of Belgian diet, was heavily taxed, while potatoes, the principal Dutch fare, escaped. Laws in general, too, tended to favour the Dutch commercial and sea-faring interests rather than the Belgian industrial ones, and inclined to the Dutch preference for free trade rather than the Belgian desire for protection. Belgian newspapers, too, were severely censored. The consequence of all this was a steadily growing state of unrest leading to monster petitions against Dutch injustice. Then came the July revolution in Paris, one or two high-handed actions by the Dutch king—and the performance of an opera dealing sympathetically with the Naples rising against the Spanish led the Brussels mob to riot in imitation. The Dutch army was successfully resisted, other towns followed the example of Brussels, and soon a National Congress had declared Belgium to be independent of Holland. A separate constitutional monarch was voted, with the usual democratic institutions of two houses of parliament, liberty of speech and worship, and so on.

This was where France and the other powers came in. Would they accept such a cancellation of one important clause in the Vienna Treaties? There was no doubt of France's answer, for the difficulty of Louis Philippe so far had been to restrain the enthusiastic French from rushing to the assistance of the Belgians. Fortunately the other powers too, in conference at London, agreed to accept Belgian independence, and offered to guarantee the neutrality of the new state—but only on condition that Belgium shouldered over half the debt of the Netherlands, did not include Luxemburg in its boundaries, and chose a king of whom the powers approved. The Belgians, annoyed at these terms, promptly invited Louis Philippe's son to be the new king—knowing that this would be highly disagreeable to everyone except France.

The Belgian Crown— Louis' dilemma

Louis Philippe was now faced with a delicate choice—if he accepted on behalf of his son he would risk involving France in another European war, while if he did not he would offend his own people. He was firm and sensible enough to refuse and to agree to the English nomination, Prince Leopold of Saxe-Coburg, the future Queen Victoria's uncle. The Belgians then accepted Leopold, and there was no European war about the matter—but there was a general feeling in France that Louis Philippe had been outmanœuvred by Palmerston, and his prestige suffered accordingly. Actually, he was able to recover a little of his reputation when, in 1832, the Dutch king, William, who had refused to accept the powers' decision, invaded Belgium. The Dutch started sweeping all before them in a brilliant ten-day campaign, and Louis Philippe was hastily authorized by the powers to intervene to protect Belgium. This he did successfully, and so was able to claim that France after all had aided Belgian independence.

Nevertheless he was obviously only going as far as England allowed him, and this cautious and pacific policy struck Frenchmen brought up on the Napoleonic traditions as distinctly inglorious.   Eventually the whole matter of Belgian independence was concluded in 1839, when the Dutch king, after some years of sulking about the matter, cleverly accepted the powers' original terms.   He thus got back Luxemburg, which the Belgians had been holding meanwhile.   A general European treaty was now signed guaranteeing the independence and neutrality of Belgium—the famous treaty which Germany, after referring to it as 'a scrap of paper,' violated in 1914.

Other instances of Louis Philippe's peaceful foreign policy were plentiful.   In spite of the urgent desires of the French (who customarily showed them by rioting), he did nothing to help the Poles in their revolt against the Russians or the Italians in their campaign against the Austrians.   Twice Thiers, as principal minister, resigned because the King would not let him carry out anything more adventurous— once in 1836 when Thiers wanted to support the Liberal side in a Spanish civil war, and once in 1840 when France's ally, Mehemet Ali, was ordered by England, Austria, and Prussia to restore Syria to Turkey.   The second occasion showed so obviously that the bolder Palmerston could humiliate France whenever he chose, by relying on Louis Philippe's anxiety to preserve the peace, that the result was widespread dissatisfaction in France with the King's foreign policy.

Further resistance to foreign adventure

When Guizot, a Conservative whose views on politics agreed very well with the King's, replaced Thiers in 1840 the same foreign policy continued.   The French annexed Tahiti— until England protested, when the annexation was cancelled.   In fact, up till 1846 the universal charge against the monarch was subservience to England.   In that year, however, Guizot and Louis Philippe carried out their only bold and successful piece of foreign policy apart from the conquest of Algeria (which, anyway, had been started under Charles X).   Both the Queen of Spain, Isabella, and the heir to the throne, the Infanta, her sister, were unmarried.   There was naturally competition among the powers to supply husbands.   Palmerston favoured the claims of a German prince, Louis Philippe a

Ministry of Guizot, 1840–1848

The Spanish marriages

French one.   Both agreed to withdraw their claims on condition the other did.   Then suddenly Palmerston revived the
claim of his candidate : whereupon Guizot and Louis Philippe
went secretly to work and within a short time astounded
England by arranging a double marriage—of Isabella to an
old nobleman who was rumoured to be incapable of begetting
children, and of the Infanta (who would thus inherit the
Throne) to a son of Louis Philippe.   For once someone had
stolen a march on Palmerston.   But while France rang with
applause over the matter and the King's popularity revived a
little, England smarted, withdrew her friendship, and two
years later watched the Orleans dynasty dethroned without
lifting a finger to save it.   Thus the King's only bold piece
of foreign policy had the unfortunate effect of losing him his
sole ally in Europe.

Home
policy. No
effort to
improve
bad social
conditions

Damaging as the foreign policy of Guizot and the King was
to the reputation of the monarch, their home policy was even
more so.   Both were highly intelligent men, and Guizot's
reputation as an orator, a scholar, and a historian-philosopher
stood second to none.   Yet both completely failed to realize
the need for state-action on behalf of France's poorer classes,
or for any political or social progress.   At a time when France,
in turn undergoing her Industrial Revolution, was beginning
to learn the horrors of factory life, slum-dwellings, and
propertyless workers, Guizot could get no further than the
fashionable doctrine of *laissez-faire*.   In his view the only
concern of the government in such matters was to keep outside
them.   Apart from a law providing elementary education
and a factory act limiting the employment of children, the
eighteen years of Louis Philippe's reign saw no real effort to
improve the conditions of the masses.   That some improvement was needed may be seen from the single fact that nine-
tenths of town-dwellers examined for the army during the
reign were rejected as physically unfit.   All this time, however,
the wealthier middle classes, the bankers and industrialists,
were prospering greatly—railways were built, while the production of French wine increased two-fold, coal four-fold, and
machinery ten-fold.   Thus the situation was doubly galling
for the working classes—to be not only poor, but poor in a
period of prosperity.   And the only contribution the govern-

ment seemed to make to the matter was to break up strikes by bloodshed, suppress trade unions and political clubs, and deny the ever-increasing clamour for an extension of the right to vote to poorer citizens.

It was the refusal of this demand which ultimately brought about the fall of the monarchy. The parliamentary system had never really functioned smoothly under Louis Philippe. The exact extent of the King's power was rather vague, and there grew up a general feeling that he was exercising more influence than he should as a constitutional monarch. Further, there had not as yet been time for the formation of two highly organized parties to assure one side or the other of a constant majority, and so even an upright man like Guizot maintained himself in power by a system of bribery. Government posts, pensions, business contracts (especially in connection with the new railways) were distributed among members of parliament. Guizot was thus supported throughout the years 1840 to 1848 by a parliamentary majority, though he was actually bitterly opposed by most of the country. While the right to vote, too, was restricted to such a small class—only 200,000 out of 35,000,000—such a state of affairs could continue indefinitely. So 'parliamentary reform' became the rallying-cry of all who were opposed to the conservatism of the King and his minister. Some, like Thiers, probably wanted to extend the franchise slightly to capture power for themselves. Others, like the Republicans, aimed at the vote for all men in order to carry out a complete reform of the social system. In any case a great campaign for parliamentary reform was begun, and against the slightest concession to this Louis Philippe and Guizot resolutely set their faces. *Parliamentary reform demanded*

By 1846 or 1847, moreover, the dissatisfied in France were able to look to certain positive programmes of reform in place of the unorganized revolutionary violence of earlier years. One of these increasingly attractive alternatives to the stagnation of Louis Philippe was the new doctrine of Socialism, propounded since 1828 by a series of brilliant French writers. Socialism claimed that by abolishing private ownership of great industries, banks, transport systems and the like, and by putting them under the control of the state, all citizens would thus be more or less equal partners in the wealth of the country, *Socialism* and the grotesque inequalities of capitalism would be avoided.

One of the foremost Socialists, Louis Blanc, in his book *L'Organisation du Travail*, tried to show how the state would begin to take over the control of industry by running national works and workshops for the benefit of the unemployed. He showed, too, how the whole unemployment problem would be solved when the state, which would not be concerned merely with private profit, acted as the general employer. His phrase 'the right to work' became a main demand of the poorer classes, who naturally saw in Socialism not only a means of avoiding the dreaded spells of unemployment, but a method of winning for themselves a much fairer and greater share in the wealth of the country than they enjoyed at the time. Socialism in various forms thus began to attract the loyalty of the town masses from the Orleans dynasty. Socialism itself underwent a rapid development from 1828, when it was full of idyllic schemes, such as the proposal that men should work in fields to the sound of grand pianos, till by 1848 it had become an almost scientific doctrine. Not only were there Blanc's proposals and hundreds of suggestions for really practical undertakings (such as the cutting of a Suez Canal), but in addition the Germans Marx and Engels were maturing the elaborate creed known now as Communism, or revolutionary Socialism.

The second alternative to which the working classes could turn was Bonapartism. It might seem difficult to understand where the attraction came in, since Napoleon had led the French to disaster. But it must be remembered first that the military triumphs of the Empire had been a great source of pride to Frenchmen and satisfied their age-long passion for 'glory,' and secondly that the principles of Bonapartism had been entirely reconstructed since 1815. In exile at St. Helena, Napoleon had cleverly edited the history of his career to show that the constant warfare was more or less accidental and caused by other nations, and that his dictatorship was intended to be purely temporary. He would have given France peace, prosperity, and Liberal institutions had Europe permitted him to fulfil his life-work, he declared. These elements in Napoleon's defence of himself were seized on and magnified

by the heir to the Bonaparte claim, Louis Napoleon Bonaparte, a nephew of the great Emperor. In a series of pamphlets he proclaimed his care for both the army and for peace, and his desire for free institutions. He outlined many schemes of public works and of agricultural and commercial reform, all designed to abolish unemployment and bring prosperity. Though he twice failed ridiculously in attempts to seize power, the cult of Bonapartism gradually developed. Unimportant at the beginning of Louis Philippe's reign, it became gradually more and more of a menace as industrial distress grew and the government still did nothing. As shaped by Louis Napoleon, it appealed to the neglected working classes, to the slighted army, to all those who disliked Louis Philippe's cautious foreign policy, and even to Liberals who swallowed the promises of free institutions. To rob the growing agitation of something of its sting, Thiers and Louis Philippe completed the Arc de Triomphe in celebration of the victories of the Empire, opened a 'Museum of Conquests' at Versailles, and had the Emperor's body brought from St. Helena to be interred in Paris. The manœuvre was unsuccessful ; they hoped to satisfy the Napoleonic clamour by a little cheap pageantry, but in fact they only caused men all the more to contrast the colourful days of the Empire with the drab existence of the present reign. The contrast was heightened by the work of a number of skilled French historians, such as Lamartine and Blanc, who in their treatment of the revolutionary period depicted the leaders of that generation as gigantic figures who completely dwarfed Louis Philippe and Guizot.

Thus by 1848 the government had very few enthusiastic supporters. It had done nothing for the workers ; it was corrupt ; it had knuckled under to England. Its very real services in keeping the peace were not appreciated. Either Socialism or Bonapartism promised more. Further, France, as Lamartine put it, was simply 'bored' with the existing régime. It was all too colourless and stagnant. The fat old King, always drawn by caricaturists in the shape of a William pear, became a figure of ridicule. His middle-class taste, shown in the new apartments at Versailles, seemed utterly unattractive when compared, in the same building, with the splendour of Louis XIV or the brilliant vulgarity of Napoleon.

General dissatisfaction with Guizot

PUT OUT!

Louis Philippe's candle is snuffed by the 1848 Revolutionaries.

Above all, the ministry of Guizot, 'the austere wirepuller,' in eight years of power had simply maintained affairs in an immovable position and barred all progress. As Lamartine, the republican poet and historian, said, "If that were all the genius required of a statesman charged with the direction of affairs, there would be no need for statesmen—a milestone would do just as well." To nearly everyone it became clear that the first step to progress was to shift the 'milestone' ministry, as Guizot's government was rapidly nicknamed.

To accomplish a real change in the direction of the government, however, it was necessary to enlarge the franchise, for the existing class of wealthy electors was quite satisfied with Guizot. The agitation for parliamentary reform grew universal ; there was not so much a desire to uproot the monarchy, weak though support of it was, as to make the government more democratic and more aware of industrial and social problems. The full result of the 1848 revolution, like that of 1830, though everything had been leading up to it, was nevertheless something of an accident.

The opposition started a big series of Reform Banquets. Reform Banquets At these, after the dinner, opposition orators would speak on the need for giving more people the vote. Gradually they developed from a request for modified electoral reform to omission of the King's name from the toast-list and a demand for a republic with a vote for everybody. In February 1848 a great Reform Banquet was announced, with a Reform Procession. Scenting danger, the government banned the banquet ; a number of complicated moves followed, and the organizers finally decided to call off the procession. Half the banqueters did not know whether the whole affair was really on or off, but by this time the Paris masses had got it into their heads that *something* exciting would happen anyway, and so turned up for the procession in force. Then the government made the fatal mistake of calling out the National Guard to disperse the crowd—fatal because the Guard simply showed their sympathy with the crowd and so encouraged it. A more ruthless man than Louis Philippe would have ordered out the regular troops to fire on the Guard, and perhaps quelled the whole matter by a brutal display of force. Louis Philippe, old and peaceful, refused to face the prospect of blood, and consented to dismiss Guizot. The next day an accidental clash between a small section of the crowd and some troops led to the barricades going up all over Paris again, and the working classes preparing to resist the troops by force. In the fighting which ensued the troops put no heart into the work, and when the King reviewed them, instead of 'Vive le Roi !' he got shouts of 'Vive la réforme !' Discouraged at the collapse of all his work, murmuring "This is worse than Charles X," the old King lost heart for the first time and abdicated. The Orleans monarchy, mourned by very few, was at an end. A temporary government was formed in Parliament, and France became a republic for the second time in her history. The Tuileries meanwhile had been looted by the mob, some of whom were drowned in the floods of wine released from the royal cellars.

The Revolution of 1848— exit Louis Philippe

I. Unadventurous foreign policy.

II. Government inattention to bad conditions.

III. Growth of Socialism and Bonapartism.

IV. Demand for Parliamentary Reform.

CAUSES OF THE DOWNFALL OF THE ORLEANS MONARCHY.

CHAPTER VI

The Second Republic and the Second Empire, 1848–1871

France ?

1. *The Second Republic, 1848–1852*

The Orleans monarchy had fallen ; what was to take its place ? No one was very clear, except that there was a general feeling among the revolutionaries that the new government must be a republic. Among those who had created the revolution, however, there were two distinct elements. There were the leaders of the intellectual middle classes, like Lamartine, who wanted a republic largely for sentimental reasons (such as admiration for the old Roman Republic, for the first French Republic of 1792, for the Girondins, for 'republican virtue,' and so on). But there were also the leaders of the working classes, like Blanc, who wanted a republic so that it could proceed to pass socialistic measures to raise the standard of the labourer's life. Further, it must always be remembered that behind these two elements lay yet another of completely different views—the peasantry and small landowners of France, conservative in instincts, deeply suspicious of republics and anything that happened in Paris, and desiring above all things law, order, and security in their property. It was never this last class which created revolutions, but it was precisely this class which provided the support first for Napoleon I to end the disorders of the First Republic and now soon for Napoleon III to triumph over the Second Republic.

A provisional government. Elections

In 1848, then, Lamartine, taking a lead, managed to secure approval by the mob of a list of names for the new government. To this list the working classes compelled him, by demonstrations, to add some of their own representatives, notably Louis Blanc. This provisional government then arranged for elections to be held. A vote was given to all—

whether they could read or not—and France's electorate suddenly leapt from 250,000 to 9,000,000. The results of the elections, by giving nearly all the seats to the moderates and only a few to the socialist extremists, showed that, whatever Paris was, France was still really a conservative country. But the Paris working classes were important, for since February they had been armed, and they were determined not to let their efforts merely serve the interests of the middle classes, as had been the case in 1830. They therefore looked especially to Blanc, some of whose ideas the government had promised to carry out.

Blanc, a Socialist, had long advocated 'National Work- National shops'—a series of state-owned enterprises not only to absorb Workshops the unemployed, but to form the first steps towards socializing all the vital elements in economic life. He had to work, however, with a government which was by no means Socialist and which therefore tried to limit the application of his ideas. The result was that, though National Workshops were set up in response to popular clamour, they were nothing like the workshops of Blanc's dreams. The work offered was almost entirely of the labouring order—replanting trees, paving roads, building railway stations—for which a rate of two francs a day was paid. The unemployed, and even many of the employed, flocked to the national works—with disturbing results. In the first place the government, very unimaginative in supplying work and frightened of offending wealthy manufacturers by setting up in competition to them, began to order the same pieces of work to be done over and over again to employ all the applicants. As this got more absurd, greater and greater numbers were placed on 'inactivity' pay of one franc a day. Taxation began to mount to pay for all this, and a financial crisis occurred. The interests of tax-paying middle classes and property-less working classes were now seen to be clearly opposed, and the government, consisting almost entirely of the former, decided to close the Workshops. To do this with- The Work-out breaking too many promises it offered the workers and shops idlers of the National Workshops the choice of joining the closed army or clearing land in the provinces—an offer summed up by one French historian as " a choice between being shot by the Arabs in Algeria or dying of fever in the swamps of

A popular
rising

Sologne." Consequently, in June 1848, the armed masses of Paris rose to a fresh revolution against their new government. Up went the barricades ; over went buses and locomotives to strengthen them.   The Paris working classes observed discipline well and fought bravely, but they were opposed by the government, the army, the National Guard, the upper and middle classes, and the whole of the provinces. Heavy artillery was used to smash the resisting streets, and the blood of over 10,000 Frenchmen flowed before the revolt was crushed. After the struggle was over, thousands more were deported. It was a dreadful experience, and it rendered certain the future downfall of the Republic, for the working classes would never forgive it and the middle classes would never feel confidence in its stability. Louis Napoleon had things made very easy for him.

The
Presidency
of the
Republic

Early
history of
Louis
Napoleon

The question of the Presidency of the Republic had not as yet been settled. The three main candidates were Cavaignac (the general who had just beaten the Paris revolutionaries), Lamartine, and Louis Napoleon Bonaparte, nephew of the great Emperor. The last-named had thus far enjoyed an amazing history. A romantic youth, believing firmly in his destiny as his uncle's heir, he had been involved in scrapes, revolutions, or love affairs in half the countries of Europe.   In 1831 he had joined the Italian Secret Society, the Carbonari, in their revolt against the Papal rule in Rome, and had eventually to escape from the Austrians disguised as a footman. Exiled from France, he wrote books on military subjects to make himself popular with the French army, and on social subjects to show his care for the French people. In 1836, with a few followers, he had endeavoured to invade France, raise the garrison of Strasbourg, and claim the throne from Louis Philippe—but had shrunk from using violence, had failed even to make a good speech to the soldiers, and consequently had seen the whole affair degenerate into a scuffle, his own arrest, and forcible ejection to the United States ! Undeterred by this miserable failure, he again landed at Boulogne in 1840, with fifty men and a captive vulture, which was supposed to represent the Imperial eagle. Again the 'invasion' developed into an undignified scuffle ; Louis Napoleon tried to escape by swimming out to a boat, but it capsized ; he was wounded and captured—and in a few hours was again the laughing-stock of France. At his trial, however, he cut a more impressive figure, maintaining stoutly that the plebiscite which had put his uncle in power had never been revoked by the French people, and that therefore a Bonaparte should still be ruling. The lenient government of Louis Philippe, anxious not to make a martyr of him, confined him in the fortress of Ham and his 'eagle' in the Zoological Gardens. At Ham, under very free conditions, he studied hard to master social problems, and had soon succeeded in producing schemes for the development of the French beet-sugar industry, for improving army recruitment, for a Panama Canal, and for doing away with poverty by making the state take over and develop all unoccupied land. The result of this labour was that he grew popular with the French working classes, was well spoken of by Blanc, and was generally looked on as a man of vision. In 1846 he decided that the time had come for his escape—so he damaged his rooms so badly that repairs were necessary, then one day disguised himself as a workman and simply walked out of the fortress with a plank over his shoulder. Safe in London he soon evidenced his passion for law and order by enrolling as a special constable during the Chartist riots, and his love of humanity by becoming the darling of the ballet girls. When the Revolution of 1848 had broken out he had gone to France, offered his services— and been asked to leave. Returning in June when the law against the Bonapartes was repealed (for the benefit of his cousins, not himself), and securing election to Parliament, he made such a poor impression that his opponents did not rate him seriously. Thiers, in fact, even began to encourage his candidature for the Presidency on the ground that "he was a noodle whom anyone could twist round his finger." But they miscalculated badly. The name Napoleon offered to the middle classes a guarantee of law and order, and the books which Louis himself had written promised a host of useful social reforms. The military dictatorship of Napoleon I was kept in the background, and only his reforms and liberal 'intentions' stressed. So it came about that, on a national vote, Louis Napoleon was elected President of the French Republic with 5,400,000 votes, while Cavaignac received

Louis Napoleon President

1,400,000 and poor Lamartine, with his ideals so swiftly outpaced by events, only 17,000.

His popularity

The new President was to enjoy a spell of office of four years. He immediately set out to combine enjoyment with popularity. One step, in particular, which the Assembly took he strove to undo—3,000,000 casual labourers had been disqualified from voting by a law that they must have resided continuously for three years in the same district. Louis Napoleon championed the cause of these men, and this, combined with his plans outlined in 1850 for railways, roads, harbours, canals, model farming, drainage, and sanitation, increased his popularity with the lower classes. His period of office would expire in 1852 and there was a law against re-election. Yet he was now planning to secure re-election by illegal methods, partly through ambition, partly because he was deeply in debt and needed a continuation of his Presidential income. At the same time some of the leaders of the Assembly were clearly plotting to get rid of the President, and Thiers, for example, openly boasted that "before a month is up, we will have Louis Bonaparte under lock and key."

The Coup d'État, 1851

It was the President who struck first. At 10 p.m. on the night of December 2nd, 1851—the anniversary of Austerlitz— after he had held his usual evening reception, a brilliantly engineered *coup d'état* began. Seventy-eight separate police officers during the night arrested seventy-eight separate leaders of the opposition—both police and prisoners being quite ignorant of the fact that they were part of a large-scale plan. Troops were posted in strategic positions and printers were forced to print proclamations announcing the change in the presidential position. Paris woke up to find Louis Napoleon supreme over his opponents. He proposed to rule as President for a further ten years, after holding a national plebiscite to confirm him in his power. After the first shock there was a little barricade-work on December 3rd and 4th—but order was restored with the loss of about 500 lives. In the provinces there were some outbreaks, which led to something like 27,000 people being arrested, of whom 10,000 were deported. The subsequent plebiscite, however, came quite up to his highest hopes, 7,400,000 voting for him and only 600,000 against. The moral was drawn by the President—"France has realized

YOUNG FRANCE'S NEW TOY.

France neglects Louis Philippe, Lamartine (with lyre), and General Cavaignac for Louis Napoleon.

that I broke the law only to do what was right. The votes of over 7,000,000 have just granted me absolution." The use of the word 'absolution' tends to show that the *coup d'état* really weighed on Louis Napoleon's conscience, as is also evidenced by the fact that he released all the prisoners by 1859. Indeed, it had some business to weigh on his conscience, since he had solemnly sworn before God to be faithful to the French Republic as established in 1848. But a politician's promises, as he himself observed, "are even more brittle than lovers' oaths."

2. *The Second Empire, 1852–1870*

The Empire   It was not long before there occurred the logical sequel, the restoration of the Empire. A year of useful reforms—housing schemes, abolition of Sunday labour, provision of baths, wash-houses, asylums—combined with pageantry and triumphal tours to impress some and wandering round slums on foot to impress others, and various public bodies began to urge him to become Emperor. The invitation did not fall on unwilling ears. On December 2nd, 1852, the second French Republic ended and the second Empire began, the ex-President assuming the title of Napoleon III. A further plebiscite confirmed the step by 7,800,000 to 250,000, while 2,000,000 did not vote. Naturally Parliament was allowed very little power, political meetings and associations were forbidden, newspapers were heavily taxed, and all steps taken to see that opposition was too weak to overthrow the Emperor. This dictatorship Napoleon III, with his queer mixture of ideals and ambitions, proposed to modify låter when France had settled down. For the moment, however, he was careful to point out that an isolated plebiscite was a different matter from perpetual democracy, and aptly expressed the difference by saying that he "did not mind being baptized with the water of universal suffrage," but that he "refused to live with his feet in it."

Reforms   The reforming zeal of the new Emperor was soon evident. For some years it was said that he never visited a town without making better arrangements for its future. In Paris, in collaboration with the Prefect of the Seine, Baron Haussmann,

TERRIFIC ASCENT OF THE HERO OF
A HUNDRED FÊTES.

Louis Napoleon climbs higher ! Boulogne and Strasbourg refer to his
two ridiculous attempts to capture the throne in Louis Philippe's reign.

he instigated the biggest slum-clearance scheme on record. Thousands of narrow, insanitary, unlit streets with verminous dwellings were destroyed, to be replaced by magnificent wide boulevards, complete with trees and lamps—a piece of reform which had the secondary object of making the erection of barricades more difficult. Water and gas-mains were laid along the Paris streets. In the improvement of the country's communications the Emperor showed an equal zeal, railway, telegraph, and steamship services all expanding through his interest. A period of prosperity, marked by great financial speculation, began for France. There were no signs as yet of the adventurous foreign policy which was to bring ruin on the Second Empire as it had done on the First, and there was every sign of Napoleon III's care for the masses. So acute an observer as the English Prince Consort soon remarked of the Emperor, "Louis Napoleon wishes for peace, enjoyment, and cheap corn."

The Court   The court life of the Emperor rapidly became notable for its brilliance. Rebuffed in an attempt to secure a bride who had the merit of royalty, since the other sovereigns of Europe for the most part regarded him as an upstart, he concentrated instead on looks. Eventually he married a beautiful Spanish noblewoman, whose love letters to him had been written, though he did not know it, by Prosper Mérimée, the famous novelist. The Empress Eugénie, as she became, was unfortunately less well equipped mentally than she was physically. This would not have mattered in itself had she not endeavoured to influence the Emperor's political policy. This, however, was reserved for the future ; for the moment all was enjoyment at Court, with spiritualistic diversions (tables talking and accordions playing by themselves), grand receptions, appearances at the Opera, visits from interesting people such as Pasteur, Verdi, Gautier, the interminable love-affairs of the Emperor, and the rather more innocent pastime of the Empress—blind man's buff. It was Napoleon III, in fact, with his love of amusement and his rebuilding schemes, who gave that atmosphere of elegance and entertainment to Paris which has made of it the Mecca of Englishmen escaped to holiday abroad.

There was something in the Napoleonic character, however,

which could not be content with either reform or enjoyment. Though by no means a hardened militarist, Napoleon III was unable to resist the traditions of his uncle and the pressure of certain army leaders. His ambition and sometimes his ideals prompted him to undertake military campaigns, but he lacked the ruthless character of the first Napoleon, and after a successful beginning his foreign policy led him to disaster.

Foreign ventures

The first foreign venture was, comparatively speaking, a success. Already possessing a personal grievance against the Czar Nicholas for refusing to address him as 'brother' in the customary manner between sovereigns, and anxious to assert French claims wherever possible, he had quarrelled with Russia. The question at issue was the guardianship of the Holy Places of Palestine, which Napoleon claimed had been accorded to Charlemagne and his French successors. When Russia not only refused to surrender this right but demanded from Turkey the protectorship of all the Sultan's Christian subjects—which would have given Russia the right to interfere widely in the Turkish Empire—Napoleon III, supported by England, prompted Turkey to refuse. The subsequent invasion of Turkish territory by Russia and the sinking of the Turkish fleet at Sinope caused England and France to ally for the purpose of reducing Russian influence. It was decided to send a joint expedition to the Crimea to compel Russia to keep her warships off the Black Sea, and thus lessen the likelihood of their threatening the Balkans and Anglo-French interests in the Mediterranean. The key to the Black Sea was the fortress of Sebastopol, and for a year English and French generals vied with each other in committing mistakes in besieging it. Eventually, when 100,000 French soldiers had lost their lives after suffering the untold miseries of campaigning in a Crimean winter, Sebastopol was taken, Russia requested peace, and the war ended.

(1) The Crimean War, 1854–1856

The Emperor had had some awkward moments : in 1855, for example, he had reached the point of wanting to take charge in the Crimea himself, a resolve from which he was persuaded only by the entreaties of Queen Victoria, whose truly feminine heart had been mildly fluttered by his expert addresses. But the end of the war compensated for

Treaty of
Paris, 1856

everything, and the Treaty of Paris of 1856, with Russia compelled to accept the neutralization of the Black Sea, gave the Emperor his first taste of the sweets of victory.

(2) Italian
intervention

The next foreign venture appeared equally successful at first, though it was before the end to involve Napoleon III in a bewildering series of difficulties, complexities, and contradictions. The enthusiasm of the Emperor as a young man for the cause of Italian unity has already been noted. The young Carbonaro of 1830 had, however, naturally to be more careful now that he was in control of the destinies of France. His problem may be briefly stated—how to aid the Italians in their struggle for national unity without (a) making an Italy which would be too powerful a neighbour, (b) offending the very important clerical circles in France, who would not wish to see the Pope's rule over the Papal States abolished, and (c) getting into trouble with too many other nations. As a further complication may be added (d) that unless he did something to help the Italians he would offend Liberal circles in France. He was thus bound to offend one of two parties in France, and probably he would have done best to go all out on one side or the other. Instead he tried to please both, and failed to satisfy either.

When he became President in 1848 he had found French troops helping the Pope against Mazzini and Garibaldi, who were trying to establish a Roman Republic. For a time he continued this policy—to please the clericals—but combined this with assurances that he would make the Pope carry out a liberal policy—to please the anti-clericals. After the 1848 episode Italian problems for a while took a secondary place in the Emperor's mind, though Count Cavour, Prime Minister of Piedmont and Sardinia, the centre of Italian hopes, staked a strong claim on the Emperor's gratitude and future services by sending a contingent of Sardinian troops to help the French in the Crimean War. At the Treaty of Paris, Cavour raised the question of Italian unity ; the Emperor, however, did nothing further till a violent incident jogged his memory.

The Orsini
attempt

In 1858 a number of fervent Italian patriots, led by Orsini, attempted to assassinate the Emperor as he was driving to the Opéra. The explosion of the bombs killed eight people and wounded 150, but to the great relief of the French the Emperor and the Empress were unhurt. At the trial Orsini conducted himself heroically, and the Emperor, strangely affected by this incident, determined to do something more to carry out his youthful vows and ideals. He would even have forgiven Orsini had not his advisers reminded him that the attempt had caused a regular massacre of innocent victims. Four months later he met Cavour at the Spa of Plombières as though by accident—his Foreign Minister even telegraphed to

L'Empire c'est la paix

[*Reproduced by permission of the Proprietors of 'Punch.'*]

THE FRENCH PORCUPINE.

He may be an Inoffensive Animal, but he Don't Look like it

" L'Empire, c'est la Paix," said Napoleon III frequently—but Europe could never quite believe it.

tell him that Cavour was there !—and concluded an alliance with Piedmont. The terms of the agreement were that Napoleon would free Italy 'as far as the Adriatic,' in return receiving Savoy and Nice, which were under Piedmontese rule, but which were predominantly French in sentiment. This meant helping Piedmont to drive the Austrians out of Lombardy and Venetia. It only remained to find the necessary excuse for starting the war.

The war begins, 1859

Shortly afterwards the Austrian ambassador was amazed to hear Napoleon III say to him, "I regret that our relations with your government are not as good as they have been"; and it was not long before Cavour, by arranging provocative frontier incidents, had tempted Austria to invade Piedmont and neglect the French warning not to do so. The war had begun, and with the French army under the Emperor's personal command two big victories over the Austrians were registered at Magenta and Solferino. Lombardy was freed—it remained to complete the task by sweeping the Austrians

Peace of Villafranca, 1859

from Venetia. Suddenly came the astounding news that the Emperor had concluded an armistice with the Austrians, leaving an infuriated Cavour and Piedmont in the lurch. Many motives have been suggested for this sudden reversal of policy, among them the fact that the Emperor, sickened with the horrors of war at first hand, had lost all stomach for the enterprise. Perhaps a more important consideration was one he himself advanced—that his victories had been by a narrow margin, and that attacking Venetia meant capturing the four tremendously difficult Austrian fortresses known as the Quadrilateral. Further there was a lurking fear of Prussian intentions in his mind, and probably too there was an increasing conviction that Italian unity might be an awkward thing for France when accomplished. At any rate he retired from North Italy, though he shortly afterwards by diplomatic means prevented Austria from annexing Modena, Parma, and Tuscany, thus allowing them to throw in their lot with Piedmont. For these services he claimed his reward of Savoy and Nice—confirmed, as usual, by a plebiscite. The whole adventure of 1859 shows up Napoleon III's Italian policy in all its contradictions—helping Italian unity in the north (while his troops still kept the Pope in power in Rome), then backing out at a critical moment—offending half France by beginning at all and the other half by stopping when he did. All the same, by 1859 Italy had provided a second field for the victories of French arms, the French army was regarded as the best in Europe, and the Emperor was at the height of his power. Successful minor enterprises in Syria and China contributed to the general effect.

The following year, however, marked the turning of the tide.

THE FIRST LESSON.

Not so bad for a Beginner!

The Amnesty to his old opponents (1859) was Napoleon III's first step towards the " Liberal Empire."

In 1859 the Emperor, true to his policy of allowing greater
An amnesty liberty as time went on, allowed all political exiles to return,
and thus laid his Empire open to attack from a number of men
who feared nothing.   In 1860, too, he allowed Parliament
more freedom to criticize and amend proposals brought before
it, which contributed to the same result.   Above all, in 1860
he provoked widespread discontent among the manufacturing
classes by concluding a commercial treaty with England
The 1860 (represented by the famous free-trader Cobden).   By this
Cobden agreement the French duties on English textiles, iron, steel,
treaty and hardware goods were lowered considerably in return for
English reductions on French wines, silks, and fancy goods.
This exposed many French manufacturers to the full blast of
English competition, and the Emperor's popularity suffered
accordingly.

(3) The A further foreign adventure, dragging on over several
Mexican years, lowered the Emperor's prestige in a serious fashion.
adventure In 1861, when the Mexican Republic defaulted on its debts
and was refusing to pay interest on bonds held by foreign
creditors, France, England, and Spain agreed to send a joint
expedition to enforce payment.   When the object of the
expedition had been obtained, England and Spain withdrew
their forces, but Napoleon III, urged on by Eugénie and the
clerical party, retained his troops there and embarked on a
far more ambitious project.   His plan, specially designed to
enhance French prestige and please the clerical elements
offended at his Italian policy, was to overthrow the anti-
religious Mexican Republic and substitute a Catholic Empire.
Maximilian, brother of the Austrian Emperor, was persuaded,
by the promise of French support, to undertake the position
of imperial claimant.   The fighting that followed was long
and expensive, but by 1864 French arms had duly installed
him on his throne.   Unfortunately for Napoleon III, however,
another power now came on the scene in full force—the
United States.   The United States, engaged in a desperate
civil war, had thus far been powerless, but on the conclusion
of the war in 1865 a warning was given to France that the
United States would tolerate no interference with the Monroe
Doctrine.   France, in other words, must keep out of Mexico—
or be prepared to fight the United States.   Napoleon, already

tired of a costly war, welcomed the excuse, and withdrew his forces. The result of the whole episode was again that both parties in France were annoyed—the liberals because Napoleon had engaged in the venture and the clericals because he had terminated it too soon. Maximilian's desperate wife, unable to extract a promise of further help from Napoleon, went mad at the thought of the sure fate of her husband, and finally when the news came in 1867 that Maximilian had been captured by his enemies and shot, Napoleon, who had led him into the whole adventure and then deserted him, was made to look particularly mean.

Napoleon III by now was meeting with considerable difficulty in restraining political opposition in France. His Italian and Mexican policies had pleased no one, his economic reforms had not gone far enough to prevent outbreaks of strikes and the growth of Socialism and Communism, and there was an increasing demand for greater political liberty. Again following his earlier theory (which he also declared to be Napoleon's intention) of 'liberalizing' the Empire as time went on, he now gave greater liberty to the press, allowed more political meetings, and granted a limited right of forming trade unions. To 'crown the edifice' Parliament was given yet more power, and in 1870 a ministry was appointed which really did reflect the views of the majority and was responsible to the Assembly. By 1870 Napoleon, urged not only by his theories but by a dreadfully painful illness, which was sapping his strength, had thus turned himself from a dictator to a constitutional monarch. The change was approved by another enormous plebiscite—7,500,000 against 1,500,000. Within less than a year the reign of Napoleon III was at an end. *The "Liberal Empire," 1869*

The death-blow to the Empire, torn as it now was by disunion, came from a state Napoleon had not sufficiently considered in the early years of his rule—Prussia. The nightmare of the growing power of Prussia under Bismarck had, however, begun to haunt him from 1865 on. The change had come with the Austro-Prussian war of 1866—the 'Seven Weeks' War.' The year before, France and England had been unable to agree in supporting Denmark against Prussia and Austria over the fate of Schleswig and Holstein. Schleswig *The rise of Prussia* and Holstein having thus fallen to the stronger side, the victors had quarrelled over the spoil, and war broke out between Austria and Prussia. Europe expected the struggle to be a protracted one, and Napoleon had visions of a strong France at the end of the war dictating policy to both of the exhausted opponents. He thus consented to remain neutral, the more especially as he was bribed to do so by Bismarck, who promised him a free hand to absorb Luxemburg. Alarmed, however, by the rapid Prussian success at the battle of Sadowa, when Austria was overwhelmed in a single defeat, Napoleon rather hysterically began to demand 'compensation' for France in German territory in the Rhine district, besides plotting to get not only Luxemburg but Belgium. Bismarck all along the line cleverly outmanœuvred his opponent, and used Napoleon's proposals for two vital ends. The first of these was to force the south and west German States, through fear of France, to ally and eventually to unite with Prussia. The second was to reveal details of the secret negotiations at two critical moments—one just at the outbreak of the Franco-Prussian war. The result was thus, by displaying Napoleon as eager to grasp surrounding territory, to throw European sympathy into the Prussian rather than the French scale, and to rob Napoleon of any possibility of English support in 1870.

The Franco-Prussian War, 1870–1871

The fatal moment for the Empire had now come. With first Denmark then Austria beaten, the south German States won over to Prussia by fear of France, Italy bribed by the acquisition of Venetia in 1866 through Prussian help, England offended with France from knowledge of her ambitions in Luxemburg and Belgium, Napoleon was isolated. At home his prestige was low ; physically, he was a dying man. Bismarck decided that the moment had come to strike. And, most foolish and fatal of all, Bismarck's plans were facilitated in every respect by France, even more anxious to come to grips with Prussia. The actual conflict arose over the candidature for the vacant Spanish throne, for which a Hohenzollern prince was, on the insistence of Bismarck, a reluctant candidate. France, nervous of Prussian progress and determined not to be again outwitted, demanded the withdrawal of the candidature. The Prussian king, William, agreed to persuade his relative to withdraw, and France's main object was satisfied. But certain circles in the Government—not so much the Emperor himself—were anxious for an even more resounding diplomatic triumph to enhance the Emperor's tottering prestige, and so a further demand was formulated that in no circumstances must Prussia ever renew such a candidature. William, who regarded the incident as closed, saw no point in seeing the French ambassador again on the subject, and his decision was explained in a despatch to Bismarck known as the Ems Telegram. Bismarck, before publishing this, slightly altered it to read so that the impression gathered was that Wilhelm deliberately refused to see the French ambassador with the express object of insulting France. A howl of wrath arose in the Paris press and a momentary war-fever—a fatally easy thing to rouse—swept over the government, which a month before had reduced the army by 10,000 men and had proclaimed that "at no epoch was the peace of Europe more assured." Again it must be emphasized that Napoleon did not share in the general French confidence or in the fatuous blindness of the commander who said that there was "not so much as the button of a gaiter missing." But the sick man gave in before the imperious will of Eugénie, who revelled in the prospect of the conflict and boasted proudly, "This is *my* war."

Disillusion was to come speedily. After a few very minor successes, the French found Alsace and Lorraine invaded by an enemy vastly better equipped and trained. Some heavy fighting sufficed to shut up the main French army in the town of Metz, where, besieged, it could help no other part of France. The Emperor, dispirited and in agony, proposed to fall back on Paris with the remaining principal force. Such a decision would have prolonged the struggle and given France a chance of drafting millions more into the conflict. But Eugénie and her advisers could not brook the temporary humiliation and forbade such a step, assuring the Emperor that his throne was lost if he retreated. So against all his own inclinations the harassed Emperor, who had now little control over his troops, moved to the relief of Metz, was caught, as was almost inevitable, in an unfavourable position, and witnessed the crushing defeat of his army at Sedan. On September 3rd came to

The fighting

Sedan

Paris the dramatic despatch : "The army of Chalons has surrendered ; I myself am a prisoner. Napoleon." Within a day the mob had invaded the Assembly with cries of 'Down with the Empire,' and Gambetta, a fiery young politician already distinguished for his daring opposition to Napoleon, had proclaimed the new Republic—the third in French history. There was no contest, not a finger lifted to save the Empire. Napoleon himself accompanied William as a prisoner into Germany, soon to be released and to die in England, whither Eugénie, escaped from Paris with the help of her American dentist, had already fled. The Empire, it has been said, 'crumbled like a castle of cards under the flick of a child's fingers.'

The end of the Empire

So the reign of Napoleon III, which opened in revolution, ended in revolution. It had been a thing of contrasts. It had combined dictatorship with democracy ; professions of peace and the first Paris international exhibitions with territorial ambitions ; support of nationalism in North Italy with opposition to it in Rome and Mexico. Beneath its 'gas-lit pomp' lay squalor, industrial and moral. And the whole contradictory nature of the Empire had been perfectly mirrored in the character of Napoleon himself, idealistic and self-seeking, reforming and reactionary, profound and superficial. Less complex in character, Eugénie had, however, done almost as much as her husband to bring about the downfall. Her influence on the Roman question, on Mexico, on the Franco-Prussian war had been decisive. She, at any rate, learnt her lesson, for in the long years of her exile, till she died in 1919 at the age of ninety-four, she never again interfered in politics. A vigorous old lady, even after the terrible blow of the loss of her son, (killed fighting for the English against the Zulus), she maintained her activity to the last, learning to ride a bicycle, buying one of the first motor-cars, and even wanting to fly at the age of ninety. But "the Empress Eugénie," she said, "died in 1870."

The Third Republic

The Empire had collapsed, but meanwhile the new Republic fought on. For four months Paris, besieged like Metz, endured heroically while Gambetta, escaped in a balloon, organized armies and resistance in the countryside. But before long Metz had to give in, on the point of starvation,

VERSAILLES, OCT. 5, 1870.

" The Royal Head-Quarters were transferred here to-day.''—*Telegram.*

HOST OF LOUIS THE FOURTEENTH (*to Ghost of* NAPOLEON THE FIRST).   " IS THIS THE
END OF ' *ALL THE GLORIES* ?' "

5*

and nearly 200,000 French soldiers laid down their arms. The Prussians thus released from conducting the siege were employed in adding to the forces before Paris or in holding back Gambetta's attempts to relieve the capital. Till the last the Parisians resisted, till everything had been eaten, including the elephant in the Zoo and the rats of the streets and sewers, and the fuel was exhausted. Then there was no alternative but to capitulate.

The Treaty of Frankfort   The terms of the treaty of Frankfort of 1871 were regarded at the time as extraordinarily severe, though they pale somewhat by comparison with the Versailles treaties of 1919, at any rate in financial details. France was to pay an unprecedented war indemnity of five thousand million francs in three years, to suffer an army of occupation, and to lose Alsace and most of Lorraine, including Metz. The last provision especially engendered a state of bitterness which speeded on the European conflict of 1914, in the usual way in which one war begets another.

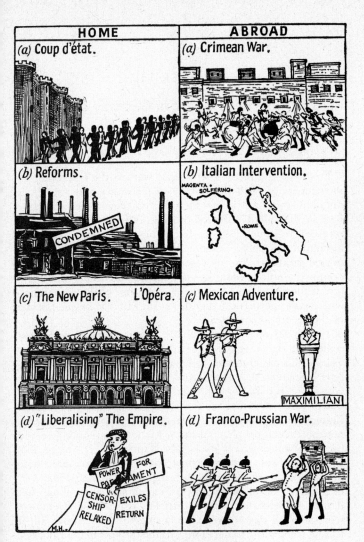

HOME	ABROAD
(a) Coup d'état.	*(a)* Crimean War.
(b) Reforms.	*(b)* Italian Intervention.
(c) The New Paris. *L'Opéra.*	*(c)* Mexican Adventure.
(d) "Liberalising" The Empire.	*(d)* Franco-Prussian War.

THE SECOND EMPIRE.

CHAPTER VII

The Metternich Period in Germany and the Austrian Empire, 1815-1851

1. *From the Congress of Vienna to the Outbreak of Revolution*

Metternich From the end of the Napoleonic wars to the revolutionary movements of 1848 the history of Germany and Austria is dominated by one man—Metternich. Few statesmen have had so difficult a series of problems to face and few have received so much blame, both then and since, for their attempted solutions. In some respects he was and is a greatly misjudged man. In any case, for more than a generation he occupied a unique position—not only as Chancellor of Austria but as the embodiment of the older Europe of the monarchies which was fighting a desperate battle with the newer Europe of the revolutionary ideals.

To understand Metternich's pre-eminence we must remember that it was he more than anyone who, within four years of his appointment as Chancellor in 1809, had successfully manœuvred Austria away from the temporary alliance with Napoleon and brought her in with the Allies. It was his skill in 1814 which inspired the manifesto of the Allies, invading France, to the effect that their quarrel was with Napoleon, not the French people. "I know Metternich : only he could have thought of that !" exclaimed Napoleon. It was he, too, whose spirit was so active at the Congress of Vienna and whose diplomacy was so successful in bringing the famous Final Act, or summary of the arrangements, to completion—a Final Act, it may be remarked, of 121 articles, which took twenty-six secretaries all day to write out a single copy. Above all, it was he who, with Castlereagh, was the inspirer of the Congress movement—the movement to establish a 'Concert' of Europe, or, in the words of a contemporary, "to put all heads under the same thinking cap."

The ideas of such a man, born the son of a count and educated from the first to fit him for an outstanding position in the Imperial Court, were necessarily fixed. He had spent all his public life thus far in striving to protect Austria from the menaces of Napoleon, who claimed to be the representative of certain ideas associated with the French Revolution. He had seen the intense nationalism of France bring untold misery to Europe. He was an enthusiastic traveller, a student and patron of art and science, whose boundaries are far from being national. He was the Chancellor of an Empire which included thirteen races and many religions, accumulated by means varying from conquest to diplomatic matrimony. It was his habit, he said, to write "to Paris in French, to London in English, to St. Petersburg in Russian, and to Berlin in German." In a word, his outlook was that of a cosmopolitan aristocrat of the 18th century. It was an outlook which in its culture, its love of peace, and its opposition to anything which smacked of the vulgarity of "the rabble," such as disorderly democratic agitation or nationalist hysteria, had much to commend it. Unfortunately it was also an outlook which concentrated on effects rather than causes, on conservatism rather than development.

It was because Metternich represented so completely and so ably the views of European aristocracy generally that he occupied such an outstanding position in the generation after Waterloo. His task was twofold—to preserve the European peace and to maintain for monarchy and aristocracy their privileged position against the assaults of the two greatest forces of the age, liberalism and nationalism. In both objects it must be admitted that he met with a fair degree of success. Although the Congress System had collapsed by 1829, no major European war occurred from 1815 till the Crimean War of 1854, and no liberal or national outbreak really shook the Austrian Empire till 1848. Even then the revolutionary movements were suppressed within a year or so, and it was not till 1859 that, in the loss of Lombardy, the dismemberment of the Empire began. At the same time it is apparent to the observer from the vantage-point of the 20th century that in the struggle against what was for the most part extremely inefficient monarchy, the liberal and national forces were bound to win. It has required the ruthless efficiency of modern dictatorship to suppress the liberal movement. Metternich himself was often acutely conscious of the fact that his task was almost hopeless. "I have to give my life to propping up a mouldering edifice," he once remarked in a moment of pessimism, while the Emperor Francis put the matter even more strongly—"My realm is like a worm-eaten house—if one part is removed, one cannot tell how much will fall." Let us see how Metternich strove to act, in his own words, as "a rock of order" in Austria and Germany.

It will be remembered that the Allies of 1813, in the War of Liberation, had taken advantage of the national fervour of Germany, aroused by the Continental System and the oppressive demands of Napoleon. As Napoleon had employed all the forces of national feeling in the early days of victories, so the Allies had later been able to use the same weapon against him with deadly effect. Napoleon himself, with his usual acuteness, prophesied that the Allies would pay for their encouragement of nationalism when it turned against their own empires. The arrangements of the Congress of Vienna, in regard to Germany and the Austrian Empire not less than elsewhere, illustrate how little importance the Allies really attached to nationalist principles.

The Austrian Empire

The Austrian Empire, as recognized by the treaties of 1815, included as its main sections Austria proper (which was truly German), Bohemia and Moravia (inhabited chiefly by Czechs, Slovaks, and Germans), Hungary (Magyar, with many minorities, notably Serb and Croat), Galicia (mainly Ruthenians and Poles, acquired during the partitions), Transylvania (Roumans, of Latin stock), Illyria and Dalmatia (Serbs and Croats), and Lombardy and Venetia (Italians). It thus contained, besides oddments like the Magyars, representatives of the great racial divisions—Teuton (the Germans), Slav (Czechs, Croats, Poles, Serbs), and Latin (Roumanians and Italians). As yet, with the exception of the Italians and possibly the Germans of Austria itself, the new wine of nationalism and democracy had not yet reached the heads, or even the lips, of most of these peoples, and thus the strength of the central government in Vienna was not in immediate

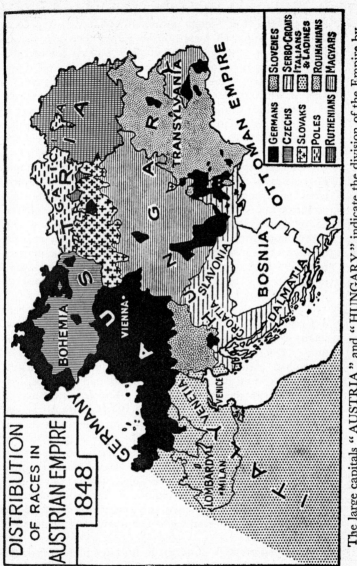

DISTRIBUTION
OF RACES IN
AUSTRIAN EMPIRE
1848

GERMANY

BOHEMIA

VIENNA•

GALICIA

AUSTRIA

HUNGARY

TRANSYLVANIA

LOMBARDY•
MILAN•

VENETIA
VENICE•

CROATIA

SLAVONIA

BOSNIA

DALMATIA

OTTOMAN EMPIRE

GERMAN EMPIRE

GERMANS · SLOVENES
CZECHS · SERBO-CROATS
SLOVAKS · ITALIANS & LADINES
POLES · ROUMANIANS
RUTHENIANS · MAGYARS

The large capitals "AUSTRIA" and "HUNGARY" indicate the division of the Empire by
the Ausgleich of 1867.

danger of being challenged. This was all the more so since the government at Vienna permitted a wide variety of local difference, employed local officials rather than bureaucrats from Vienna, and generally allowed a very considerable degree of liberty—provided that no political agitation of any kind took place. Hungary enjoyed a separate parliament, or Diet, in which its intensely feudal nobility frequently asserted their privileges against Vienna. It was, further, no part of the policy of Metternich to attempt to 'Germanize' or 'Austrianize' the whole of the Empire—he was not keen enough on nationalism to enforce his own particular brand of it, while he correspondingly denied the right of the other brands to break away from his 'international' Empire. The government of Vienna, however, while well-meaning and not unduly tyrannical, was for the most part inefficient. It was badly in need of reorganization, and Metternich made several efforts, notably in 1811 and in 1817, to induce his imperial master to accept schemes of reform. Purely internal matters, however, were the subject on which he possessed least influence : "I have sometimes ruled Europe," he once remarked, "but I have never governed Austria."

Germany   In the matter of race alone, Germany presented a very different picture from the Austrian Empire, as it was inhabited solidly by Germans. Politically, however, it had even less unity. Before the Napoleonic wars some hundreds of petty states had existed, acknowledging the authority in name, though not at all in fact, of the Holy Roman Emperor, who coincided with the ruler of Austria. Napoleon's campaigns in Germany, however, had broken down many of the old divisions and substituted new and much greater units, such as the Confederation of the Rhine. In these a great deal of reform had been carried out in administration, and large sections of Germany had thus been released from cramping mediæval restrictions for the first time. The peacemakers of Vienna could naturally not allow such Napoleonic creations to survive—they had collapsed, anyway, with the breakdown of Napoleon's power—and consequently a fresh settlement was necessary in 1815.

The German Confederation   The Congress of Vienna made no attempt to revive the long-since obsolete Holy Roman Empire, which had long ago been styled by Voltaire "neither Holy, nor Roman, nor an Empire." Austria herself readily consented to the abandonment of the shadowy title whose history had begun with Charlemagne in 800, because she had set herself the task of consolidating a real Austrian Empire centred round the Danube. At the same time she was not prepared to see the growth of a powerful northern rival, and this fact, taken together with the claims of the various royal houses of Germany, made it certain that there would be no strong German state created. The hundreds of states had, indeed, now, by the force of circumstances, been boiled down to a mere thirty-nine, but the Confederation into which these were formed was deliberately kept as weak as possible. Its Diet consisted purely of ambassadors of the various states, not representatives elected by the peoples. Its members undertook not to declare war on one another and to furnish protection if attacked, but no law was binding on any member-state unless that particular member-state approved of the law in question. This alone, with the fact that unanimity was necessary for any change in the constitution, rendered the Confederation quite powerless. The monarchs of Austria (in virtue of her German lands, not the others), England (in virtue of Hanover), Denmark (Holstein), and Holland (Luxemburg) were all represented in the Diet, and it would certainly be to their interest to stop a strong Germany emerging.

At the same time while we can see that this was bound to prove a disappointment to those Germans who had hoped for a greater measure of national union, we must admit that there was no agreement on any particular form of union, and that the powerful forces of local patriotism were all against any possible central government. We must remember, too, that though the Confederation was left weak, its members were enjoined by the Vienna Act to grant constitutions to their subjects. Germany might thus look forward to a period of liberalism, though not of nationalism.

In actual fact, however, all that the Confederation did, Liberalism though it perhaps served as an inevitable step to something protests bigger, was to grant Germany 'an unlimited right of expectaton.' Only two or three rulers carried out their promise to

grant a constitution. The natural consequence was an outbreak of liberal agitation, particularly among the numerous
university students and their professors. In 1817 occurred
the 'Wartburg Festival,' a meeting to celebrate the battle of
Leipzig and the tercentenary of the Reformation, and to form
a closer union among German university students. The
students marked the occasion by burning a number of selected
'guys,' some books and periodicals whose views they resented,
and a few emblems of Prussian militarism, which was disliked
both for itself and for having adopted French fashions. The
emblems concerned included a corporal's cane, a pig-tail,
as worn by the infantry, and a pair of corsets, as sported by the
cavalry. It was only a student demonstration, but its spirit
was unmistakable, and Metternich took good notice of it,
the more so since he suspected the still liberal Czar Alexander
of fomenting similar trouble throughout Europe.

(1) The
Wartburg
Festival

Two years later occurred a much more sensational student
act, the murder of Kotzebue. He was an unpopular author
of reactionary views and a spy in Russian pay who was
regarded as poisoning the mind of Alexander against liberalism.
At once Metternich seized his opportunity. He won over
Alexander so completely from the last of his liberalism that in
1820 the Czar said to him : "To-day I deplore all that I said
and did between 1815 and 1818. I regret the time lost ; we
must study to retrieve it. You have correctly judged the
condition of things. Tell me what you want and what you
want of me, and I will do it." It was a remarkable admission
—but then, as Metternich said, "Alexander's mind never could
pursue one line of thought for long." More important still,
he used the occasion to secure the passage through the Diet
of the Confederation of a series of laws designed to crush all
political agitation. These, originally propounded in Carlsbad,
were known as the Carlsbad Decrees. By them a strict
censorship was everywhere set up, 'investigators' of recent
activities were appointed, student societies were suppressed,
political meetings were forbidden ; by their operation
professors were dismissed, Liberal leaders sentenced to years
of imprisonment. The result was for Metternich a triumph ;
liberalism in Germany and Austria was crushed for nearly a
generation to come. The German race, robbed of the right

(2) The
murder of
Kotzebue

The 'con-
version' of
Alexander

The Carls-
bad Decrees

of political expression, had to find scope for its genius in the fields of such strictly non-political subjects as science and music.

The stranglehold which Metternich thus secured was 1830 remarkably complete. Though the fall of the Bourbons in France in 1830 produced repercussions all over Europe (including revolutions in Belgium, Poland, and Rome), the Austrian Empire and Germany remained free from serious disturbance. In South Germany, indeed, the inhabitants of four states succeeded in wringing constitutions from their rulers, but that was all. In fact, from the Carlsbad Decrees till the revolutionary movements of 1848, there was no event of outstanding interest for the future of German nationalism.

There was, however, one movement, primarily economic, The Zollverein which was destined to have the greatest results. In 1818 Prussia had abolished a remnant of hampering mediævalism when she repealed all her internal customs duties and made the transit of goods from one district of Prussia to another quite customs-free. She also invited neighbouring states to join her in forming a single large customs-area, within which no duties would be payable. The invitation was made a little more pressing by putting enormous tariffs on the goods of those who did not accept. This 'Zollverein,' or Customs Union, as it soon became, showed remarkable signs of success —so much so that it was resented by other German states, who formed opposition groups. The opposition groups, however, found themselves forced by economic pressure to link up with the Prussian one, so that by 1829 the Union centring round Bavaria had joined and by 1834 that round Saxony. By 1844 the Zollverein covered nearly all Germany. Thus though Germany still lacked any effective political union, it was on the way to economic union, and the importance of this fact must not be overlooked. Moreover, through the Zollverein Prussia rather than Austria appeared to be taking the lead in Germany. Nor was economic advancement, especially in Prussia, confined to matters of customs. New roads had been built, a modern postal system initiated, railways constructed, steam-power introduced, while side by side with this, great developments in education, such as the founding

The develop-
ment of
Prussia

of polytechnics, schools, gymnasia, were apparent. After a period during which Prussia seemed to lose all desire to follow the tradition of her great reformers of the 1806 period, Stein, Hardenberg, and Scharnhorst, she began to revert to her policy of equipping herself as a really modern state.

A change of
monarchs

The changes on the thrones of Austria and Prussia during these years are matters of some importance. In 1835 the Emperor Francis, steady, conservative, far from brilliant but trusting implicitly in Metternich, died. He was succeeded by Ferdinand, described by Palmerston in his usual round terms as "the next thing to an idiot." Henceforward Metternich's advice was not always followed, and from about 1840 on he had constantly to intrigue to secure his position at court. The presence of an opposite party to the Chancellor's at court encouraged liberalism in Austria to hope once more.

(1)
Ferdinand
in Austria

(2) Fred-
erick
William IV
in Prussia

In Prussia, too, the greatly respected old man, Frederick William III, like Metternich and Francis a survival from Napoleonic days, also died, and was succeeded in 1840 by Frederick William IV. The character of the new king, who was known to be religious, humane, and anxious to avoid all forms of persecution, caused a great revival of the partly neglected aspirations for constitutionalism and a greater degree of national union. The composition in 1840, for example, of the famous patriotic song 'Die Wacht am Rhein' ('The Watch on the Rhine') showed which way sentiment was moving. The appointment of well-known patriots and even Liberals as the principal Prussian ministers, together with a relaxation of the censorship, seemed to confirm Prussians in the opinion that their king was indeed of democratic opinions. Unfortunately, however, it is obviously difficult for a king (or a pope) to be democratically inclined when the increased demands resulting from his encouragement begin to outrun what he himself desires. Frederick, who was in truth no democrat at all but a religious autocrat who had humane sympathies, rapidly found himself in this position. He soon terminated the experiment of a milder censorship. He did, however, agree to do something towards the establishment of the constitution which Frederick William III had promised Prussia as far back as 1815, when he permitted a Parliament or Diet to meet for Prussia in 1847. As he allowed it no more

Revival of
Liberalism

than mere debating rights, however, it was of little use to enthusiastic Liberals.   In fact, the idea of a written constitution which truly limited his power shocked his religious feelings as well as his political instincts, for he had a strong conception of the Divine Right of his position.   "Never will I consent," he said, "that a written paper should intrude like a second Providence between our Lord God in Heaven and this country, to govern us through its paragraphs."

The demand for a more representative form of government in both Austria and Germany, however, was soon to enter a new phase.   In Germany the failure of the potato crop of 1846, the doubled price of wheat in 1847, the thousands dying of hunger-typhus, had all reacted powerfully on the government.   In 1846 Poland gave an example of rebellion. Then in 1847, too, the more democratic Swiss cantons overthrew the more autocratic section, known as the Sonderbund, which had been formed under Austrian patronage.   Finally, in February 1848, the Orleans monarchy of Louis Philippe fell in France, and, like fireworks touched off one from the other, liberal revolutions broke out all over Europe—and not least in Austria and Germany.

2. *The Revolutionary Movement in the Austrian Empire*

The revolutions of 1848 are remarkable for their dramatic suddenness.   The news of the fall of the Orleans monarchy reached Vienna on March 1st ; by March 13th Metternich, the statesman of forty years' experience, was fleeing from the capital with a forged passport 'like a criminal' and rulers were making frantic concessions all over Germany to save their tottering thrones.   It is difficult to tell the story of these events separately, for the revolution in Germany was profoundly affected by the revolution in Austria, but for the sake of clarity it may be well to follow first the revolutionary movements in the Austrian Empire.

The section of the Austrian Empire which was most highly Hungary organized in its expression of national feeling was Hungary. Here a separate Diet had long existed, in which the proud Magyar nobility frequently endeavoured to assert independent claims against Austria.   At the same time Hungary itself, like most of the Austrian Empire, was in an intensely backward state, with the nobility still preserving mediæval feudal privileges over the peasantry and enjoying complete exemption from taxation. Already in Hungary, led by the fiery young journalist Louis Kossuth, a movement to introduce democratic reforms had arisen. His first demand was that the debates of the Diet should be held in Magyar, not Latin. Imprisoned for his insistence on reporting parliamentary debates, Kossuth, emerging after four years, continued the campaign with heroic determination. In his efforts to outwit the police and the law he was reduced to having his pamphlets lithographed instead of printed, and then finally to having them copied out by hand. In 1847 this ardent democrat was elected as member for Budapest to the Hungarian Diet, where though the nobility disapproved of most of his ideas, all could accept his championing of Hungary as against Austria. Immediately on receipt of the news of the 1848 revolution in France, sensing that the hour of democracy had struck, Kossuth on March 3rd came out with a flaming speech in the Hungarian Diet. "From the charnel-house of the Viennese system," he said, "a pestilential breath steals over us which paralyses our nerves and deadens our national spirit." He demanded not only that Hungary should be equal to Austria in all respects, enjoying a separate Hungarian ministry, but that the nobles' privileges should be abolished and a constitutional system established, with liberty of the press, of meeting, and of association. Support of Kossuth's policy was not lacking from the populace of Budapest, who succeeded in making their own nobles accept a 'People's Charter.' In March and April a series of laws (the 'March and April Laws') were carried, and the triumphant democrats were ready to force their acceptance at Vienna.

Meanwhile in Vienna itself events had moved in the same direction. Taking their cue from France and from Hungary, a number of students and professors held a great demonstration on March 12th. The mob cheerfully developed this the following day to fighting and an invasion of the palace, and secured important promises from a paralysed and inefficient government. The outcry naturally began with yells of 'Down with Metternich,' and the government could think of nothing

Kossuth [margin note]

Vienna [margin note]

better to do than sacrifice the aged Chancellor to the storm. When it called troops into Vienna they only fraternized with 'the rabble' (to use Metternich's expression).   On March 15th the government promised a constitution and the formation of a National Guard, and then on March 17th had to accept the Hungarian demand for a separate ministry responsible to the Hungarian Diet alone. *The fall of Metternich*

These events were rapidly paralleled in other sections of the Empire.   Before March was out the Austrians had been driven *Revolutions in Italy and Bohemia*

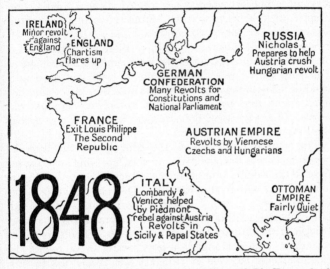

out of Milan and Venice, and the King of Piedmont had declared war with the intention of expelling them from the entire Italian peninsula.   At Agram in Croatia the Croats demanded the restoration of their ancient rights, while at Prague, capital of Bohemia, the Czechs framed constitutional demands similar to those of the Hungarians.   To all these a nerveless Imperial government agreed.   Only in Italy, where war was deciding the issue, and in Galicia, where the energetic Austrian governor, Count Stadion, kept the Poles in check, was there any real resistance.   In April a single liberal constitution for all the Empire was announced.   Hungary was to enjoy a separate arrangement. *A constitution granted*

The salvation of the Austrian monarchy, however, soon came in spite of itself. In May it touched its lowest depths, when, after a feeble effort to oppose further demands by Viennese agitators, the Emperor and his family suddenly left Vienna for Innsbruck, on the frontier. At the beginning of June, too, a great Congress of the different branches of the Slav race opened in Prague to discuss possible ways of organizing their racial kinship, a movement which seemed dangerous to an Empire of which the ruler was not by race Slavonic. But just when things seemed at their worst for the Empire, the tide began to turn. From Italy came news of the first success of the Austrian commander, Radetsky. In Prague itself the Austrian Governor, Windischgrätz, resisted the demand of the mob for armaments, and after a struggle in which his palace was attacked and his wife shot dead at a window, he withdrew with his troops from the city, bombarded it all night, and by morning had completely subdued the rebels. The Czechs of Bohemia had failed and one part of the Empire at least was saved.

The solution of the rest of the difficulty for the Imperial government was to come from the very fact which had caused most of the trouble—the existence of such a welter of different nationalities within the Empire. The important point to bear in mind is that not only was the Empire so composed, but each state within the Empire was practically a smaller edition of the Empire in its varying races. The Croats and Roumans under Hungarian government now found, for example, that the rule of Hungary was rather less to their taste than that of their previous and more distant masters, the Austrians. When they claimed from the Hungarians the same liberty as the Hungarians claimed from the Austrians, they were denied it. Before long the Croats, under their beloved leader Jellaçic, who was a great hater of the Magyars and a loyal servant of the Emperor, were at war with Hungary. They trusted Jellaçic's optimistic view that loyalty to the House of Austria would earn them more concessions than revolt. It was the obvious if unsavoury policy of the Imperial government to accentuate these national jealousies, and then sit back and watch its various enemies rend each other in pieces. Fresh hope gleamed for the monarchy, the more so since

The Slav Congress

Recovery in Italy

Recovery in Bohemia

The Croats quarrel with the Hungarians

Jellaçic

Radetsky had, in July, won a great victory over the Italians at Custozza and was soon to re-enter Milan.

Spurred by this success and stung to action by Kossuth's extreme financial measures, which were budgeting for Hungary as a purely separate state, the Austrian government now definitely urged Jellaçic and his Croats to invade Hungary. For a while he was held in check and part of his army had to surrender. But a use was soon found for his troops. When another and more violent democratic outbreak occurred in Vienna itself, the government called in Jellaçic to advance there, and at the same time summoned help from Windischgrätz in Prague. So in October Windischgrätz arrived to bombard Vienna into submission as he had done Prague, while Jellaçic defeated a force of Hungarians sent by Kossuth to the rescue of the Viennese democrats. The Imperial government was thus now in control not only of the Czechs, the Croats, and the Italians, but of the Austrians themselves. With the abdication of Ferdinand in December 1848 because of his mental condition, a new Emperor, Francis Joseph, a youth of eighteen, succeeded unencumbered by any promises about constitutions. It remained for the fast-reviving monarchy to deal with Hungary.

Jellaçic and Windisch-grätz save the government

Francis Joseph

The Hungarians, of whom Kossuth was now virtually the dictator, soon found themselves paying the price of their intolerance to their minorities. All round Hungary the different races were hostile, and in January 1849 it proved a fairly simple matter for Windischgrätz and Jellaçic to advance and capture Budapest. Kossuth and the government, however, who fled, organized resistance to the Austrians from the provinces. Much to the surprise of Europe, this proved very successful, the Hungarians defeating the racial risings on their frontiers and compelling the Austrians to withdraw from Budapest. Kossuth had by now cut the last ties asunder, and declared Hungary, in March 1849, an independent republic, of which he was 'Governor-President.' The decisive moment had now arrived. The Austrian government appealed to a source from which they knew they could, in the last resort, derive help—Russia. The Czar Nicholas, a great hater of revolutions and republics, was only too willing to aid the young Francis Joseph. Palmerston protested against the

Hungary declares its independence

Russia
intervenes

The
collapse of
Hungary

intervention, but in vain. By July an advance by Russia
from the east, the ruthless Austrian general Haynau from the
west (fresh from triumphant barbarities in Italy), and Jellaçic
from the south rendered the result a foregone conclusion.
The frantic Hungarian government's belated concessions to
its minorities were useless. Kossuth and the Hungarian
generals quarrelled senselessly, and finally Kossuth abdicated
and fled into Turkey, burying the Iron Crown of St. Stephen
on the way.   The last Hungarian army now laid down arms
and surrendered to the Russians. The Russians handed
control over to Haynau, who found the task of ordering the
scores of executions and hundreds of imprisonments so
congenial that at last even Vienna grew ashamed and recalled
him.   It is a matter of minor importance but of some interest
to note that both Kossuth and Haynau later paid visits to
England. Kossuth won a tremendous welcome from the people
and a reception by Palmerston in spite of the opposition of the
entire Cabinet. Haynau, however, who had received the nickname of 'Hyena,' on a visit to a London brewery was chased by
liberal-minded draymen. They would have undoubtedly
administered a little of the chastisement in which the distinguished visitor specialised had he not been rescued from
them in the nick of time.

Reaction
triumphant

It remained for Austria to take advantage of her escape.   In
Italy, with the decisive defeat of the Piedmontese at Novara
and the suppression of the Venetian Republic, the anti-
Austrian movement had collapsed. The Imperial government was there restored in doubled firmness. Roumans,
Croats, Czechs, Hungarians, Poles, all underwent for their
varying activities a tightening-up of control. By the end of
1851 the government felt sufficiently secure in Vienna to
abolish the constitution for the Empire wrung from it in April
1848, and reaction was everywhere triumphant. But while
no portion of the Empire received greater national independence or constitutional freedom as a result of the events of 1848
to 1851, it must not be forgotten that the feudal privileges of
the nobility and the serfdom of the peasantry had disappeared
never to return.   Just as the first French Revolution, in spite
of the dictatorship of Napoleon, preserved the benefits it had
won for the peasantry, so did the revolutionary movements of

"HE WENT AWAY WITH A FLEA IN HIS EAR."—*Old Saying.*

KETCH OF A MOST REMARKABLE FLEA WHICH WAS FOUND IN GENERAL HAYNAU'S EAR.

A humorous presentation of one of the draymen who 'rough-housed' Haynau on his famous visit to Barclay's Brewery. The 'flea's' remark refers to a threat of disciplinary action against the draymen. It is obvious where Punch's (and England's) sympathies lay.

1848 achieve the same result in spite of the re-establishment of Hapsburg power.

3. *The Revolutionary Movements in Germany*

The story of the revolutionary struggles of these years in Germany must now be told. It must first be noted that the German demands were bound to differ somewhat from those in the Austrian Empire, since German liberal feeling was not complicated by racial differences. Consequently, whereas the subject nations of the Empire wished to weaken the central government to gain greater local liberties, most German Liberals rather wished to set up a stronger central government to give expression to their national pride.

Liberal demands

Frederick William IV's accession to the throne of Prussia was, as we have seen, the signal for revival of German liberalism, and he had so far kept the promise of Frederick William III that in 1847 he had called a parliament for his kingdom. With the bad harvests, starvation, and typhoid epidemics of 1846 and 1847 the liberal demands had become more urgent and the Prussian parliament had framed requests for freedom of expression, trial by jury, an income tax, and a single National German Parliament, elected by the people for the whole of Germany. They were prepared to let the old powerless Confederation Diet exist side by side with this. Frederick William, however, had quite other ideas—he had refused a written constitution, and he had, instead of setting up a democratic Parliament for all Germany, wished simply to enlarge the powers of the Confederation Diet. He was in particular concerned with the problem of Austria, for her lands being chiefly non-German might lead to her exclusion from an all-German Parliament. "Germany without Austria," he said "would be worse than a face without a nose." It is not kings of this stamp who get the big things done in history, and Frederick William was throughout extremely nervous of allowing Prussia to take the lead. He thus soon fell out with his newly called Prussian parliament and dissolved it.

A National Parliament

The attitude of Frederick William

The fall of Louis Philippe in February 1848—"going out by the same door as he came in by," as the Czar Nicholas bluntly put it—aroused the same ferment in Germany as it did in the

Austrian Empire. Popular movements at once occurred in dozens of states, and everywhere the rulers after singularly little resistance granted their subjects constitutions or at least appointed liberal ministers. As one historian puts it—"the fruit fell from the trembling tree at the first shock." But a local state constitution was not enough—some wider form of German union must be attained. Already by March 5th fifty leading Liberals, chiefly from South Germany, met and debated plans for summoning a preliminary parliament (Vorparlament) which should establish a constitution for all Germany. Most of the state governments knew better than to oppose such a scheme at such a moment, and even the old Diet contrived not to get too much in the way. So on March 31st the Vorparlament actually met at Frankfort. The Vorparlament That could not have happened, however, unless not only the minor governments but Austria and Prussia had been seriously weakened by revolution. Austria, we have seen, was out of action by March 15th, when Metternich fled. Prussia's turn, as we shall now see, came on March 18th and 19th.

Following the news of the fall of Metternich in Vienna an outcrop of public meetings, addresses for reform, and the like occurred in Berlin until soldiers were eventually called on to fire to clear the streets. This policy, however, Frederick William, a great lover of peace, sincerely hated, and on March 18th he agreed to a constitution and parliament for the whole of Germany. He also abolished the censorship in The rising in Berlin Prussia. But in the afternoon another, almost accidental, clash between crowd and troops took place, and in two or three hours Berlin was up in barricades and revolution. The poor King went nearly frantic deciding whether to order the troops to attack the barricades or not. Finally, on the morning of the 19th, after a tortured night, he decided to withdraw his soldiers and even to go one step further by granting the mob's request for arms. Later in the day a new Liberal ministry was appointed and the King and Queen had to appear on the balcony of the palace to salute the corpses of citizens killed fighting against the royal troops. On the 21st he issued a proclamation in which he employed the famous phrase that "henceforth Prussia is merged in Germany," and "Prussia merged in Germany" was compelled to spend the day riding round promising nearly everything demanded. He afterwards referred to it as the most terrible day in his life.

When the German Vorparlament met at Frankfort on March 31st it thus felt confident in the fact that the monarchs of both Austria and Prussia were too weak to oppose the national movement. The Vorparlament (a hundred and forty-six members of which came from Prussia, but only two from Austria) was thus able to order elections to be held for a real parliament, or National Assembly, and to dissolve itself.

The National Assembly at Frankfort

By May this National Assembly had met, also at Frankfort. It was an extraordinarily talented body, containing most of the well-known names in literature and scholarship at the time. Many of its members, like those of the parliament of the first French Revolution, were lawyers ; many were state officials ; landowners and manufacturers on the one hand, and working-class citizens on the other, however, were sadly lacking. It was essentially representative of the professional middle classes.

The tasks and work of the Assembly

A number of tremendously difficult tasks confronted the Assembly, the first one being the construction of a constitution which would be at once liberal and acceptable to the various state governments. It was not too hard to draw up a list of citizens' rights, such as equality in law, freedom from arbitrary arrest, freedom of speech, of press, and of public meeting— the French 'Declaration of the Rights of Man' has always served as a classic example of this sort of thing. It was, again, quite easy to announce that all German states should have a constitution and a really representative government. All this was actually pronounced as law in December 1848. What was not so simple, however, was to get it all carried out by Austria, Prussia, and the other governments, even if they were temporarily weak. Yet a far more serious problem arose when the position of Austria was considered. Before this happened the Assembly had already lost prestige when it reluctantly approved Frederick William's withdrawal of support from the German party in Schleswig-Holstein, who were fighting against the incorporation of these two duchies into the Danish monarchy. (An attempted explanation of this, one of the most complicated questions in European history, will occur in a later chapter.) A day of bloodshed and riots in Frankfort

The difficulty about Austria

The difficulty about Schleswig-Holstein

had followed, extremists in the mob demonstrating in favour of continuing the war and if necessary fighting the King of Prussia too. Consequently by the time the Assembly came to tackle the vexed question of who or what was to be the central authority in the new Germany and what exactly Austria's position was to be, much of the early confidence had departed.

The difficulty about Austria was the fact that most of the Austrian Empire was non-German. The Assembly was thus faced with three possible solutions—to admit all the Austrian Empire into the new Germany, to admit only the German part of it, or to admit none of it. All of them had fatal objections. It would be nonsensical to admit Austria's thirteen different races into a state specially formed to express German nationalism, but to exclude them would be to offend Austria. The third possibility, of omitting Austria entirely, was viewed with horror by Frederick William and by many other Germans—a sentiment still visible nearly a century later in the refusal of the Nazis to tolerate an Austria separated from Germany. Thus the solution eventually favoured was the second, that of inviting Austria to be a part of the new state in virtue of Austria proper, but to exclude her Empire. This could not be acceptable to Austria, as it would mean that she would be split into two different states. The Austrian government, therefore, naturally refused such an invitation, and maintained that the whole Assembly should be abolished and the old Confederation restored, possibly with larger powers. As yet, however, she could not take any more active steps in opposition, for with the Empire crumbling on account of the various nationalist movements she was powerless. *(margin: Proposed solutions of the Austrian difficulty)* *(margin: The attitude of Austria)*

The opposition of Austria to the ideas of Frankfort thus compelled the Assembly to look to the next greatest state, Prussia, for leadership. It was not by any great majority that the Crown of the new 'German Empire' was offered to Frederick William, for by this time there were few illusions on the subject of his views and character. He had, too, by now recovered his position in Prussia somewhat by granting a constitution which still preserved a great deal of monarchical power. Nevertheless if it could not be Austria it must be Prussia, and so the invitation was duly tendered to Frederick William (March 1849). *(margin: The Assembly offers Frederick William the German Crown)*

The attitude of Frederick William

That monarch, now feeling more confident, had little hesitation in refusing the 'crown of shame' offered by a revolutionary assembly—or rather declaring that he would not accept it until it was offered by the various kings and princes of Germany, which was an impossibility. Further, he knew that Austria was entirely opposed to the whole movement and equally to Prussian leadership of it, and that acceptance of the crown might mean war. The Czar Nicholas too was almost equally likely to pour troops into Germany to stop a nationalist liberal movement. There was, moreover, his historic duty as King of Prussia—would it not be better from that point of view to follow the ideas of a young politician named Bismarck, and aim at absorbing Germany into Prussia rather than sinking Prussia into Germany? So Frederick William kept to the path of conservatism and prudence, admitting frankly that "Frederick the Great would have been the man for such an occasion—as for himself, he was not a great ruler." He followed this up by refusing the consent of Prussia to the whole laboriously compiled national constitution,

The withdrawal from Frankfort

and by withdrawing the Prussian delegates from Frankfort. Prussian troops, too, were employed to put down any consequent insurrections in Germany. Austria had already withdrawn her delegates, the other monarchs soon followed suit, and by the end of 1849 the last vestiges of the Assembly and its constitution had disappeared. Thus ended in failure a great design to combine German nationalism and democracy, nobly planned but fantastically difficult of execution. It is one of the greatest tragedies of 19th-century history that Germany could eventually achieve union not by the idealism of Frankfort but only by the Machiavellian realism of Bismarck.

An alternative Prussian union

The story has one tail-piece. In 1849 Frederick William gave his assent to the creation of some more acceptable and less democratic alternative in the form of a union of any willing states under Prussian leadership. This started promisingly, receiving the adhesion of several petty states and a few of the larger ones, besides the approval of a large group of the late delegates to Frankfort. A constitution was even drawn up, elections held, and a parliament called—but at the critical moment, owing to the opposition of Austria and the largest states, Frederick William abandoned this his latest offspring,

I. Racial Jealousy in Austrian Empire.

II. Hostility of Czar Nicholas I to Revolutions.

III. Frederick William's reluctance to assume leadership.

**THREE REASONS FOR FAILURE OF AUSTRIAN AND
GERMAN REVOLUTIONS.**

which accordingly perished. For a moment he thought of resisting when the old Confederation was resurrected by Austria and encouraged to support one notorious German tyrant in his quarrel with his subjects. But at the last minute, after Prussian troops were mobilized, he again gave way, and at Olmütz agreed to the Austrian demands. Nothing was left but to consent to the revival and the activities of the Confederation in its 1815 form.

So Austria, secure again in its own house, triumphed all along the line, not only over revolution but also over Prussia. Of all the turmoil of 1848 in central Europe the only notable gain for liberalism, apart from the freedom won by peasants from their lords in the Austrian Empire, was the watered-down constitution which survived in Prussia. Monarchy was 'on top' again, the various 'rabbles' subdued, nationalist claims frustrated. In 1851, as though to complete the restoration of the old Europe, shaken but still supreme, there returned to Vienna, to live for some years yet as a revered 'Elder Statesman'—Metternich.

CHAPTER VIII

The Unification of Italy, 1815–1870

1. *From the Congress of Vienna to the 1848 Revolutions*

In considering the hysterical nationalism which marked
Mussolini's Italy and Hitler's Germany, we are often apt to
forget that Italy and Germany are such recent creations.
England was already a single national state in the Middle
Ages, but both Italy and Germany consisted of many different
states until only two generations ago. Further, in the case of
Italy some of these states were under foreign rule. Nationalism
to both Germany and Italy is thus rather a new and exciting
thing, while the first flush of enthusiasm for it has somewhat
worn off in older states like France and England. With so
much by way of general comment, let us now follow the
process by which, during the 19th century, the *country* Italy
(or 'geographical expression,' as Metternich put it) became
the *state* Italy.

The arrangements of the Congress of Vienna affected Italy
no less than the rest of Europe. Napoleon in his first and
subsequent Italian campaigns had played havoc with the then
existing divisions, and now it was necessary to put something
in their place. He himself had aroused at first the enthusiasm
of Italians by his promises of reform and freedom, and indeed
the French government had everywhere introduced modern
ideas and improvements in administration. He had reduced
the divisions of the country to three, established the enlightened
French legal codes, constructed roads and bridges. Ultimately, however, as with all territories he conquered, Napoleon
had betrayed the trust of the inhabitants by repressive police
measures and taxation. He had, too, robbed Italy of its most
precious works of art. His 'Kingdom of Italy,' moreover, had
included only the north. Nevertheless he had inspired many
Italians with a genuine desire for freedom and reform, and the

*The work
of Napoleon*

Congress of Vienna might have seemed a suitable moment for giving shape to these aspirations.

Unfortunately, as we have seen pretty frequently by now, the Congress of Vienna had little realization of the importance of either nationalism or reform.   Consequently when Italy was reorganized in 1815 most of the old political divisions were restored and the power of Austria was doubled by her acquisition of Venetia.   This meant that in all there were some thirteen states set up in Italy, which, with some unimportant exceptions, fell into five main groups.   These, reading from south to north, were :

(A) *Naples and Sicily*, or the 'Kingdom of the Two Sicilies,' poverty stricken, infested with brigands, and ruled with cruelty and inefficiency by Ferdinand I, a member of the Spanish Bourbon family.

(B) *The Papal States*, ruled by the Pope, and therefore by now invariably by an Italian, but disputing with Naples and Sicily the claim to be the worst-governed section of the country.   The clergy had a stranglehold over freedom of thought, and the Inquisition and torture were employed against those whose politics were liberal or whose ideas in general were at all modern.   It was dangerous to proclaim the theory that the earth revolved round the sun, since the mediæval Church had thought otherwise.   Only about 2 per cent. of the rural population could read.   The development of communications was somewhat hindered by the fact that before long the Pope prohibited the introduction of the railway and the telegraph into his domains.

(C) *Modena, Parma, and Tuscany*, in Central Italy, were three independent duchies.   All of them were better governed than the states of the south, as their rulers were more mildly disposed and more concerned with the cultural welfare of their subjects than were the Pope or Ferdinand.   This applied especially to the Duchess of Parma, Napoleon's second wife, the easy-going Marie Louise.   But all three rulers, as far as the Italians were concerned, were tainted with one unforgivable sin—they were Austrians.

(D) *Lombardy and Venetia* were the sections directly under the rule of the Austrian Empire.   Lombardy, with its capital Milan, was the most fertile district in Italy, and Venetia, with

Venice as its chief port, was probably the richest trading centre. The Austrian government was again far better than that of the south. Nearly every town had an elementary school and most had secondary schools. But the most efficient department of government was unfortunately the police, whose supervision was terribly strict. Austrian spying was most highly organized—as one lady indignantly remarked in Vienna at the time of the Congress : "My daughter cannot sneeze but Prince Metternich will know of it." Every modern history-book was sent to Vienna for censorship, and no freedom of discussion on political matters, either in public or in the press, was for a moment allowed. Thousands of political prisoners soon filled the gaols. Such a system, too, naturally cost a great deal to maintain, and Lombardy and Venetia, though only an eighth in population and an eighteenth in area of the Austrian Empire, had to provide a quarter of the taxes. In such circumstances the other merits of the Austrian government earned it no gratitude.

(E) Finally, there was the *Kingdom of Sardinia*, including Piedmont and Savoy, which we will call Piedmont, for the sake of brevity. None of these territories was prosperous— Sardinia was a barren island and Savoy a mountainous region inhabited largely by French. Piedmont itself was rather better, but the only district of any wealth was Genoa— and that was hostile because it had been forced to forgo its republican status when it was merged in the kingdom in 1815. The king then restored, Victor Emmanuel I, was a hopeless old reactionary, who even had parks torn up and gas-lighting abolished because they had been introduced by the French. Nevertheless to Italians he had the supreme merit—in an age of national feeling—of being an Italian.

To understand the situation in 1815 it is necessary to bear in mind, however, the fact that Austrian influence was not confined to Lombardy and Venetia, or even to the Duchies as well. There was a treaty between Ferdinand and Austria that no alteration should be made in the government of Naples without Austria's consent ; and equally the Papal States relied on the long arm of Austria to support the Pope's despotic government. Thus Austria, determined to maintain existing conditions everywhere as a barrier against revolution, was

The extent of Austrian influence

regarded by the Italians with detestation throughout the
length and breadth of the peninsula. To those who hoped
for better things, it seemed that improvement could come,
unless the Papacy should suddenly reform its whole administration, only from the one really Italian state—Piedmont.
Accordingly it came about that men's eyes gradually focused
on Piedmont as a possible nucleus of Italian unity. That,
however, was later ; the first step was not union, but merely
local independence from foreign or despotic rule. Meantime
in 1815 it was true that 'Italy could no more be called a nation
than a stack of timber could be called a ship.'

The
Carbonari
and their
revolt in
Naples,
1820

It was not long after the Congress of Vienna that the first
explosion occurred. Italy was honeycombed by secret
societies aiming at independence. There were many of them,
but the most important was the Society of the Carbonari
(literally 'charcoal-burners'). In 1820, following a momentarily successful revolution in Spain, some leading Carbonari
in Naples raised the standard of revolt against Ferdinand,
and being either unopposed or assisted by the royal troops,
managed with absurd ease to force that monarch to issue a
constitution. The constitution concerned was a re-issue of
the Spanish one of 1812, a very advanced document involving
the abolition of nobles' and clerical rights and privileges,
including the power of the Inquisition, and the setting up of
a democratically elected parliament. The King swore a
great oath to observe it faithfully : "Omnipotent God—if I
lie, do thou at this moment annihilate me." Then he obtained
permission from his ministers to go to the conference of Laibach "to obtain the sanction of the powers for our newly
acquired liberties." At Laibach he promptly proceeded to
disown the whole movement and to beseech Austria to send

Suppression
by Austria

troops to restore him to the full height of his former powers.
This, as we have seen in the chapter on the Congress System,
was soon done by Metternich, and the first effort had failed.

The
Carbonari
revolt in
Piedmont,
1821

Meanwhile in Piedmont a similar outbreak had occurred,
to wring a constitution from the old King. Again the
Carbonari took the lead and endeavoured to link up the
movement with a revolt against the Austrians in Lombardy.
After the King of Piedmont had abdicated and Prince Charles
Albert, acting as regent, had granted a constitution, the new

king revoked this measure. The result was a civil war in which the forces of absolutism, aided by the Austrians, beat the Liberals at the battle of Novara (1821). Thus no constitution was gained in Piedmont, and in Lombardy the Austrian fetters were riveted on more strongly than ever. Collapse at Novara, 1821

The year 1830, with its revolutions in France and Belgium, naturally evoked similar tremors in Italy. Again under the influence of the Carbonari, the Papal States came out in rebellion. As usual the distressed ruler's appeal to Austria fell on ready ears, and the Pope had the pleasure of seeing the Austrian whitecoats suppress his rebellious subjects. A new complication now arose, for the French, jealous of Austrian interference in the Papal States, also sent an army there. So yet another rising had failed, and the inadequacy of Carbonari conspiracies against absolutist armies was apparent to all. Something greater, some more national movement was needed before anything could be done. 1830 Revolt in Papal States

It was the work of Mazzini to supply this need. In the unification of Italy there are three great names which stand out, all of them subjects of Piedmont—Mazzini, Cavour, and Garibaldi. Of these Garibaldi was the soldier, Cavour the statesman, and Mazzini the prophet. From his childhood onwards Mazzini never ceased to think of the woes of his country—in fact, he always wore black as a sign of mourning for it ! As soon as his student days were ended he joined the Carbonari, and sacrificed his visions of earning fame as a great writer for the even more thorny paths of political agitation. Indeed, he came to the conclusion that no great art *could* be produced by Italians until Italy was free. Arrested and imprisoned for conspiracy after 1830 by the Piedmontese government, he was soon exiled from his native land. The accession of the more liberal Charles Albert to the throne of Piedmont in 1831 brought a great appeal from Mazzini, in exile at Marseilles, to the King to assume the leadership of the movement for freedom. "All Italy waits for one word— one only—to make herself yours . . . place yourself at the head of the nation and write on your banner, 'Union, Liberty, Independence'—proclaim the liberty of thought—liberate Italy from the barbarians—on this condition we bind ourselves round you, we proffer you our lives, we will lead to your Mazzini banner the little States of Italy—we will preach the word that creates armies.   Unite us, Sire, and we shall conquer."   But Charles Albert was not ready for such a programme, and Mazzini had to fall back on organizing the society of 'Young Italy.'   This famous association was an effort to improve on the work of the Carbonari, by appealing to a wider number of people, including the lower classes, and by supplying a great ideal which would have the force of a religion.   Its watch-word was 'Unity and Independence.'   As a fervent preacher of the necessity of education, self-sacrifice, and rebellion, Mazzini was so successful, and the 'Young Italy' Society took such a hold that he was eventually exiled from France too.   From Switzerland, his next home, he organized an invasion of Savoy in 1833 which failed hopelessly and only brought terrible punishment on the Liberals by the frightened Charles Albert.   Exiled from Switzerland, he found refuge in England, whence he continued to direct the affairs of his Society.   It may be noted that he was by now a convinced republican, having naturally long since ceased to hope any-thing from the King of Piedmont.   While Mazzini's mis-sionary work, however, advanced to a remarkable extent the desire for unity and freedom among Italians, his strict republicanism was later to prove an obstacle when a King of Piedmont appeared who was willing to lead the national movement.

'Young Italy'

The next moment of importance in the making of Italy occurred in the year 1846, when a new Pope, Pius IX, was elected.   The personality of Pius IX proved to be a matter of extreme importance.   He was kind-hearted, hated the tortures he had witnessed in the Papal States, was prepared for con-cessions in a muddle-headed way, but was temperamentally unstable owing to fits of epilepsy and not at all the whole-hearted liberal he was at first taken for.   But the fact that there was now a Pope who was not an out-and-out reactionary, and above all that this Pope, as the first act of his régime, released all the hundreds of political prisoners in the Papal States, was bound to make Italians expect more of him than he could give.   Popular enthusiasm for the Pope rose to a great height, and intelligent Liberals, such as Gioberti, planned a great union of Italy, not under Piedmont but under

A 'liberal' Pope—Pius IX

the Papacy. Metternich, like the rest of Europe, was astounded. "We were prepared for everything except a liberal Pope," he said ; "now we have got one there is no answering for anything."

2. *The Movements of 1848 and the Preparations of Piedmont*

The year 1848, so momentous in France and Central Europe, inevitably involved Italy in the ferment. It was Italy, in fact, who gave the lead, for in January 1848 the practically unarmed population of Sicily rose and within a fortnight expelled Ferdinand II's garrison and defeated a relieving force. Once more the old 1812 constitution was proclaimed, and perforce accepted by the king, who had rapidly to extend the same concessions to the other half of his realm, Naples. The agitation spread like wildfire through the rest of Italy. In March 1848 Charles Albert, anxious to have the Liberals with him in the war with Austria he had at last decided on, published a constitution for Piedmont ; in the same month Pius IX reluctantly followed suit. On March 17th came the news of Metternich's flight from Vienna, and March 18th at once saw a desperate rising in Milan, where in 'the five days' of street fighting the Milanese expelled Radetsky's 20,000 troops. There was nothing for the veteran Austrian general to do but retire to the Quadrilateral, the district bounded by two rivers, the mountains, and four fortresses. On the 22nd Venice rose, expelled its Austrian garrison, and under Manin proclaimed an independent republic.

The moment was obviously favourable for Charles Albert to declare war on Austria. For a few precious days he hesitated, then marched an army into Lombardy to assist the inhabitants against the Austrians. From the new government of Naples came a force to assist him, but Pius IX denounced the war and refused henceforth to aid in any way the national cause. It was quite natural, as Pope, that he should hesitate to fight a major Catholic Power, Austria, but the decision proved a bitter disappointment to those who had hoped so much of the Pope, and it cost him the leadership of the reform movement. It was a leadership he was more than willing to surrender.

Margin notes: Revolt in Sicily · Constitutions in Piedmont and Papal States · Expulsions of Austrians from Milan and Venice · Charles Albert attacks Austria · Pius IX disappoints

6*

Charles
Albert
defeated at
Custozza
and Novara

A few minor successes greeted the opening of Charles Albert's campaign in the north, but after Radetsky had received reinforcements the chances of the Italians, fatally handicapped by divisions between Piedmontese, Lombards, and Venetians, were slight.   At last desperately attacking one wing of the Quadrilateral, Charles Albert was defeated at Custozza, and had to retire.   By August Radetsky was back in Milan.   In March 1849, following a renewed outbreak in Vienna, Charles Albert was again encouraged to march his forces into Lombardy, but once more he was beaten—this time on the battlefield of Novara, already before fatal to Italian unity.   Having in vain sought death on the field, the

Abdication
of Charles
Albert

unfortunate monarch abdicated in favour of his son Victor Emmanuel II, and retired to Portugal, where he died heart-broken within a few months.

Re-estab-
lishment of
royal power
in Naples
and Sicily

Meanwhile exciting events had been taking place in the southern states.   In Naples King Ferdinand had succeeded in taking advantage of the chaos brought about by inexperienced Liberal ministers, and had recovered his authority.   By May 1849, following intense and most cruel bombardment of Sicilian towns, which earned for Ferdinand the nickname of 'King Bomba,' Sicily too gave way.   Stouter resistance, however, occurred in the Papal States.   Here, in February 1849, after the murder of the Papal prime minister, Rossi, the refusal of the Pope to grant real democracy and his

The
Roman
Republic

consequent flight to seek Ferdinand's protection, a republic had been declared.   It soon fell under the influence of Mazzini, who hurried there to advance the movement, and who initiated a series of great reforms in the Papal States. The Pope, however, had appealed to the powers of Europe, and had found in Louis Napoleon, President of the French Republic, a source of aid.   It was not, of course, that Louis Napoleon, a man of the modern world, wished simply to restore the temporal power of the Pope—it was only that he

French
inter-
vention

was anxious to placate opinion at home, which at that time appeared to him predominantly pro-clerical.   In any case the French force eventually overcame the heroic resistance of Rome, and by July 1849 the Roman Republic was at an end and the Pope restored.   So Venice alone was left as a centre of resistance to absolutism, and by August

IN FOR IT—HOW TO GET OUT OF IT.

ONCE on a time there was a gentleman who won an elephant in a raffle.

It was a very fine elephant, and very cheap at the price the gentleman paid for his chance.

But the gentleman had no place to put it in.

Nobody would take it off his hands.

He couldn't afford to feed it.

He was afraid of the law if he turned it loose into the streets.

He was too humane to let it starve.

He was afraid to shoot it.

In short, he was in a perplexity very natural to a gentleman with—moderate means, a small house, common feelings of humanity—and an elephant.

France has won her elephant at Rome.

She has brought back the Pope.

She is at her wits' end what to with him.

She can't abet the Pope and the Cardinals, because she interfered in the cause of Liberty.

She can't abet the Republicans, because she interfered in the cause of the Pope and the Cardinals.

She can't act with Austria, because Austria is absolutist.

She can't act against Austria, because France is conservative and peaceful.

She can't continue her army in Rome, because it is not treated with respect.

She can't withdraw her army from Rome, because that would be to stultify herself.

She can't go forward, because she insisted on the Roman people going backward.

She can't go backward, because the French people insist on her going forward.

She can't choose the wrong, because public opinion forces her to the right.

She can't choose the right, because her own dishonesty has forced her to the wrong.

In one word, she is on the horns of a dilemma, and the more she twists, the more sharply she feels the points on which she is impaled, like a cockchafer in a cabinet, for the inspection of the curious in the lighter and more whirligig species of political entomology.

Poor France—will nobody take her precious bargain off her hands ? Rome is her bottle imp. She bought it dear enough, but can't get rid of it " at any price."

Napoleon III's eternal difficulty about Rome is well expressed in the above.

1849, faced with starvation, cholera, and ceaseless bombardment, Manin had at last to give in.   The triumph of despotism was complete—Naples, Sicily, Rome, Venice, Lombardy, had all rebelled and failed.   For the cause of Italian unity the year 1848 seemed to be entirely negative.

Collapse everywhere

Yet if nothing positive was achieved during the revolutionary movements of 1848 in Italy, at least two steps forward were gained.   In the first place a bold, patriotic king, determined on national unity, had succeeded in Piedmont—Victor Emmanuel II.   He was a fiery little man, revoltingly ugly, with coarse tastes and passions, but his devotion to the national cause was never in doubt—a great advance over any previous king of Piedmont.   Secondly the defence of Rome against the French had not only provided an epic of resistance and proved that Italians could be heroic in the service of their ideal, but it had brought to the fore another of the real makers of Italy—Garibaldi.

Victor Emmanuel II

This remarkable man, Garibaldi, born at Nice, in Savoy, had run away from his parents at the age of fifteen and had taken up a career on the sea.   Won over to the society of 'Young Italy,' he deliberately entered the Piedmontese navy with the object of inducing it to mutiny in favour of Mazzini's 1833 plot.   The first time he saw his name in print was when, escaped to France, he read that he had been condemned to death ; and having thus made Italy too hot to hold him, he disappeared to South America for twelve years.   Here he fought for Uruguay against the Brazilian Empire and Argentina, and learned in the wild South American conditions the arts of intrepid horsemanship and guerilla warfare.   He also acquired a wife, Anita, who shared his dangerous life in the saddle and on the battlefield ; he had seen her from his ship through a telescope, gone straight to her house, said 'You must be mine,' and stolen her from under the nose of a baffled rival !   As well as a wife he acquired a political or military uniform—the famous red-shirt.   Originally they were probably the shirts worn by Argentine slaughter-house workers, who adopted such a costume to make the blood of the cattle less noticeable, but they were soon to become in Europe the sign of one of the most remarkable guerilla forces ever created, Garibaldi's volunteers.

Garibaldi

His early experiences in South America

Returning to Italy in 1848, he threw himself into the struggles of that year with all his enthusiasm, fighting at first for the Lombards against the Austrians and next for the Romans against the French. He achieved one notable defeat of the attacking French troops, but eventually had to retire before overwhelming forces, who perjured themselves by breaking an armistice before the agreed period elapsed. Hunted across Italy, he succeeded in bringing his faithful followers to the Adriatic coast, whither he intended to embark to assist Venice in her struggle. Here, however, his wife Anita, who had insisted on joining him in all the dangers of Rome, was taken mortally ill, and he had to land prematurely to watch her die in his arms. With one companion, followed at every track and turn, he won his way across again to the other side of Italy, and finally re-embarked opposite Elba. Italy's guerilla chief was safe for another campaign—as long as he stayed outside Italy.

Garibaldi and the Roman Republic

Though 1848 had passed in vain, at least one corner of the peninsula had taken a step towards liberty. The constitution granted to Piedmont by Charles Albert still held good, and the young King, Victor Emmanuel II, whatever his defects in taste, morals, and personal appearance, was ardently patriotic. The most interesting and significant development of the next few years was the process by which Victor Emmanuel's kingdom was transformed into a modern state. Not only was the 1848 constitution adhered to, but the problem caused by the excessive power of the Church was boldly confronted. In 1850 a series of laws was passed by which the Church was deprived of its special courts, its right of sanctuary for criminals, its right to inherit property without the consent of the government, and its monopoly of performing the ceremony of marriage. The result was not only modernization and a quarrel with Rome which lasted till Mussolini's time, but the emergence into the limelight of a great supporter of these proposals, Cavour.

The reorganization of Piedmont

Cavour, perhaps greatest of the makers of Italy, was, unlike Mazzini and Garibaldi, born an aristocrat. Trained for the army, he rapidly tired of military routine, and after coming into conflict with the authorities for supporting the French Revolution in 1830, he resigned his commission. For some

Cavour

His early career

years he then devoted himself to agriculture on his estates, and gained knowledge which he was later to use for the benefit of Piedmont. He became, too, a great student of English affairs, hailing with approval Catholic Emancipation and the passing of the great Reform Bill of 1832. On his travels he spent many an evening in the Strangers' Gallery of the House of Commons, following the debates and making himself familiar with every detail of parliamentary practice and government. Economic subjects, like the Poor Law, Free Trade, Communism, Railways, he studied above all. By 1847 he had founded a paper in Piedmont, the *Risorgimento* ('Resurrection'— the name usually applied to the whole process of Italian unification). Its main object was of course to advocate constitutional government and the independence of Italy. Not unnaturally, therefore, Cavour was one of the members of Piedmont's first parliament, called after the

Prime Minister of Piedmont granting of the constitution in 1848. By 1850, following his skill in pushing the ecclesiastical laws, he was created Minister of Commerce and by 1852 Prime Minister. In these positions he began a work of the greatest importance—building up the prosperity of Piedmont. He removed duties, concluded trade treaties, built railways, started a service of Atlantic mail steamers, passed important laws about companies, co-operative societies, and banks, and reorganized the army. Under his skilful guidance Piedmont, by transforming itself into a modern state, acquired the essential equipment for the coming conflict.

3. *The Unification of Italy, 1859–1870*

The strength of the modern state Cavour was creating was soon to be tested. Always a schemer of the very deepest kind, Cavour calculated, when the Crimean War broke out, that it

The Crimean War would advance the cause of Italy if Piedmont were to aid France and England against Russia. Not only would it prevent any possible Russian supremacy in the Mediterranean, but it would establish a claim to the gratitude of England and France and bring Piedmont into the limelight at the peace conference. The result was highly successful. The Piedmontese troops distinguished themselves in the Crimea, and at the conference of Paris in 1856 Cavour drew attention to

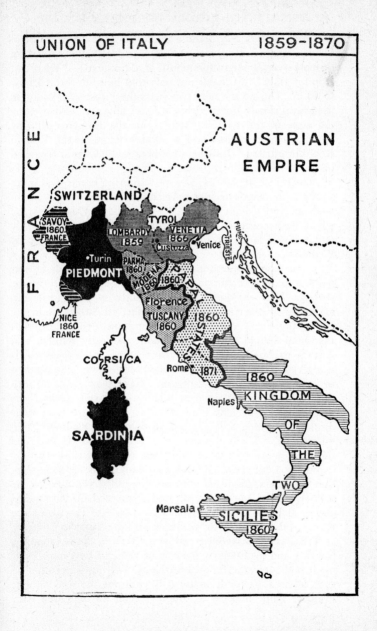

UNION OF ITALY   1859-1870

FRANCE

SWITZERLAND

AUSTRIAN
EMPIRE

SAVOY
1860
FRANCE

TYROL

LOMBARDY
1859

VENETIA
1866

•Turin

Custozza

Venice

PIEDMONT

PARMA
1860

TRIESTE

FIUME

MODENA
1860

NICE
1860
FRANCE

Florence

TUSCANY
1860

CORSICA

PAPAL STATES

Rome 1871

1860

SARDINIA

Naples

KINGDOM

OF

THE

TWO

Marsala

SICILIES
1860

the woes of Italy and pointed to Austria as the main cause of them. Further, in answer to Napoleon III's famous question (a most strange one in the mouth of a diplomat)—"What can I do for Italy?"—Cavour not only told him but showed how to do it. During the next two years the Franco-Piedmontese friendship slowly matured towards an alliance. Then came the news of the terrible attempt on the Emperor's life by Orsini, a great patriot and a notable figure in the Roman Republic of 1849. Italy held her breath and Cavour regarded his life-work as ruined; but the strange consequence, as we have seen in Chapter VI, was only to bring home even more strongly to Napoleon the necessity of aiding Italy. So in 1858 he and Cavour concluded the pact of Plombières, by which France was to help drive the Austrians from Lombardy and Venetia in return for the cession of Savoy and Nice by Piedmont.

It was now a question of securing a declaration of war without putting Piedmont and France too obviously in the wrong. This was done all very skilfully by piling up arms, arranging frontier incidents and the like, till Austria, suddenly losing patience, sent a fatal ultimatum demanding that Piedmont should disarm. Piedmont naturally refused, and Austria declared war, thereby appearing the aggressor. It was all against the advice of the aged Metternich, who pleaded in vain to the Austrian Emperor: "For God's sake no ultimatum!" But Cavour was joyful—"The die is cast," he said; "we have made some history: now let us have some dinner." France duly stepped in to protect Piedmont, and by June 1859 Victor Emmanuel and Napoleon III had won the two great battles of Magenta and Solferino, thereby capturing Lombardy. It was at this stage, as we have seen, that Napoleon, disgusted with the bloodshed, daunted by the strength of the Quadrilateral, and frightened by the clerical outcry at home and the menacing attitude of Prussia on the Rhine, suddenly made an armistice with the Austrian Emperor at Villafranca. Cavour's rage was terrible: he resigned his position and meditated suicide as he thought how near Piedmont had been to even greater things. In his desperation he even advised Victor Emmanuel to continue the war without France's help—a piece of counsel which the monarch with

The Alliance with Napoleon III

The war with Austria, 1859

Magenta and Solferino

Napoleon III withdraws at Villafranca

great good sense rejected. Victor Emmanuel concentrated on the fact that Lombardy had been won, even if Venetia still remained in Austria's hands. Further, in 1859, when the Austrians were in the midst of their difficulties, the three Duchies of Central Italy, Modena, Parma, and Tuscany, had exiled their Dukes, and one of the Papal States, Romagna, had revolted. These territories now determined to unite with Piedmont. Napoleon, true to the principle of the plebiscite by which he himself had risen to power, agreed to allow them to do so if the populace wished. The populace did wish, and since France supported them, Austria could do nothing. In return for this service Napoleon claimed the full reward originally agreed on, and Savoy and Nice, also approving the decision by plebiscite, were transferred to France. Thus the result of Napoleon's intervention in 1859 was the addition not only of Lombardy but of Central Italy to Piedmont. Obviously, in spite of the unrelenting opposition of the republican Mazzini, who plotted desperately against Cavour, union with Piedmont was the only practical way of achieving Italian unity, now fast becoming a fact.

Lombardy, the Duchies, and Romagna to Piedmont; Savoy and Nice to France

The excitement of 1859 was scarcely over before another decisive move occurred, this time in the south. Since the failure of the movements of 1848 the Kingdom of Naples had had quite an amount of unenviable publicity. Mr. Gladstone, who had visited some of the Neapolitan prisons during a holiday, had startled the world with the publication of his findings. Over 20,000 political prisoners were, he said, kept by King 'Bomba' in dungeons whose atmosphere was worse than that of a London fog. Men of the highest character and education were kept chained to ferocious criminals by couplings which were never on any occasion removed, night or day. Perjured evidence and unfair judges were the regular thing at trials. It was, thundered Mr. Gladstone, "the negation of God erected into a system of government." In vain France and England had protested, and finally recalled their ambassadors. 'Bomba's' name remained a byword for cunning and cruelty ; even his more playful moments were marked by a fondness for coarse practical jokes, such as surreptitiously withdrawing a chair from a guest about to sit down on it. In 1859 he died, still king, but not before he

Conditions in Naples under 'Bomba'

[*Reproduced by permission of the Proprietors of 'Punch.'*]

BABES IN THE WOOD.

The two 'bad men,' Napoleon III and the Austrian Emperor, duel to settle the fate of the Babes (Italy and Victor Emmanuel II of Piedmont)

had bequeathed to his unfortunate successor a legacy of hatred which was bound to break out in rebellion before long.

The rebellion duly came in 1860, in the southernmost half of the Neapolitan kingdom, Sicily. It was the opportunity which Garibaldi, whose thoughts had long dwelt on the southern tyranny, had been waiting for. Following his escape from Rome in 1849 when he eluded 'four armies and ten generals,' he had wandered round Europe and the New World, and earned his living as a candle-maker, a sea-captain, and finally, in a little island, Caprera, off Sardinia, as a farmer. In the war of Piedmont and France against Austria in 1859 Cavour had employed him as a guerilla captain, and he had carried on a very successful little campaign in the Alps. But he, like Mazzini, was infuriated by Cavour's cession of his native Nice to France—"They have made me," he said, "a foreigner in the land of my birth." Napoleon was to him 'a vulpine knave' and Cavour 'a low intriguer.' He was even planning a raid on the ballot boxes to stop the Nice plebiscite, when fortunately the greater task of an expedition to aid the Sicilian revolt attracted his imagination. The enterprise, originally suggested by Mazzini, proved to be one of the biggest romances of history. A thousand picked volunteers gathered at Genoa, ready to sail at a moment's notice. Cavour and Victor Emmanuel had to play a tricky game, encouraging Garibaldi in secret but publicly hindering and disavowing him, to avoid official Piedmontese complicity, which might have meant war with Austria. They stopped him getting recruits from the Piedmontese army ; they stopped him getting the modern rifles a patriotic fund had paid for. But in the long run, frightened though they were that he would, if successful, go on to attack the Papal States, which would bring about a fatal clash with France, they let him sail. Firearms—old converted flintlocks, though Cavour may not have known their condition—eventually arrived, registered as 'books.' Above all, in spite of official orders issued, nothing was done to prevent the volunteers embarking, though futile telegrams were later despatched by Cavour to order Garibaldi's arrest "if he put into a Sardinian port." But Cavour knew, like the rest of the world, that he was going to Sicily.

Garibaldi and The Thousand, 1860

The con-
quest of
Sicily

The landing at Marsala (Sicily) was amazingly fortunate.
The governmental batteries and troops could easily have
prevented it, but the two little steamers arrived together with
a powerful detachment of the British navy. There was
actually no connection between them—the British ships had
turned up to enforce respect for British property at Marsala—
but the garrison thought there was, and frightened at the
prospect of taking on the might of England, refrained from
firing at the Thousand, who coolly disembarked. Even the
red shirts at first were taken for British uniforms, and when at
length the commander realized his mistake it was too late—
the force had been landed with the net loss of one man
wounded in the shoulder and one dog wounded in the leg.
From that romantic beginning, the Thousand, brilliantly led
by their chief and supported by the sympathy and finally the
physical force of the inhabitants, soon conquered Sicily.
Perhaps the peak point was when Garibaldi's force, with only
370 muskets left between them, watched 20,000 defeated
Neapolitan troops march away. It had all been accomplished
inside a couple of months.

The con-
quest of
Naples

The elated Garibaldi now proposed to cross the Straits of
Messina, land in South Italy, and continue the good work on
the mainland of the Neapolitan kingdom. This was very
satisfactory to Cavour as long as Garibaldi continued to forget
his old republicanism and remained faithful to his new watch-
word of 'Italy and Victor Emmanuel.' But would he? And
would he take the dreaded step of attacking Rome? Cavour
was highly nervous, but again he decided to risk it. The
ability of Garibaldi to cross the Straits depended in the last
resort on the dominant naval power in the Mediterranean—
England. If England ranged her battleships there, he could
not get across. Napoleon III, frightened of an attack on
Rome and disturbed at the rapid growth of Piedmont, proposed to England that a joint Anglo-French force should close
the Straits to Garibaldi. The leaders of the English cabinet
were three very good friends of Italian unity, Palmerston,
Russell, and Gladstone, and they appealed to Piedmont to
know what were Cavour's wishes. Cavour, again acting
cleverly, openly requested England to join with France in
stopping Garibaldi—and privately sent a special envoy to

beseech Russell to do no such thing. So England let it be
known that she would resent the presence of French ships England gives indirect help
there ; and with the way cleared, Garibaldi was on the main-
land by September 1860. Victor Emmanuel, incidentally,
had as part of the same double game sent him a public message
forbidding him to cross and a private one suggesting he should
disobey ! As Cavour not inaptly remarked : "If we had done
for ourselves the things which we are doing for Italy, we should
be great rascals."

Once on the mainland Garibaldi's progress resembled a
triumphal march. His welcome on all sides was such that
the king fled his capital to a more easily defensible position,
and Garibaldi was thus able to enter Naples without any
opposition. Now came the critical moment—would he remain
faithful to Victor Emmanuel or, if he now swept into the Papal
States, would he declare some sort of republic ? The republican Mazzini was in Naples ; Cavour, after desperate thought,
took the biggest decision of his life. Risking the chance of Cavour invades Papal States
Austria's declaring war on Piedmont, he sent the Piedmontese
army to invade the Papal States, thereby forestalling Garibaldi. His object was twofold : first it was to stop Garibaldi's
fame overshadowing Victor Emmanuel's too completely ;
secondly it was that, while capturing most of the Papal States,
he could do what Garibaldi would never do—stop short of
Rome itself and thus avoid falling out with France. The
move was again brilliantly successful. Plebiscites held in the
newly liberated districts showed enormous majorities for
annexation to Piedmont. Garibaldi, with a Piedmontese Naples, Sicily, and Papal States (except Rome) annexed to Piedmont, 1860
army next door, had to recognize the inevitable. In October
Victor Emmanuel arrived in Naples to take possession of his
new realms. By November the last resistance was crushed.
It remained for Garibaldi to surrender his dictatorship, to
introduce Victor Emmanuel to the city of Naples, to hear
with pain the monarch's inevitable decision to disband his
volunteers, and to sail off to retirement in Caprera. He had
refused all honours ; he took with him only a few hundred
francs of borrowed money and a bag of seed-corn.

The union of Italy was now an established fact. Following The "King-dom of Italy"
the addition of Lombardy and the Duchies in 1859, Naples,
Sicily, and most of the Papal States had now joined with

Piedmont.   In 1861 a new parliament for all the realm met at
Turin, the Piedmontese capital.   Yet there remained two
sections of Italy still outside the fold—two gaping wounds still
unhealed.   They were Venetia and Rome itself—the one held
by the Austrians, the other by French troops on behalf of the
Pope.   The untimely death of Cavour in 1861 robbed the

[Reproduced by permission of the Proprietors of 'Punch.'

THE MAN IN POSSESSION.

V—R E—M—L. "I WONDER WHEN HE WILL OPEN THE DOOR."

Will Garibaldi surrender Sicily and Naples to Victor Emmanuel ?

new Italy of the man who might have prevented the chaos of
the next few years.   In 1862 Garibaldi, impatient as ever,
with some volunteers from Sicily made a dash for Rome.   He
had to be held up by Piedmontese troops, and while trying to
prevent civil war was shot in the foot.   It was a terrible
humiliation.   Another was to follow in 1866, when Italy
allied with Prussia in a war against Austria.   The Italians

ITALY IN ROME.

The inclusion of Rome in the Italian kingdom, and the disappearance of the Papal States, ended the Pope's temporal power but left his spiritual authority untouched.

were beaten by the Austrians at Custozza and suffered a crushing disaster at sea.   Only Garibaldi in the Alps was successful.   The war, however, was won by the overwhelming **Venetia joined to the Kingdom** Prussian victory at Sadowa, and in spite of the Italian failure Bismarck contemptuously tossed Italy her promised reward of Venetia.

The acquisition of Rome   So only Rome remained.   In 1867 Garibaldi made another dash for it, but his forces were badly beaten by the French with their new 'Chassepot' rifles.   Finally in 1870, when the Franco-Prussian war broke out, Napoleon III in his need for troops had to withdraw the garrison from Rome, and the Pope's last stronghold could fall to the Italians without the danger of a war with France.   In protest the Pope retired as a voluntary prisoner to his palace of the Vatican, whence no Pope ever emerged until a treaty was arranged with Mussolini in 1929.   By this the Pope was allowed sovereign rights over the 'Vatican City'—a territory a mile and a half square.

By 1870 Italy was thus united and free.   It had been a stirring story, yet disillusion was already beginning.   Perhaps the country was made too quickly—without the guiding hand of Cavour it soon proved to have little skill in managing parliamentary affairs or even in suppressing beggary and brigandage.   Disgusted with the events of the last few years, Garibaldi dashed off to France to fight for freedom and the new French republic against the Prussian military machine. (It was a tradition his descendants maintained, for six of his grandsons raised a volunteer Italian regiment to help France in another hour of need in 1914.)   Mazzini, in exile, was heartbroken about it all.   The free republic of self-sacrificing patriots he had dreamed of was far from a fact.   Garibaldi, who could have achieved it, had in Mazzini's opinion been fooled all the time by Cavour and Victor Emmanuel.   The great guerilla chief, said Mazzini, had "a heart of gold and the brains of an ox"—a similar impression to that made on the English poet Tennyson, who spoke of Garibaldi's possessing "the divine stupidity of a hero."   At any rate, to Mazzini, brilliant as Cavour's tactics had often been, the whole process of unification had been carried out by the wrong means, by double-dealings and shifty diplomacy bound to end in demoralization.   "Unity," he said already by 1860, "you may

I. MAZZINI – PROPHET.

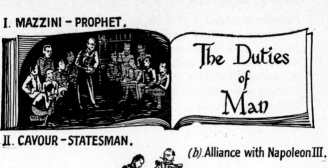

The Duties of Man

II. CAVOUR – STATESMAN.

(b). Alliance with Napoleon III.

(a) Economic Progress.

(c) Capture of Papal States by Piedmontese Army.

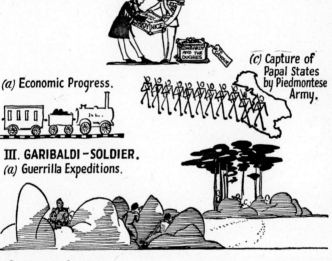

III. GARIBALDI – SOLDIER.
(a) Guerrilla Expeditions.

(b) Longing for Rome.

THE MAKERS OF ITALY.

consider as settled, and so far, so good.   The rest is all wrong."
Or again—"I shall have no more joy in Italy. . . . The
country, with its contempt for all ideals, has killed the soul
within me."   The unification of Italy, like that of Germany,
illustrates the eternal tragedy of politics—that great ends can
often be achieved only by means which rob the ends of a great
deal of their worth.

CHAPTER IX

Bismarck and the Unification of Germany, 1851–1871

The great ideal of a united and liberal Germany for which the Frankfort Parliament strove had come to nought within two years. Frederick William of Prussia had refused to accept the leadership of the national movement, and without Prussian leadership it was lost. By 1851 the supremacy of Austria in Germany was again established, the old powerless Confederation of 1815 was revived, and everything seemed to be as before the revolutions. Yet within twenty-years Germans of all states were united in the new German Empire, proclaimed at Versailles in 1871. Such a transformation, such an achievement was the work of one man above all others— Bismarck.

Bismarck, one of the most brilliant diplomatists of all time, Bismarck dwarfed every other politician in Germany, outbluffed even Lord Palmerston, and outwitted Napoleon III so completely as to make the French Emperor rather a pathetic figure. By origin he was a Prussian 'Junker,' or landed gentleman, whose family had enjoyed the rank of nobility and shared in local government from the fourteenth century. He inherited an estate of which he was passionately fond, a magnificent set of brains, a tremendous physique, indomitable will-power, and the political principles of his class. These were naturally highly autocratic, intensely conservative, and distrustful of new ideas, especially those of a liberal tendency. It was nevertheless this aristocrat who despised both the ideals and the political capacity of the majority who succeeded where the Liberals of 1848 had failed.

After a conventional university education, in which His early duelling and beer-drinking occupied the greatest prominence, life he entered the Prussian civil service and served his year in the

167

army.   His civil service career, however, was too monotonous
to absorb his restless energies, which tended to find a surplus
outlet in gambling and general dissipation.   In 1839 he retired
from the service to devote himself to his estates, studying the
science of agriculture as hard as another maker of destiny,
Cavour.   He rapidly gained a demonic reputation locally for
his vices, his physical energy, his enormous consumption of
drink and cigars, and for playful little pranks such as awakening
guests by firing pistol shots through their windows.   But he
was, too, devouring books of all kinds, making himself the
master of many fields of knowledge.   With his belief in religion
at length restored and a happy marriage to tame his wildness,
by 1848 Bismarck had acquired the stability to be on the
threshold of great achievements.

Bismarck
in 1848

The Liberal revolution of that year found in Bismarck one
of its bitterest opponents.   As an aristocrat he disagreed with
the idea of democracy ;   as a Prussian he hated the thought
of Prussia being merged in Germany.   In the Prussian
Parliament of 1847 he opposed with all his force the Liberal
schemes, speaking against them with a stinging and reckless
eloquence.   His attitude was so extreme that Frederick
William feared to promote him to office, regarding him as
'only to be employed when the bayonet reigns.'   In truth
Bismarck believed that nothing could be done without force :
he therefore strove to preserve the greatest force available in
Germany, the extremely militarist state of Prussia.   Though
he was not called to office in the critical days of 1848, his advice
made its impression on Frederick William.   In 1851, when the
Prussian monarchy, at the expense of humiliation before
Austria and desertion of the national movement, had regained
its power in Prussia, Bismarck was appointed Prussian
representative at the revived Confederation Diet.

Bismarck
as Prussian
representa-
tive in the
Diet

As the representative of Prussia in the Diet from 1851 to
1858, Bismarck developed a different viewpoint.   Hitherto
his ideas had been purely conservative ;   now he became aware
of the fact that there was a real problem in the weakness of a
divided Germany.   He resolved on uniting Germany, but
not at the price of surrendering the tradition and the power
of Prussia.   His solution of the German problem was thus
not the Liberal one of a free union under a Prussian king

stripped of his autocratic powers, but a virtually dictated union under a Prussian king with his power intact. "The God of battles," he had already said, "will throw the dice that decide."

Against this growth of Prussian power, he saw clearly in his experience as representative, Austria would fight with all the weapons at her disposal. She would exploit the ascendency which she had gained over Frederick William to remain the dominant power in Germany. As it was easier to dominate over a number of small states than over a single great one, Austria would block any schemes for German unification. Bismarck accordingly saw in Austria his first enemy. His attitude was soon shown in the famous stories of the cigar and the shirtsleeves. At the Diet only the Austrian delegate as a special sign of honour ever presumed to smoke—Bismarck as soon as he took his place promptly lit up a cigar. Secondly, when an Austrian representative received him informally in his shirtsleeves, Bismarck promptly threw off his own jacket with the remark : "I agree. It's a very hot day." Before long he had defeated an attempt by Austria to break up the Zollverein. Obviously such a man would never rest till Austria was deposed from her place of supremacy in Germany.

Yet before Austria could be tackled, there were other enemies nearer home to defeat—the Liberals of Prussia. By 1858 the reign of the unfortunate Frederick William IV had at last terminated in madness, and his younger brother, William I, occupied his throne as Regent. William, king by 1861, was by training and temperament a soldier. He had appointed two keen military minds, both violently anti-Liberal, to the key positions of the Prussian army. Roon became Minister for War and Moltke Chief of the General Staff. It did not take Roon long to decide, in collaboration with Moltke and the King, that the Prussian army must be greatly increased. Together they planned to raise its strength, including reserves, from just under half a million to just over three-quarters of a million men. This, with its creation of new regiments, would naturally involve considerable expenditure. Here was the crux of the matter—would the Liberals in the Prussian parliament agree to these military items in the budget ? It soon became apparent that they would not.

His fight against the Liberals

William

The Army Reforms

The reason for their attitude was not so much that they disapproved of a large Prussian army, but that they wanted, by making the King agree, for example, to a two-year instead of a three-year period of training, to assert the control of Parliament over the King and his ministers. Obviously a matter which concerned everybody in two ways—military training and finance—was a suitable issue over which to take up the struggle. The conflict, in fact, began to run on similar lines to that between Charles I of England and his opponents—who, at base, was the real ruler, king or parliament ? Meanwhile the King went ahead and created the new regiments by money which was not voted for that purpose. A Parliament overwhelmingly against him threw out the budget prepared by his ministry. The situation was becoming perilously near civil war or the surrender and abdication of William.

Bismarck 'Minister-President' of Prussia

It was at this stage that the King turned, like Charles I to Strafford, to the strong man whose appointment meant no compromise. The difference was that, while Charles and Strafford had no army, William and Bismarck had one of the finest fighting machines in Europe at their disposal. In 1862 Bismarck, who since 1859 had been more or less out of the way as Prussian ambassador first at St. Petersburg and then at Paris, was summoned to Berlin by a telegram from Roon. It read : "Come. The pear is ripe. Danger in delay." Hastening to the capital he persuaded the King to tear up a document of abdication the monarch had prepared and to carry out the struggle to a finish. On the same day as the budget was again rejected by Parliament, Bismarck was appointed Minister-President. The destiny of Prussia was at last in his hands, and with it the destiny not only of Germany but of half Europe.

Bismarck's conception of force

The appointment created the greatest surprise throughout Europe, where statesmen betted how long the new minister would last, and the greatest consternation throughout Prussia, where it was regarded as a deliberate affront to the Liberals. Hardly anyone realized either the enormous ability of Bismarck or the growing strength of the state he was to govern, with its army, its devoted civil service, its advanced educational system, and its expanding commerce. Bismarck himself seemed to go out of his way to slap the Liberals

soundly in the face by such remarks as the famous : "Germany
has its eyes not on Prussia's Liberalism but on its might.
The great questions of the day will not be decided by speeches
and resolutions of majorities, but by blood and iron."   The
phrase 'blood and iron' ever afterwards stuck to Bismarck ;
and however much we may dislike the fact, the events of the
next few years proved that Bismarck's prophecy was completely accurate.   He had, in fact, penetrated to the heart of
European politics, that affairs were arranged not by right but
by might, and he therefore simply determined to carry this
out to the logical conclusion by making Prussia mightier than
any possible enemy.   It was the old policy of Frederick the
Great.   Bismarck argued that in the long run people always
thought those who were successful were also right.   In any
case the word 'right' had for him no meaning in international
politics, though it possessed some in private life.   So Bismarck
believed, not like Cavour that wrong must sometimes be
committed in the interests of the state, but that nothing committed in the interests of the state could be wrong.   Bismarck
was later to suffer many sleepless nights from indigestion, but
none from a guilty conscience.

The first step towards the creation of the great Prussia and Anti-Liberal measures
Germany he dreamed of was to crush the Liberal opposition
to the army reforms.   This was done by advising the King
to carry on in spite of the rejection of the budget and to collect
necessary taxes all the same.   The press was gagged, Liberals
were driven from official positions, and Bismarck's unpopularity reached such heights that he could say later of it—
"Men spat on the place where I trod in the streets."   But
Bismarck had rightly judged that the leading German Liberals
shirked an appeal to physical force and he calculated that
everything would be forgiven him when he had achieved
something great for Prussia.   He deliberately aimed, in other
words, at successes in foreign policy in order to win the battle
at home.   Yet his foreign adventures were always strictly Victory at home to be sought through foreign policy
and closely connected with his main aim, Prussian leadership
in Germany, and never, like Napoleon III's, merely designed
to dazzle a discontented populace.

The main steps by which Bismarck achieved his desired Bismarck's wars
result were three in number.   Each was marked by a war—

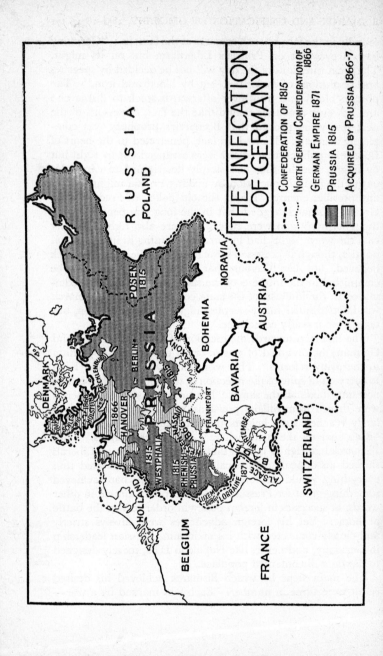

THE UNIFICATION OF GERMANY

Confederation of 1815
North German Confederation of 1866
German Empire 1871
Prussia 1815
Acquired by Prussia 1866-7

RUSSIA

POLAND

POSEN 1815

PRUSSIA

BERLIN

MECKLENBURG

DENMARK

1866 HOLSTEIN

1866

1815 HANOVER

WESTPHALIA 1815

RHENISH PRUSSIA 1815

HOLLAND

BELGIUM

LUXEMBURG

LORRAINE 1871

ALSACE

FRANCE

SWITZERLAND

BADEN

WÜRTEMBERG

NASSAU 1866

FRANKFORT

BAVARIA

SAXONY

BOHEMIA

MORAVIA

AUSTRIA

in turn against Denmark, against Austria, and against France. It is proof of the brilliance of his statesmanship that in spite of the obviously growing power of Prussia, he succeeded in preventing his enemy from allying with any major power. His first aim in any war—the isolation of the enemy—was always achieved. Let us follow the process by which the union of Germany was accomplished along Bismarck's lines. *His diplo-matic skill*

In 1863 a question which had long troubled German nationalists became once more acute. The King of Denmark ruled over two Duchies, Schleswig and Holstein, not as King of Denmark but as their Duke. Holstein was largely German in character, was a member of the German Confederation, and resented the Danish connection. As the nationalist movement developed in the 19th century, keenly national Danes wanted to absorb the two Duchies completely into the Danish kingdom. On the other hand, keenly national Germans wanted to save them from that, so that they could later be brought into a united Germany. Already there had been fighting over the matter in 1848 and a disputed succession. In 1852 a conference of the great powers at London had settled the succession in favour of the King of Denmark. On the bigger question, however, it had simply decided that the Duchies should be kept as they were, part of the lands of the King of Denmark, but not subject to the laws of the Danish kingdom. Unfortunately this did not satisfy either the Germans or the Danes. By 1863 the intricacies of this situation were such that Palmerston maintained that only three persons in Europe were completely acquainted with the truth—the Prince Consort, who was dead ; a German professor, who was in a lunatic asylum ; and himself, who had forgotten all about it. In 1863 the Danes came out with a new constitution which would separate Schleswig from Holstein and absorb it in Denmark. At once violent protests arose from the Duchies, which clung to their traditional semi-independence, and from all Germany. The Danes were undoubtedly breaking the London treaty of 1852, and the eyes of Germans turned to Prussia to see if she were going to act as leader of Germany in the matter. Would she represent German feeling and install the rejected candidate of 1848, a true German, as ruler of the duchies ? *The Schleswig-Holstein question*

7+

Bismarck's attitude

It was Bismarck's first opportunity. How could the situation be so manœuvred that Prussia would take the lead on behalf of Germany, but finish up in possession of the Duchies? A glance at a map shows that Schleswig and Holstein are of immense strategical importance to Prussia, particularly since Schleswig could be used as the base of naval operations against her. No one as yet, however, saw through Bismarck's policy of annexation, for the simple reason that Prussia had no more 'right' to the Duchies than had China or Japan. Europe had not yet realized that the real attitude of Prussia was represented by Roon, who remarked that the question of the Duchies was not one of right or law, but of force, and that Prussia had it.

Prussia and Austria fight Denmark, 1864

Bismarck's handling of the question was consummately skilful. He first secured the friendship of Russia by helping the Czar in every possible way short of war to subdue the Polish rebellion of 1863. Then he secured an alliance with Austria to settle the future of the Duchies by joint agreement between Austria and Prussia; then he demanded that Denmark should submit the whole matter to a European congress. When, encouraged by England, Denmark refused, the Duchies were promptly invaded by Austrian and Prussian armies. Bismarck had seen that France and England were not on good enough terms to agree in stopping the invasion, had bribed Napoleon by a promise of future 'compensation' to keep out, and had called Palmerston's bluff that "if Denmark

and take the Duchies

had to fight, she would not fight alone." England was soon humiliated before all Europe, and after the Danes had been soundly beaten Schleswig and Holstein were handed over to Austria and Prussia.

The affair at this stage, however, was far from ended. Public opinion in Germany and the Duchies expected that the unsuccessful claimant of 1848 would now be installed as Duke. Bismarck, however, proposed that he should be installed on conditions which left him completely under the power of Prussia. Eventually, after they had nearly come to war, it was agreed by the two powers, though not by the unfortunate claimant, who now faded out of history, that Austria should

The Convention of Gastein

administer Holstein and Prussia Schleswig. The 'Convention of Gastein' (1865), as this agreement is called, simply, in

THE PROMISSORY NOTE.

MR. JOHN BULL (DENMARK HAVING PRESENTED THE NOTE FOR PAYMENT). " NOW, THEN, MR. KNOUTEM AND MOUNSEER FROGGY, WHAT ARE YOU SKULK-ING OFF FOR ?   YOUR NAMES ARE TO THE NOTE AS WELL AS MINE, AND YOU'RE AS MUCH BOUND TO PAY YOUR SHARE AS I AM."

England complains that no one joins her in supporting Denmark against Prussia over the Schleswig-Holstein question.   Actually a little before England had refused to co-operate with France on the matter, and now France had her revenge.

Bismarck's phrase, "papered over the cracks." He knew that he could now before long pick a quarrel with Austria over the government of Holstein and smash the Austrian army as the Danish had been smashed. Thus he would finish up with Germany under Prussian control and Austria forever driven from her dominant position. It was subtle and immoral statesmanship, and for it to appeal to certain essential persons with more delicate consciences than himself, such as William, Austria must first be put 'in the wrong.' At these finer aspects of the diplomatic game Bismarck was a past-master.

Bismarck plans war with Austria

In preparation for the war against Austria he had now decided on, Bismarck took two important steps. Again he secured the neutrality of Napoleon by a promise of future compensation—Napoleon for his part imagining he would step in after months of conflict and make off with the lion's share of the spoils ! Then he secured an alliance with the new Kingdom of Italy to attack Austria in the rear if war should come within three months. It only remained to make certain it did come. Failing to provoke Austria by sending Prussian troops into Holstein, Bismarck proposed a reform of the Confederation by which Austria would be entirely omitted from German affairs. Austria naturally objected, and proposed that the members of the Diet should jointly attack the insolent Prussia. The other main German States agreed. The war had come—and Bismarck had managed to convince William and the Prussians that it was purely defensive !

He secures: (a) France's neutrality

(b) Italy's alliance

He picks the quarrel

The course of the 'Seven Weeks' War,' as it is called, astonished Europe. Against the minor states the Prussian army had little more to do than to walk in and take possession, while against Austria and Saxony everything was settled in one overwhelming victory at Sadowa in Bohemia. Even the fact that the Austrians were entirely successful against the Italians could not alter the result in the main seat of the war. Prussian training, tactics, and the breech-loading needle-gun had done their work. Everything was over before Napoleon could reap any advantage from it—when he frantically tried to claim territory Bismarck simply threatened hostilities against France as well. "It is France that is beaten at Sadowa," said Thiers.

The Seven Weeks' War, 1866

Sadowa

HONESTY AND POLICY.

BRITANNIA. "WELL! I'VE DONE MY BEST. IF THEY WILL SMASH EACH OTHER, THEY MUST."

NAP. (*aside*). "AND SOME ONE MAY PICK UP THE PIECES!"

Napoleon III hopes for 'pickings' from the Austro-Prussian War.

The lenient
Treaty of
Prague

The wisdom of Bismarck's statesmanship is nowhere seen more fully than in the conditions he imposed after the Prussian victory in the Seven Weeks' War.   The King and the army were anxious to march in triumph to Vienna and rob Austria of all that could be got.   Bismarck instead called a halt.   His object was not to make of Austria a permanent enemy, but simply to expel her from German leadership.   Consequently, by the treaty of Prague, 1866, he insisted that not a yard of Austrian territory should be annexed by Prussia, the only loss suffered by Austria being Venetia, which had been promised to Italy.   Outside Austria Prussia acquired a certain amount of territory—Holstein as well as Schleswig and some of the

Prussia's
gains

smaller states, such as Hanover.   These gave her an extra four and a half million inhabitants and an important outlet to the North Sea.

The North
German
Confedera-
tion

The main change effected, however, was the abolition of the old Confederation and the substitution of a new body to ensure the supremacy of Prussia.   From this new North German Confederation, as it was called, Austria was excluded. Most of the defeated German States were compelled to enter, including the Kingdom of Saxony.   Certain South German territories, however, including Bavaria, Baden, and Würtemberg, had to be left outside owing to strong local feeling and the attitude of France.   The King of Prussia was the President,

Bismarck
Chancellor

Bismarck the Chancellor of the new organization.   Home affairs were left almost entirely to the individual states, but matters of foreign policy were placed in Prussian hands by the stipulation that Prussia controlled the armies of all the members.   A concession to democracy was made by allowing all men a vote for the Parliament or Reichstag—though, as the Chancellor was responsible to the King and not to the Reichstag, this concession was more apparent than real.   The feelings of individual states, too, were considered by the setting up of a Federal Council, or Bundesrath, consisting of their representatives, in which it was possible for all combined to outvote Prussia.   This meant that the North German States, while definitely acknowledging the supremacy of Prussia, did not lose all the liberty of action and prestige they would have surrendered by definite annexation, and thus their relations with Prussia were not unfriendly in spite of

KÖNIGSSTRASSE !

PEACE—AND NO PIECES !

BISMARCK. "PARDON, MON AMI ; BUT WE REALLY CAN'T ALLOW YOU TO PICK UP ANYTHING HERE."
NAP. (*the Chiffonnier*). "PRAY, DON'T MENTION IT, M'SIEU ! IT'S NOT OF THE SLIGHTEST CONSEQUENCE."

Napoleon III's expectations from the Austro-Prussian War are disappointed.

defeat in the war. Further, Bismarck cleverly secured a military alliance with the remaining South German States by revealing to them Napoleon's plans of expansion at their expense. He linked them up with the Northern Confederation, too, in a new customs parliament in place of the old Zollverein. Thus by the arrangements following the war Bismarck achieved the remarkable feat of expelling Austria from her old leadership and uniting most of Germany under Prussia without making permanent enemies of any of his victims. This leniency was absolutely essential to Bismarck's policy. He knew only too well that the day of reckoning had to come with Napoleon III, and when it did it was important to have Austria and South Germany as friends rather than foes. Like a good chess-player, Bismarck thought several moves ahead.

The Seven Weeks' War, greatly as it turned for the benefit of victorious Prussia, was not without advantage for defeated Austria. Driven out of Germany and Italy, she at last recognized her real mission as an Empire centred on the Danube. Realizing that if reorganization was to be successful something must be done to satisfy racial feeling within the Empire, Austria decided on a large measure of compromise with Hungary. This agreement of 1867, known as the 'Ausgleich' ('Compromise'), divided the Austrian Empire into two halves—Austria, which included Bohemia and the northern provinces, and Hungary, which covered also the South Slav states and Transylvania. Each section recognized Francis Joseph as Emperor, but preserved its independent parliament for most matters. Three subjects, however—foreign affairs, war, and finance—were to come under a joint body representative of the two divisions, and meeting alternately in Vienna and Budapest. Thus the Austrian Empire was reorganized as a dual monarchy, or Austria-Hungary, under which name it continued to be known until it broke up into its various racial fragments at the end of the First World War.

For Bismarck there remained one more stage in the unification of Germany under Prussia. Austria had been displaced from her supremacy and the North German Confederation formed. In Prussia itself the old opposition of the Liberals, dazzled by his success, had died down, and he had been forgiven everything. Yet the South German States, Bavaria, Würtemberg, and Baden, although now bound by military and economic alliance, still remained outside. Bavaria especially clung to her independence and her local peculiarities. Bismarck, however, possessed all the trump cards. He knew that if war between Prussia and France broke out these lands, uncomfortably situated between the two combatants, could not remain neutral. As Germans and as military allies of Prussia they must oppose France. Once let them fight side by side with Prussia against the historic enemy, once let Prussia take control in the emergency of war, and Bismarck knew that the Prussian hold would not be lightly shaken off again. Accordingly he deliberately willed and prepared for war with France to complete the unification of Germany.

Bismarck plans war against France to unite Germany

This fact, however, must not blind us to the equal truth that France, on her side, gave Prussia every provocation Bismarck desired. Ever since Sadowa, terribly alarmed at the growth of a new power on her eastern boundary, France had striven might and main to stop the completion of German unity. Ill-feeling grew when Napoleon, desperately trying to secure his throne by successes in foreign policy, endeavoured to absorb Luxemburg. This move, which Bismarck himself had promised to accept since it did not greatly affect Prussia, was thwarted by an outcry in Germany. A conference of the powers decided on the neutralization of Luxemburg under its Grand Duke. Baulked of lands on the Rhine in 1866 and Luxemburg in 1867, humiliated in Mexico and in a contradictory position in Italy, Napoleon could not risk another rebuff. The many enemies of his régime at home would have used the occasion to dethrone him. So Roon and Moltke prepared the Prussian armies and Bismarck laid his diplomatic plans, secure in the knowledge that at the right moment France could be manœuvred into threatening war. South German States would then fight gladly side by side with Prussia to protect Germany from danger—and Bismarck would know how to deal with the opportunity. Like Cromwell, he believed that it was a good thing to strike while the iron was hot, but a better thing to make the iron hot by striking.

The errors of France

7*

[*Reproduced by permission of the Proprietors of 'Punch.'*]

"TO BE SOLD."

EMPEROR NAPOLEON. "I—A—HAVE MADE AN OFFER TO MY FRIEND HERE, AND——"

THE MAN IN POSSESSION. "NO, HAVE YOU, THOUGH?—I RATHER THINK I WAS THE PARTY TO APPLY TO."

EMPEROR NAPOLEON. "OH, INDEED! AH! THEN IN THAT CASE I'LL—BUT IT'S OF NO CONSEQUENCE."

Prussia stops Napoleon III buying Luxemburg from the King of Holland.

The opportunity came in 1870. The throne of Spain being The Hohenzollern candidature in Spain vacant, a Hohenzollern relative of William's was encouraged by Bismarck to stand as a candidate. Bismarck knew perfectly well that France, already frightened of the growth of Prussia to the east, could not accept a German on the throne of Spain to the south. William and the prince concerned knew this too, and not wishing to cause a European outcry were unwilling to advance the Hohenzollern candidature. Bismarck, however, overrode them both and almost compelled the prince to go forward. The announcement of the news caused the reaction in France that Bismarck had expected—intense indignation and a demand that the candidature should be withdrawn. Acting now on his real inclinations, William agreed—and France had won a striking success. Unfortunately France had had experience of Bismarck's double-dealing, and was suspicious that the prince's son might become the candidate instead. She was, too, anxious for an even more resounding diplomatic triumph. Consequently the French ambassador now demanded also that the Hohenzollern candidature should never in any circumstances be renewed. This demand William refused as a reflection on his good faith and an attempt to pick a quarrel. How Bismarck, who had thought his chance was slipping from his hands, seized the opportunity by editing the King's decision from Ems to read most offensively has already been told in the account of the War breaks out Second Empire. In face of the fury of France Bismarck persuaded William to order the mobilization of the Prussian army. In face of the mobilization of the Prussian army, France declared war.

The Franco-Prussian war, as we have seen, astonished The Franco-Prussian War, 1870–1871 Europe by the ease with which the much vaunted French military prowess crumpled before the ruthless efficiency of the Prussian troops. Strasbourg, Sedan, Metz—France was at Prussia's feet. But the organization of the Prussian armies, Sedan, 1870 the work of Roon, Moltke, and the King, would have been in vain had not Bismarck first secured the requisite political conditions. The secret of it was that France had been isolated from all possible help. Italy was no more than half a friend while France occupied Rome, and had recently fought as an ally of Prussia. Russia was bribed not to interfere by the

Bismarck's
diplomatic
brilliance

suggestion that she should repudiate the clauses of the 1856 treaty restricting her right to warships on the Black Sea. England was alienated by Bismarck's publication at the critical moment of Napoleon's proposal of 1866 that he should annex Belgium. Austria and the South German States had been partly reconciled by the lenient treatment after the Seven Weeks' War. France had no friend in Europe, and left alone in a state of internal dissension to face the Prussian armies she was powerless. It was Bismarck's master-stroke.

The
German
Empire
created,
1871

Already before the war was over and the treaty of Frankfort signed, by which Prussia was to strip France of Alsace, Lorraine, and an indemnity, Bismarck's main object was achieved. In the flush of enthusiasm for the common cause the South German States had been persuaded to unite with the North German Confederation into the German Empire. Special concessions were given to Bavaria in the way of independence, and the Bavarian king then undertook to invite William in the name of the princes to accept the Emperorship of the new Germany. So on January 18th, 1871, in the Hall of Mirrors at Versailles, the German Empire was solemnly proclaimed, with William as the first Kaiser. The setting was appropriate. Versailles stood more than anything else for the historic, aggressive glory of France. Now, in Versailles, while Paris lay starving ten miles away, a triumphant Germany rose by and through the humiliation of the most brilliant civilization in Europe. But Empires, even when they are the work of a Bismarck, are not seldom built on shifting sands. Overbearing Germany and heart-broken France could not know that before fifty years were out the Hall of Mirrors would reflect another scene of equal importance—with the rôles reversed.

BISMARCK'S VICTIMS.

CHAPTER X

The Eastern Question, 1815–1878

1. *The War of Greek Independence and the Syrian Question, 1820–1841*

The Ottoman Conquests (14th–17th centuries)

From the 14th to the 17th century the Ottoman Turks, a Central Asiatic race, built up by unremitting conquest a Mediterranean Empire. After Armenia and Asia Minor had fallen to the ruthless invaders from the East, the Balkan peninsula came next. The capture of Constantinople in 1453 and the break-up of the old Eastern Roman Empire, which had endured a thousand years, sealed the fate of Serbians, Bulgarians, Albanians, Roumanians, and other tribes and kingdoms in South-eastern Europe. Even Hungary was conquered, and the victorious host advanced twice to the walls of Vienna itself (1529 and 1683). Meanwhile, too, the North African coast—Egypt, Tripoli, Tunis, Algeria—had been compelled to acknowledge submission, together with islands like the Ionian Isles, Cyprus, and Crete. Even large stretches of South Russia, including the Crimea, came under Turkish sway.

The Ottoman Empire in decline

At length, however, the tide of conquest spent itself and began to recede. Through the might of Austria the Turks were compelled to relinquish Hungary, through that of Russia the Crimea. At the end of the 18th century the Ottoman Empire, though still enormous in extent, was a power in decline. The efforts of the various subject nationalities in the Balkans to secure independence, together with the ambitions and policies of states such as Austria, Russia, and England in relation to the decaying empire, constitute the 19th-century Eastern Question.

The Eastern Question

In the general approach to the question it is possible to discern certain main trends. The traditional English attitude was the preservation of the power of the Sultan as a bulwark against a possible Russian advance to the Mediterranean. England supports Turkey to check Russia The fact of Turkish misgovernment did not greatly matter to most English statesmen compared with the advantages of keeping a great military power like Russia from capturing Constantinople, one of the most strategically important cities in the world. They hoped, quite in vain as it proved, to secure better conditions for the subject races by 'representations' to Turkey. Russia, on the other hand, felt strongly for the Balkan peoples, who were mostly, like herself, Orthodox in religion and Slavonic in race. Her attitude thus became to break up the Ottoman Empire and free the subject races, while securing concessions and privileged positions for herself in the bargain. These broad lines of policy were sometimes departed from, but in general they held true for most of the 19th century.

The first phase in which this perennial problem vexed the minds of our ancestors was in connection with the War of Greek Independence (1821–1827). The Greeks, like all the subject nations of the Turks, enjoyed certain privileges which made their lot more tolerable than might have been expected. They were allowed complete educational and religious freedom, the head of their Church, or Patriarch, being afforded a recognized governmental position. They were exempt from military service, which was theoretically a great dishonour and in practice a considerable advantage, as they thus monopolized commerce and became wealthy. Such concessions, however, did not alter the fact that they were in reality an enslaved race, subject to the arbitrary will of local governors. Much depended on the character of the governor, for the whole Turkish system had become extremely loose in the way of central control. As long as the governor got in the requisite amount of taxation—provided almost entirely by the subject peoples—and sent along a few detruncated heads as a sign of his efficiency, he administered his province practically as he pleased. This meant that Turkish rule might vary enormously in severity from one district to another : for the most part, however, it was light, but inefficient and corrupt, and punctuated by periods of savage repression whenever there were signs of revolt.

The early years of the 19th century witnessed a great

TURKEY IN DANGER.

England's constant view of Russian ambitions in the Balkans.

development in the Greek national spirit. The modern Greeks, through admixture of races, were a far cry from their classical forbears. Yet with the birth of a new literary language in the early 19th century, midway between peasant speech and classical Greek, Greeks of various kinds, hitherto sundered by the differing dialects, experienced a greater national consciousness. The educated classes recalled 'the glory that was Greece' and felt a responsibility to revive the heroism and the culture of the days of antiquity. A society known as the 'Hetairia Philike' was founded to spread this form of enthusiasm among the Greeks. The first step was obviously to expel the Turks from the sacred soil of Greece, and to this end in 1820 Hypsilanti, a Greek officer in the Czar's army, raised a revolt. This did not occur in Greece itself, but in the districts of Moldavia and Wallachia, two Turkish provinces inhabited by Roumanians. The idea was, after these two provinces were liberated, to invade Greece and free that too. Hypsilanti claimed to have the support of the Czar, for Russia, with her Orthodox Church, naturally felt a religious kinship with the Greeks. Alexander, however, disowned him completely, and his name anyway was soon besmirched when he allowed his forces to perpetrate barbarous massacres. By 1821 Hypsilanti had been hopelessly defeated, for the Roumanian population gave him very little support, and he fled to Austria, where he was imprisoned for seven years. *Hypsilanti's plan, 1820–1821*

Scarcely had this first revolt been suppressed when a second, far more serious, broke out in Greece itself, in the district known as the Morea. The local Greeks, who were chiefly illiterate peasants and brigands, fell on all available Mohammedans and massacred them. Whole batches of prisoners, sometimes two thousand in number, were butchered, the grand total running into something like fifty thousand. Within a short time there was not a single Mohammedan left in the Morea. Naturally the Turks retaliated in kind. The Patriarch and two other bishops in Constantinople were hanged, their corpses being tipped into the Bosphorus in the traditional fashion, and the Turkish soldiers matched atrocity with atrocity. All Europe now began to take an interest in the matter. The Russians, infuriated at the outrage on the *The Revolt in the Morea* *The Turks retaliate* bishops, demanded intervention against the Turks. Men of liberal sympathies everywhere gave their support, in spite of the massacres, to a small nation struggling to be free—the outstanding example of this type being Lord Byron, who hallowed the Greek cause by his death at Missolonghi. It says much, too, for the classical education of the English upper classes that they now reacted strongly in favour of, and not against, Greece. As yet, however, though private individuals volunteered, no government actively intervened, for Metternich persuaded Alexander that he must not assist 'revolution.'

The Turks call in Mehemet Ali

The turning-point in the rebellion came when the Sultan, unable to make an impression on the Morea because the Greeks of the surrounding isles had the mastery at sea, called on his vassal, Mehemet Ali of Egypt, for help. Mehemet Ali had a strong fleet, and by means of this an Egyptian army under the command of his son Ibrahim Pasha was landed in the Morea. The previous barbarities now appeared insignificant before the conduct of Ibrahim, who set his troops to wipe out ruthlessly the entire Greek population. The Russian demand for intervention soon grew irresistible, and was strengthened by the death of Alexander and the accession of Nicholas I, who was determined to protect his fellow Christians.

Russian intervention

Canning's attitude

At this point, seeing that Russia was bound to intervene before long and anxious that she should not acquire too much influence in the Balkans in the process, Canning decided to join in the intervention with the object of supervising Russia.

The Treaty of London, 1827

A meeting of the powers was held, and the Treaty of London (1827) concluded, by which England, France, and Russia agreed that Greece should be independent, though under Turkish overlordship. Austria and Prussia refused to sign. When the Turks declined to accept this settlement a joint naval force was promptly despatched to cut off Ibrahim from his supplies in Egypt. Its instructions were to enforce an armistice, preferably by peaceful means. In the course of

Navarino Bay, 1827

staging a 'demonstration,' however, at Navarino Bay, before the assembled Egyptian and Turkish fleets, the allied squadrons encountered some Turkish vessels which refused to move out of the way. An exchange of shots gradually led to a general battle, at the end of which the Egyptian and Turkish navies were at the bottom of the water. Although Wellington, Prime Minister on Canning's untimely death, disapproved of this anti-Turkish activity and apologized for the battle of Navarino as an 'untoward event,' the effect of it remained. Ibrahim had to evacuate the Morea, and the war was won for Greece.

It required a further development to complete the liberation of Greece. Disregarding the views of England, which was anxious to preserve the strength of the Ottoman Empire as much as possible, Russia drove on her troops in a hard-fought advance southwards. With Constantinople at Russia's mercy the Turks had to agree to the Treaty of Adrianople (1829), by which Greek independence, though under Turkish overlordship, was recognized. In addition Moldavia and Wallachia were to enjoy a similar independence and Russia acquired some Turkish territory in Asia. But England and Austria feared that a semi-independent Greece would give Russia further excuses for intervention ; so they determined on complete independence or nothing. They confined the new Greek state within the narrowest of boundaries, but the defeat of the Tories in 1830 and the accession to the Foreign Secretaryship of Palmerston meant a more generous attitude on the part of England, and in the end wider boundaries were permitted. In 1832 a final treaty was signed by which Greece became an independent monarchy, the king chosen being Prince Otto of Bavaria. The first phase of the Eastern Question in the 19th century was over : the first great hole had been made in the rotting fabric of the Ottoman Empire.

The next phase began almost immediately—the question of Syria. Mehemet Ali, bribed by the Sultan with Crete at the beginning of the war of Greek Independence, was dissatisfied. Syria, Damascus, and the Morea had been promised him for his help during the conflict—and now the Greeks had the Morea, while the Sultan, already alarmed at the power of his vassal, naturally refused to hand over the other covetable districts in view of the Turkish failure to win the war. Knowing that the Sultan was reorganizing the Turkish army and that it might soon be directed against himself, Mehemet Ali decided to forestall the danger and claim his due at the same time. Accordingly in 1831 Ibrahim Pasha was once more

Marginal notes:
Russo-Turkish war

The Treaty of Adrianople, 1829

Greece a completely independent kingdom, 1832

Phase II. The Syrian Question, 1831–1840

despatched with an Egyptian army, and within a very short time had completely overrun Syria. Two or three Turkish forces were overwhelmed, and within a year Ibrahim was in a position to threaten Constantinople itself.

Ibrahim invades Syria

In his extremity the Sultan turned for aid to an unexpected source. Nicholas of Russia had since the Treaty of Adrianople come to the conclusion that Russian influence might perhaps be better served by maintaining a weak Turkish Empire than by setting up strong national Balkan states—especially if he thus avoided falling out with England. Accordingly he offered to help the Sultan against Ibrahim, and at the moment the Sultan's danger was such that he had no option but to accept the proposal. "A drowning man," a Turkish minister remarked, "will clutch at a serpent." Russian intervention, deeply distrusted not only by Turkey but by England, saved the situation for the Sultan. All the same, he had to abandon Syria, Damascus, and Palestine to Ibrahim, while the new friendship with Russia was expressed in the Treaty of Unkiar-Skelessi (1833). This document contained officially only a treaty of alliance between Russia and Turkey, but secretly another clause promised that Turkey would close the Dardanelles to the warships of all nations at Russia's demand—a provision which would enable Russia to carry out an aggressive Mediterranean policy, and then, if need be, retire securely into the Black Sea. The secret clause was betrayed to England by a Turk who objected to his master's surrender to Russia, and the consequent outcry was immense. Russia, it seemed, had stolen a very obvious march on England.

The Sultan appeals to Russia

The Treaty of Unkiar-Skelessi, 1833

England's opportunity for a reversal of this verdict came before very long. In 1839 the Turks, whose Sultan had devoted his life to vengeance on Mehemet Ali and the recovery of his lost provinces from Ibrahim, invaded Syria. But their armies met with the same lack of success as before, and the Sultan's cup of bitterness overflowed when the Turkish navy, sent to attack Mehemet Ali's fleet, simply surrendered to the Egyptians on the ground that the ministers at Constantinople were in the pay of the Russians ! At this stage the powers of Europe intervened once more, England and Russia for once taking up a similar attitude. The solution agreed on by England, Russia, Austria, and Prussia was that Mehemet Ali

Turkey invades Syria

The powers intervene

should be given the hereditary title of Pasha of Egypt and that he should retain the southern half of Syria, while surrendering his other conquests. This proposal, however, met with great opposition both on the part of Mehemet Ali and on the part of France, who cherished a strong sympathy for this introducer of Western organization. France, too, undoubtedly hoped to establish her influence in Egypt—always a centre of attraction to her since Napoleon's expedition—through support of Mehemet. When the latter, backed by France, refused to agree to the loss of half Syria, the powers withdrew even that concession and determined to limit his power simply to Egypt. A force sent to Syria soon cleared out Ibrahim, who had become very unpopular with the local peasantry, while the appearance of the British fleet off Alexandria induced Mehemet Ali to submit. For a moment it seemed that France would declare war on England, but the wiser counsels of Louis Philippe prevailed against the firebrand activity of Thiers, and France climbed down. The Sultan, of course, seeing things go so well, now wanted to take Egypt too from Mehemet Ali, and had to be restrained from this course by the powers.

France supports Mehemet Ali and Ibrahim

Syria restored to Sultan

France climbs down

To close the incident, after Syria had been completely restored to the Sultan and Mehemet confirmed in his position of Pasha of Egypt, a new treaty was entered into by the powers, France too giving her signature. This, known as the Straits Convention, guaranteed that in time of peace Turkey would close the Dardanelles and Bosphorus to the warships of all nations. It was thus a great triumph for Palmerston and England, since Russia could not, as she had schemed to do by Unkiar-Skelessi, regulate the Straits purely at her will and send battleships into the Mediterranean. In actual fact it was soon broken, in a direction favourable to England, when, just before the Crimean War, English and French vessels were ordered up the Dardanelles to Constantinople. At any rate the latest trick in the game was Palmerston's, who had maintained the power of the Sultan against his rebellious vassal and thereby brought back Turkey to reliance on England rather than Russia. The ambitions of France, too, had been checked. No wonder 'Pam' was a popular foreign minister—in England.

The Straits Convention, 1841

2. *The Crimean War, 1854–1856*

Phase III.
The
Crimean
War

Causes :
(a) distrust
of Russia's
attitude to
Turkey

The third and thus far the most acute phase of the Eastern Question led to the first war between the great powers since the days of Napoleon.   Something has already been said of the Crimean War in the account of the Second Empire, but here the main causes must be recalled and amplified.   The main general cause leading to war was undoubtedly the distrust of Russian intentions with regard to the Ottoman Empire.   There was a justifiable fear among the powers that Nicholas's recent policy of friendship with Turkey and preservation of the Empire was only a cloak for some dark design.   Both in 1844 and later in 1853 the Czar had broached schemes of partition with England—for instance, in the former year he had suggested that Russia should take Constantinople, while England 'compensated' herself with Egypt and Crete. The proposal was not entertained, partly because England feared to be trapped in some way, partly because there seemed no legitimate excuse for the whole business, and partly because England did not agree that Turkey was as weak as Nicholas implied.   Indeed, the Czar's favourite phrase in connection with the Sultan was a reference to him as 'the sick man of Europe.'   So early as 1833 he had employed it in negotiating with Metternich on the subject—"Prince Metternich, what do you think of the Turk—is he not a sick man ?"   To which that astute diplomatist had countered—"Is it to the doctor or to the heir that your majesty addresses the question ?"   At any rate England decided it was wiser not to strike a bargain of the sort suggested—though in actual fact forty years later Egypt was duly occupied by British troops and in 1915 England, at war with Turkey, at last promised Russia Constantinople.

(b) the right
to protect
the 'Holy
Places'

It was the general atmosphere of distrust of Russia which made what appeared to be an unimportant quarrel develop into a great war.   Round Jerusalem there were certain 'Holy Places' connected with the life of Christ which were traditional centres of pilgrimage for Christians.   The protection of these Holy Places had been granted by an ancient treaty to France, but that country had long since ceased to trouble herself about them.   Accordingly Russia, a nearer neighbour, had fulfilled the functions neglected by France, repaired the shrines, and generally stepped into the vacancy caused by French lack of interest. In 1850, however, Louis Napoleon, soon to be Napoleon III, in order to please the clerical party revived the French claim—to which the Sultan agreed. Russia protested strenuously, and the Sultan was in the unfortunate position of being bound to offend one of the two powers. As though to make things as awkward for Turkey as possible, in 1853 the Czar added a fresh claim, that Russia should exercise a general right of protection over all the Orthodox Christians in the Ottoman Empire.

(c) the Russian claim to protect all Christians in Ottoman Empire

These two demands on the part of Russia now led on to the war. The danger was that Russia might use such privileges to interfere continually in every part of the Ottoman Empire purely for her own benefit. Turkey, however, would possibly have given way to so powerful a foe, but the Sultan was unofficially encouraged by the British ambassador at Constantinople, Lord Stratford de Redcliffe, to reject the Russian demands. This meant that England accepted some responsibility for the consequences, for the ambassador's action was upheld by the British Cabinet. Diplomatic complications followed, but the most positive move was the occupation of Moldavia and Wallachia by Russian troops, as a kind of guarantee. Turkey, probably again prompted by Lord Stratford, now delivered an ultimatum calling on Russia to evacuate the two territories. When she did not, the Turkish armies marched north and a state of war gradually set in.

Russia occupies Moldavia and Wallachia. War with Turkey begins, 1853

As yet, however, diplomatic efforts to arrange the dispute were still being pursued by the powers, and the war was of a rather unofficial character. To be prepared for any eventuality, England and France (whose Emperor, Napoleon III, had also a personal quarrel with Nicholas about the latter's non-recognition of his title) ordered their warships up the Dardanelles. This broke the Straits Treaty of 1841, and Nicholas, thinking the two powers would reinforce the Turkish navy unless he acted quickly, ordered the Russian fleet to attack a Turkish squadron on the Black Sea. This action at Sinope was for some peculiar reason regarded in England and France as an unjustifiable massacre, and war-feeling immediately ran high. It must be remembered throughout,

Turkish fleet destroyed at Sinope

by way of explanation, that the working- and middle-classes of both England and France were delighted at the prospect of striking a blow against the most despotic monarch in Europe, who in addition to allowing his own people no liberty, had also deprived the Poles and the Hungarians of theirs.

Popular sentiment against Russia

[*Reproduced by permission of the Proprietors of 'Punch.'*]

WHAT IT HAS COME TO.

Aberdeen. " I MUST LET HIM GO ! "

Aberdeen, a peaceful Prime Minister, tried to restrain the English anti-Russian fury in 1854. The following year he was replaced by the more warlike Palmerston.

Swept on by public enthusiasm, England and France now demanded that Russia should withdraw her troops from Moldavia and Wallachia and recall her ships from the Black Sea to their naval base, Sebastopol. When this was refused, war followed.

The Crimean War begins, 1854

The first object of the war was rapidly attained when the Turkish armies were successful in driving the Russians from Moldavia and Wallachia in 1854. This, however, brought little prestige to England and France, who scarcely felt that they had yet enjoyed a war at all. Accordingly the Allied governments decided to destroy the great naval base, Sebastopol, and to this end they landed an expeditionary force in the Crimean Peninsula.

— STOP

The Crimean campaign which resulted will live for all time as a fantastic exhibition of military inefficiency and political futility. A recent historian of Europe has termed it "a contest entered into without necessity, conducted without foresight, and deserving to be reckoned from its archaic arrangements and tragic mismanagements rather among mediæval than modern campaigns." The object of the Allies in itself was scarcely worth wasting a man on—even if Sebastopol were destroyed and Russian warships driven from the Black Sea, that state of affairs could not be made permanent. As soon as the English and French force was removed—for the Sultan would not want the presence of such embarrassingly powerful allies for all time—Russia was bound to build up a Black Sea fleet once more. It was about as sensible as for Russia to hope to prevent England or France building a fleet on the Atlantic.

The futility of the war

As though the object of the war were not senseless enough, the conduct of it reached the very height of absurdity. After the successful landing in the Crimea and the allied victory on the River Alma which immediately followed, the obvious move should have been an attack on Sebastopol itself, which was not well fortified. To a land attack on the south it could offer little resistance, though from the sea, especially since the Allies had allowed the Russians time to block up the harbour by sinking ships, it was almost untakeable. Accordingly the allied army was marched round to the south of the town, the generals being so confident of rapid victory that orders were given for knapsacks, clothes, tents, and the like to be left behind—with a Crimean winter approaching. When the commanders seriously examined the place, they decided that a preliminary bombardment was necessary. Since the guns had now to be fetched and since it had not occurred to the

The investment of Sebastopol

British War Office to make arrangements for the construction
of the necessary five-mile railway from the base, the artillery
took three weeks to arrive. During this period the only
commander in the district of any pronounced ability, the
Todleben Russian Todleben, designed and constructed an elaborate
series of earthwork defences round the town. In fact, by the
time the Allies had finished their bombardment Sebastopol
was infinitely stronger than when they first arrived outside it.
Not only that, but the Russians had by now brought up a
further army of 100,000 men, which gave them in all about
140,000 against 60,000 of the Allies. A more disastrous
military decision than that of Marshal St. Arnaud and Lord
Raglan to postpone the original assault it would be difficult to
find.

The battle of Inkerman, which followed in November, gave
the Allies a taste of victory, while Balaclava a week or so
beforehand had shown in the famous charge of the Light
Brigade that not even the criminal blunders of their own
commanders could shake the courage of the British troops.
In the words of the French, it was magnificent but it was not
war. The engagements were not productive of any important
results, and the Allies had to settle down to winter in the
War Crimea. The men had no cold-weather equipment ; snow
conditions blocked the roads and made it impossible to bring up ammuni-
tion, food, or forage. Horses died of starvation, making the
transport problem still worse. With inadequate nourishment
and disgraceful sanitation the army suffered dreadfully from
cholera. Owing to the complete lack of any but local dressing-
stations, casualties had to be shipped right across the Black
Hospital Sea to the nearest big hospital at Scutari—a journey which in
conditions war conditions often took three weeks. And there, too, chaos
at Scutari reigned. The hospital, converted from a barracks without
any thought or preparation, was built near great sewers and
cesspools. It was rotten with vermin. The most elementary
necessities were lacking—not enough beds or blankets, only
coarse canvas sheets, no bedroom furniture at all except empty
beer-bottles for candlesticks, hardly any basins, towels, soap,
brooms, trays, plates, knives, forks, spoons, fuel, scissors,
stretchers, splints, bandages, or drugs. Even when materials
did arrive they were lost in the Turkish Customs House or held

up by departmental regulations and War Office red tape. To treatment in such conditions those who were maimed in the Crimea could look forward ; and meanwhile the dreary siege of Sebastopol dragged on.

Fortunately for the Allies an unofficial observer, the correspondent of *The Times*, let the English public have an account of much of the ghastly mismanagement. An inquiry was moved into the conduct of the war. Lord Aberdeen, who had never been in favour of it, was replaced as Prime Minister by the more vigorous Palmerston, and in the spring of 1855 the Allied army was reorganized. Meanwhile at Scutari too, Florence Nightingale, an English gentlewoman who had come out with some volunteer nurses, had effected a transformation. Using money collected by her friends and by *The Times*, she succeeded, against the bitter opposition of many of the regular authorities, in reorganizing the nursing, the laundry, the sanitary conditions, the food and the clothing of the wounded. On one occasion when she was visiting the Crimea the chief medical officer even tried to starve her into submission by ordering that no rations should be supplied to her and her nurses—a manœuvre the prudent Miss Nightingale forestalled by arriving with a great quantity of provisions ! After six months' heroic struggle she had succeeded in reducing the death rate of the wounded from forty-four per cent. to two per cent. The one good result of the Crimean war, and that a lucky by-product, was the permanent reform in military nursing effected by this remarkable woman—who gained the reputation of a saint by the ruthless persistence of a demon.

At last, in the June of 1855, after the Allies had been reinforced by the Piedmontese, the southern half of Sebastopol fell. Even now Palmerston was for continuing the war and winning a more resounding victory. Eventually, however, Napoleon III drove him to agree to peace by announcing that if the French continued the war they would do so to liberate Poland and other subject nationalities of Europe—a development so great that Palmerston quailed at the limitless possibilities involved. The conclusion of peace, too, was aided by the death of Nicholas and the accession of his son Alexander II, more liberally inclined, with no personal enmity towards the French Emperor and willing to concede

Reorganization of Allied effort, 1855

Florence Nightingale

Capture of Sebastopol 1855

most of the points at issue. So an armistice was arranged between the powers and one of the most futile of wars was over.

The Treaty
of Paris,
1856
The Treaty of Paris, which fixed the final terms, gave the Allies all they had fought for. The Black Sea was neutralized —*i.e.* both Turkey and Russia were forbidden to have warships on it. The Russian demand for a protectorate over the Balkan Christians was dismissed and a simple promise accepted from the Sultan that he would treat this section of his subjects on an equality with his Mohammedans. In addition, Moldavia and Wallachia were given complete independence, except that Turkish overlordship had to be formally acknowledged, and the same arrangement was made for Serbia. Thus, on paper at least, the Allies had registered a victory. In fact, however, none of the objects achieved by the war on which the victors so congratulated themselves had the slightest permanence.

Temporary
nature of
the settle-
ment
The Black Sea clause was repudiated by Russia while France was busy fighting Prussia in 1870. The Sultan never showed the least sign of carrying out his promise about the Christians. Moldavia and Wallachia, it is true, prospered and soon became the kingdom of Roumania, but that was more or less accidental, as was the development of Serbia—it was not for them that over half a million men had died. All the results which really counted were ones rather apart from the issues both of the war and the peace—results such as Florence Nightingale's reforms and the impetus given to revolution in Russia by the inefficiency of Czardom so clearly revealed by the war. If the war did in any sense check the policy of Russia, the check was purely a temporary one and along lines not destined to endure. Not the preservation of the power of the Sultan but the formation of new national states in the Balkans was to provide the best barrier against a Russian advance to Constantinople. That, however, was for England to discover in the future. Meanwhile the Crimean War had illustrated the truth that war is a risky instrument of policy. The terms inserted in peace treaties at such cost of men and money have a habit of proving completely unimportant compared with some result of which nobody ever dreamed at the beginning of hostilities.

3. *The Balkan Nations to the Congress of Berlin, 1878*

The main developments of the next few years in the Eastern Question concerned rather the small Balkan nationalities than the great powers. In 1862, for example, the Greek King Otto, whose reign had been one long period of misgovernment, had to abdicate, a successor being found in Prince George of Denmark after the throne had been practically hawked round Europe. The goodwill of England was shown to the new dynasty by the cession of the Ionian Isles to Greece. In Serbia difficulties also occurred with the ruler, partly as a result of a long-standing and bloody feud between two rival families who claimed the throne. The Serbs, after losing their independence in the 14th century, had remained under direct Turkish rule till the beginning of the 19th century, when a chieftain known as Kara George started a successful rebellion. He was, however, in 1817 murdered by a rival, Milosh Obrenović, whose title as prince was recognized by a National Assembly and by Turkey. The country now enjoyed a great deal of administrative independence, but was subject to a Turkish garrison and payment of tribute. Three Obrenović princes followed in succession, of whom two were compelled to abdicate, the last, Milosh Obrenović, in favour of a son of Kara George, Alexander Karageorgović. The latter, however, pleased the Serbs no more than Milosh Obrenović, and in 1859 the Karageorgović prince was deposed for Milosh to return. This Box and Cox alternation continued, for though Milosh Obrenović's son, Michael Obrenović, succeeded him, he did not last long. In spite of his reforms in military and educational matters and his successes in getting all Turkish troops withdrawn (only the Turkish flag now remaining), he was murdered in 1868 by Karageorgović assassins. An Obrenović still continued on the throne for a while, however, though the deadly rivalry, as we shall soon see, was by no means done with. Perhaps the best indication of the nature of this royal gangsterdom is the single fact that of the Serbian rulers of the 19th century only one was allowed to die in his bed in his native land—and he was insane.

The two districts of Moldavia and Wallachia, at the mouth of the Danube, had, as we have already seen, received virtual

The Balkan nations

Greece

Serbia

Virtual independence of Turkey

Obrenović and Karageorgović

Moldavia and Wallachia

independence at the end of the Crimean War, only a tribute being still payable to Turkey. As outposts of the Turkish Empire they had constantly been occupied by Russian forces when war threatened between the two powers. They had, however, always manifested a strongly national spirit and shown pride in their descent from the old Roman colony of Dacia. Revolutions had occurred, notably in 1848, but little progress was made until in 1856 the powers allowed the

Their virtual independ- ence provinces independence with the idea of creating a buffer-state between Turkey and Russia. The two territories were given separate assemblies and forbidden to unite, but this difficulty was ingeniously overcome by the two assemblies each choosing the same prince—a development which was

The two principali- ties unite eventually agreed to by Turkey and the powers. A favour-able opportunity had been seized, for it was while France was at war with Austria over North Italy. From the year 1861, when the prince concerned, Alexander I, united the two separate assemblies in defiance of the powers, the new state of Roumania may be said to date. This name, however, was not given to it until 1866, when Alexander, a native, was forced to abdicate in the usual Balkan fashion. His reign had

They become "Rou- mania" produced great advances in the way of free compulsory education and the liberation of the peasantry, but he had offended too many vested interests. Prince Charles of Hohen-zollern now accepted the throne. He promised to rule by the terms of a new constitution, a very democratic one except in its neglect of the rights of the Jewish population—the Jewish question in Roumania being for long after a matter of the greatest moment. The selection of Prince Charles, a close relative of the King of Prussia, William I, gave the future German Empire a useful ally on the Danube, and Roumania began to revolve in Bismarck's orbit.

Montenegro Of the other Balkan peoples Montenegro, under a separate prince, had for centuries enjoyed the same virtual inde-pendence as Serbia, an effort by the Sultan to increase his authority having been defeated by the vigour of Montenegrin resistance in 1858. Close relations were pursued with Serbia, and it might be reckoned that if the Sultan ran into any difficulties Montenegro and Serbia would take the opportunity to increase their territory and destroy the last remnants of

The BALKAN NATIONS
1878

HUNGARY

BESSARABIA
1812

MOLDAVIA
1822

TRANSYLVANIA

(TO RUSSIA)

ROUMANIA
1861

WALLACHIA
1822

BOSNIA
1878
(TO AUSTRIA)

HERZEGOVINA

SERVIA
1817

BULGARIA
1878

BLACK
SEA

MONTENEGRO

EASTERN ROUMELIA

BOSPHORUS

ADRIATIC
SEA

OTTOMAN

CONSTANTINOPLE
SCUTARI

SEA OF
MARMORA

EMPIRE

MACEDONIA

GREECE
1832

NAVARINO

CRETE

MEDITERRANEAN SEA

TURKISH FRONTIER IN 1789
TURKISH FRONTIER IN 1878
TURKISH FRONTIER IN 1914
PROPOSED BULGARIAN BOUNDARY
by TREATY OF SAN STEFANO.

Turkish authority over them.   Thus by 1870 of all the main Balkan peoples only the Bulgarians had as yet no taste of independence.   It was precisely in this quarter that the next acute phase of the Eastern Question developed.

Revolts against Turkey. Bosnia and Herzegovina

In 1875 Bosnia and Herzegovina, two provinces inhabited by Serbs but not yet united with the Serbian principality, rose against their Turkish masters.   The trouble was the unfavourable position of the Christians, who were employed in no governmental positions, and their heavy taxation by the Turks, who took some two-thirds of the peasants' crops, even in a year of bad harvest.   When the revolt showed signs of

Serbia and Montenegro support the Bosnians, 1876

establishing itself, Serbia and Montenegro joined in to help their brother Serbs, war being declared against Turkey in 1876.   It was this situation which encouraged a small section

The Bulgarians also revolt

of the Bulgarians to revolt simultaneously while the going was good.   The Turks, in a fright at being confronted with four sets of foes, now behaved with the utmost ferocity.   In one village of Bulgaria, for example, the inhabitants surrendered on a promise that their lives would be spared—only to be

"The Bulgarian Atrocities"

slaughtered to a man, or rather to a woman and child.   Those who were not simply butchered like cattle were collected in the school and the church, there to be burned alive as the buildings went up in a flare of petroleum.   For two months no one could approach the village, so nauseous was the stench of the five thousand rotting corpses.   The news of these massacres startled and shocked the world, though as yet the details were but imperfectly known.

Russia takes a hand

It was hardly surprising in the circumstances that Russia decided to intervene, the more especially since the Serbs were being badly beaten by the Turks.   The powers compelled Turkey to restore the captured Serbian territory, and then demanded that all Christian subjects of the Sultan should enjoy equal treatment with Mohammedans, and that Bulgaria, Bosnia, and Herzegovina should be granted home-rule.   The

Abdul Hamid announces a constitution, but refuses the powers' demands

new Sultan, the wily Abdul Hamid II, foiled this, however, by the clever manœuvre of announcing a constitution for all subjects, complete with a parliament of approved Western type, etc.   As no one, not even the English Prime Minister, Disraeli, who was more strongly pro-Turk than anyone, could see the Sultan carrying out this promise, an ultimatum was

THE DOGS OF WAR.

BULL A 1. " TAKE CARE, MY MAN ! IT MIGHT BE AWK'ARD IF YOU
WAS TO LET 'EM LOOSE ! "

Russia's supposed control of the small Balkan States and England's anxiety to
preserve Turkey are both well shown here.

8+

sent requiring some guarantees and Turkish disarmament.

When this was refused, Russia, soon supported by Montenegro, Roumania, and Serbia, to say nothing of the Bulgarian peasants, declared war on Turkey. Before this onslaught the Turks rapidly wilted. The Russians, with their Cossack troops rivalling the Turks in barbarities, penetrated south as far as Adrianople, and it seemed that by January 1878 nothing could prevent the fall of Constantinople.

At the critical moment, however, two other powers had their say. Though the Liberal opposition under Gladstone and even a section of his own Conservative party by no means agreed with him, Disraeli had all along minimized the extent of the Turkish atrocities in Bulgaria. Now, alarmed at the rapid Russian advance on Constantinople and anxious still

to cling to Palmerston's traditional policy of preserving the Ottoman Empire, he ordered the British fleet to the Dardanelles. With this force he now threatened Russia if she advanced further. The same sort of attitude was taken up by Austria, who had ambitions of her own in the Balkans. Indeed, in 1876 she had concluded a secret agreement with Russia to occupy Bosnia and Herzegovina, and if the war went on much longer Russia and Serbia would be so powerful that they would not permit it. Accordingly Austria demanded that an armistice should be signed, and Russia, with no fleet as yet rebuilt after the Crimean war, decided she could not face the combined hostility of England, Austria, and Turkey.

The treaty of San Stefano of March 1878, now dictated by the Russians to the Turks, contained clauses to enlarge Serbia and Montenegro and to secure their complete independence. Russia herself was to take territory in Asia and the valuable district of Bessarabia at the mouth of the Danube— to be ceded by her unfortunate ally Roumania, who was to get in return a barren strip of Turkish territory. Bosnia and Herzegovina were to enjoy home-rule. Most important of all,

however, were the clauses concerning the Bulgarians. A great new state of Bulgaria was to be set up, including the district of Macedonia, which would cut Turkey off from her remaining possessions in the Balkans. Many Greeks and Serbs, besides the Bulgarians, were to be included in it. It was to be independent, but to be 'advised' in its first tender years by Russia.

The terms of this settlement immediately aroused the hostility of England. Though the English government had gone a certain way with Russia and though the Sultan had rendered English support difficult by his behaviour, Disraeli was not prepared to see the Ottoman Empire carved up so completely. It was particularly the size of the new Bulgaria to which he objected, for he persisted in regarding it as simply a Russian puppet-state. In this he was supported by the usual anti-Russian feeling in the country, well exemplified in the famous song which now swept the music-halls—

> We don't want to fight, but by jingo if we do,
> We've got the men, we've got the ships, we've
> got the money too

—a song incidentally which gave the word 'jingoist,' meaning an extreme patriot, to the language. Accordingly Disraeli now threatened Russia with war unless she consented to a revision of the terms of the Treaty of San Stefano by a European Congress. Austria supported England, her help having been assured by a promise that England would not object to Austrian occupation of Bosnia and Herzegovina. Faced with this combination Russia again gave way, and the powers met at Berlin under Bismarck's 'honest brokerage' to revise the treaty.

He and Austria compel Russia to submit the treaty to revision by a congress

The Congress of Berlin was at once Disraeli's greatest success and his greatest failure. Everything went much as England wished it. Certain of the Russian terms were recognized—the complete independence of Serbia, Montenegro, and Roumania, for example, and the Bessarabia arrangement. The 'big Bulgaria' of San Stefano, however, was drastically reduced. It was, in fact, trisected, part forming the new state of Bulgaria, part forming a separate district with semi-independence known as Eastern Roumelia, and part being handed back to Turkey. Moreover, when Russia claimed her Asiatic conquests, Disraeli produced a private agreement with the Sultan by which England was to receive Cyprus from Turkey to offset Russian power in Asia Minor. This, then, was the price of England's aid ! Austria, too, was allowed to occupy Bosnia and Herzegovina and

The Congress of Berlin, 1878

The "big Bulgaria" reduced

England takes Cyprus ; Austria "administers" Bosnia and Herzegovina

another strip of territory which severed Serbia from Monte-negro. The Sultan, of course, promised his usual reforms in connection with his Christian subjects, and Disraeli and Salisbury were able to return to England in triumph. As far as they could see, Russia had been checked, Turkey strength-ened once more, and though some millions of Bulgarians had

[*Reproduced by permission of the Proprietors of 'Punch.'*]

FIGURES FROM A "TRIUMPH."
(*A RELIEF—ON THE ROAD TO BERLIN.*)

Disraeli and Salisbury return from the Congress of Berlin bringing ' peace with honour.' There is a good pun here in the word ' relief '—a form of sculpture and a relief from the fear of a European war.

been restored to the Sultan's rule, there was no danger of further massacres because he had given promises of good behaviour ! England, too, had acquired a valuable Mediter-ranean outpost—and all without a war ! No wonder Disraeli claimed to have returned bringing 'peace with honour'—and no wonder that historians, examining the real nature of the Berlin settlement, have sometimes waxed a little sarcastic at the phrase.

"Peace with honour"

"HUMPTY-DUMPTY!"

"HUMPTY-DUMPTY SAT ON A WALL;
HUMPTY-DUMPTY HAD A GREAT FALL:
DIZZY, WITH CYPRUS, AND ALL THE QUEEN'S MEN,
HOPES TO SET HUMPTY-DUMPTY UP AGAIN."

Thanks to Disraeli, Turkey regains part of the 'big Bulgaria' at the Congress of Berlin.

Results of
the Con-
gress quite
transient

Bulgaria
unites with
Eastern
Roumelia

More
Turkish
massacres

Increase in
Serbian
hostility to
Austria

For indeed, if we examine the nature of the Berlin settlement, we find that most of Disraeli's work either collapsed rapidly or else contributed to later disaster. Within seven years Bulgaria had carried out a union with Eastern Roumelia in spite of all the work of the powers. The Sultan, of course, neglected his promises of reform, and the Armenians were later to know the barbarity of systematic massacre—against which England's occupation of Cyprus proved no guarantee. Perhaps worst of all, Montenegro and Serbia were bitterly offended by the Austrian occupation of Bosnia and Herzegovina. These provinces, with their mainly Serbian population, so inflamed relations between Austria and Serbia that in the long run there was bound to be a conflagration. When it came, in July 1914, all Europe was involved in the blaze. Further, it became obvious within a few years that the new Balkan states, with their strongly nationalist feeling, were a far more effective barrier against Russian aggression than a decadent Turkish Empire. Even Salisbury, co-author with Disraeli of the Treaty of Berlin, confessed before long that in supporting Turkey England had "backed the wrong horse." When a politician admits error we may well agree with him—and meantime the Eastern Question remained unanswered.

I. War of Greek Independence.

GREECE TURKEY RUSSIA ENGLAND FRANCE

II. Syrian Question.

TURKEY SULTAN SYRIA ENGLAND MEDITERRANEAN FRANCE EGYPT IBRAHIM

III. Crimean War.

ENGLAND FRANCE SARDINIA

IV. Congress of Berlin.

TREATY OF SAN STEFANO WASTE PAPER

DISRAELI TURKEY RUSSIA BULGARIA

THE EASTERN QUESTION, 1815–1878.

CHAPTER XI

Russia and Poland, 1789-1914

1. *To the End of the Reign of Alexander I, 1825*

The unique character of Russia
Baffling alike to our ancestors as to ourselves, in the east of Europe lay the enormous state of Russia. Living almost in a different world of civilization from the west of Europe—a world in which, as the century wore on, literature, music and the ballet mingled strangely with tortures, floggings, drunkenness, and corruption—Russia had a tremendous series of problems all her own. Perhaps the main clue is simply the size of the country, stretching by the end of the century from the Arctic to the Black Sea, from the Baltic to the Pacific. Indeed, the first fact to remember is that most of Russia is not in Europe at all. The immense difficulty of communication in such circumstances, especially before the development of the railway, inevitably kept Russia in an extremely backward condition compared with states like England or France. This fact, of course, as we have seen, did not prevent her pursuing a foreign policy calculated to increase her area at the expense of Turkey and the Asiatic tribes, and thus add to her difficulties.

Russia turns westward. Peter the Great
Though signs of Western influence had appeared before, Russia's real importance in European history dates from the reign of the Czar Peter the Great (1689–1725). This brutal, intelligent ruffian, who enjoyed birching a woman or carrying out an execution personally, conceived a great admiration for the efficiency of his Western neighbours. His journeys to Europe, in one of which he actually worked as a shipwright to improve his knowledge of ship-building, are famous. The effect of his policy was to direct Russia's attentions westward—his successful war against Sweden for Baltic supremacy and his foundation of St. Petersburg ("the window to the West", now known as Leningrad) being good

indications of this. In order that the policy might survive, he had his own son and heir, who disapproved of it, done to death after unspeakable tortures.

The results of this Western bent were reflected in Peter's home administration as well as his foreign policy. He did not, of course, desire his people to enjoy political liberty : what he did desire was to improve the deplorably low standard of Russian material civilization. Needless to say, with his floggings and killings, his drunkenness and immorality, he was hardly a shining light of culture himself, but he struck hard at certain Russian customs symbolic of the conservative East—the Oriental seclusion of women, the power of the priests, the beards and gowns of the men. Above all, since enormous force was needed to carry through such a policy, he strove to create the three things which he accurately divined to be the basis of European state-power—an army, a navy, and a civil service. For the rest, his reforms were short-lived and spasmodic, but they included the institution of the first Russian newspaper, the first Russian hospital, and the first Russian museum.

The rough lines of this policy were continued by Catherine the Great (1762–1796). Before the excesses of the French Revolution produced their inevitable effect on her, as on even the best-intentioned monarchs, she had shown a disposition to introduce reforms of a Western character. In the matter of education and medicine, for example, some steps forward were taken, and if it was not achieved a codification of the chaotic Russian laws was at any rate contemplated. Catherine's German ancestry and French culture brought the Russian upper classes more into touch with European thought generally—she had, for example, a notable correspondence with Voltaire. But the most outstanding feature of her development along Peter's lines—apart from the scandal of her private life—was in her foreign policy. Here, like Peter, she waged successful wars against Sweden and Turkey, from the second of whom the Crimea was wrested. The greatest expansion of her reign, however, was directly westward in the partitions of Poland. *Catherine the Great*

The ancient kingdom of Poland, one of the largest of European states, had since the 17th century presented a remarkable *The partitions of Poland*

8*

picture of governmental anarchy. Almost alone of Continental states it had preserved its mediæval parliament—not, however, as an instrument of liberty but as a battleground of the nobility. The nobles possessed the surprising privilege of the *liberum veto*, or power for any single individual to stop the passage of a proposed law by his disagreement. The monarchy, too, had been made elective, which meant a general scramble for the kingship whenever the position became vacant. Under such conditions efficient government was impossible, and the state of Poland, hopelessly weak through its internal dissensions, was a great temptation to its stronger neighbours. The complete lack of morality inherent in the foreign policy of states in general is nowhere shown more nakedly than in the partitions of Poland. In three stages covering less than twenty-five years, a state which had existed for centuries completely disappeared from the map. After the first partition between Russia, Prussia, and Austria (1772), Catherine even encouraged the other two powers to intervene against the French Revolution so that their attention might be diverted while she absorbed the unswallowed portions. When the Poles, frightened at last into good sense, tried to reform their constitution by making the monarchy hereditary and abolishing the *liberum veto*, Catherine ordered a force into Poland. Not to be outdone, the Prussians, who had had their eye on Catherine's movements and had therefore avoided being too deeply involved in the French Revolutionary war, also occupied part of Polish territory. Thus a second partition, this time with Austria omitted, took place in 1793. It only remained to administer the *coup de grâce*, which was duly given in 1795 when Catherine seized the most valuable section of what remained and left Austria and Prussia to divide the rest. With most of Poland under her control Russia was indeed now deeply involved in the fate of Europe.

The first partition, 1772

The second partition, 1793

The third partition, 1795

Paul I

The Napoleonic wars were soon to exhibit how strong was Russia's interest in Europe. As we have seen, Catherine's son Paul, who was, it is true, half crazy, had brought Russia into the second coalition (1799) against revolutionary France. His main reason was the freakish one of resentment against Napoleon for occupying Malta, for the Knights of St. John had recently made the Czar their protector. He had also been one of the inspirers of the 'Armed Neutrality' of 1801 The 'Armed Neutrality' against the British 'right of search,' but this anti-English policy and his personal acts of tyranny, such as exiling complete regiments to Siberia for failure to comply with some minute regulation concerning uniform, caused a palace revolution. Paul was murdered and his son Alexander succeeded him on the throne.

A considerable amount has already been said of the Alexander I, 1801–1825 character and aims of Alexander I (1801–1825) in connection with the Napoleonic wars, the Congress System, and the career of Metternich. Deeply interested from the first in foreign policy, his natural move was to join England in the third coalition against France. The defeat of the Russians at Austerlitz and Friedland, however, and annoyance at being denied a loan by England brought him for a time into the French camp. The Treaty of Tilsit (1807) seemed to promise Tilsit, 1807 him great advantages—a kind of agreement to share the domination of Europe with Napoleon, the first instalment for Alexander to be found in Turkey. Since Napoleon, however, did nothing to fulfil this hope and non-industrialized Russia badly needed the cheap British goods excluded by the Treaty of Tilsit, Alexander soon recovered from the Napoleonic spell. The result was the fatal Moscow campaign and the beginning The Moscow Campaign, 1812 of the end for Napoleon. Thus far the story is familiar ; what is perhaps less well realized is the extraordinary extent of Alexander's wars during this period. Apart from China, by 1815 every neighbour of Alexander had felt the weight of the Russian Army, so that his territorial additions—notably The expansion of Russia Finland from Sweden, Bessarabia from Turkey, Georgia and three other districts from Persia—increased the Russian population by twelve millions. Yet all this time, so complex is human character, Alexander the conqueror had been at heart Alexander the liberator, anxious to free mankind from the French, from despotism, from barbarian savagery, from anything save his own shifting and uncertain ideas.

The 'liberal' phase of Alexander's life is usually reckoned to Alexander in his 'liberal' phase run from his youth, when he was profoundly influenced by his Swiss tutor Laharpe, a disciple of Rousseau, till about 1819, when he succumbed to the views of Metternich. In 1814, for example, on the collapse of Napoleon, he was not at all anxious to rivet the shackles of the old Bourbon monarchy on France. He actually wanted Laharpe to design the perfect constitution for the French—a touching instance of the impression a schoolmaster may make on even (or especially) a Czar. Again Finland, conquered from Sweden in 1808 and recognized as Russian territory by the Vienna treaties, was allowed its own separate customs and constitution. Finns were almost exclusively employed in administration, and for some years Alexander did everything to make the Russian overlordship congenial.

The 'Kingdom of Poland'

But perhaps the most outstanding example of this trend in Alexander's mind was his attitude to Poland. He really was sincerely desirous of restoring a considerable degree of their ancient freedom to the Poles. His generosity, however, did not run to granting complete independence ; instead he aimed at uniting all the Poles in one constitutional monarchy, to be ruled by himself, but to be quite separate from his other possessions. Consequently he was bitterly disappointed when the opposition of Austria, Prussia, and England prevented his gathering the remaining Polish territory into this new kingdom —the powers naturally being suspicious of any scheme which gave Russia such valuable acquisitions, and not less because they were demanded in the name of liberalism. However he proceeded with the scheme in respect of what he had recently acquired of Napoleon's Grand Duchy of Warsaw. This, however, comprised only about one-sixth of the old Polish state. The new Kingdom of Poland was given

The liberal Polish constitution

a constitution in some respects the most liberal in Europe. Freedom from arbitrary arrest, freedom of religion, freedom of the press were all guaranteed, while the right of voting was extended to a far larger class than that possessing it at this time in England or France. Only Polish citizens could occupy posts in the army and civil service, and the Polish language was to be employed for all official purposes. Moreover, in the first few years of the kingdom a new code of laws was introduced, education was encouraged, the university of Warsaw was founded, Warsaw itself was partly rebuilt, and considerable improvements were made to roads, canals, and the great navigable rivers like the Vistula. The Poles were encouraged in all respects, and notably by the prospect of having Lithuania (which covered a much larger area than it does to-day) included in their kingdom. In 1818, when Alexander opened the first Diet, he announced his complete satisfaction with what had been done. "You have proved yourselves equal to the task," he said to the assembled Diet, and went on to announce that the success of this liberal experiment in Poland had encouraged him to extend similar privileges to Russia.

Indeed, there was room for improvement of various kinds in his own more immediate domains. The work of Peter and Catherine, in so far as it had been reformist at all (for in some respects they had subjected the peasantry still more completely to the nobility, and in particular by great grants of state serfs to favourites), had barely scratched the surface. The root trouble was possibly the institution of serfdom, by which peasants were 'bound to the soil'—*i.e.* they had to supply work-services on the estates of the local lord some days in the week, and were not allowed to leave their given district. The peculiarly barbarous part of Russian serfdom was not so much the liability to give labour service—though this was what the peasantry most resented, since they claimed that all the land historically belonged to themselves—as the fact that the lord had more or less complete power over the body and soul of his serfs. They might be compelled to work in a factory, for example, if the lord should start one. Or they might be sold—the official price at this time ranged from 22 roubles for a baby boy to 1000 roubles for a full-grown peasant. Girls, of course, were less valuable and changed hands at about two-thirds of this rate. Ghastly punishments, such as confinement in chains or flogging to death with the knout, were frequently inflicted by the orders of vindictive lords or stewards. Alexander's favourite minister, for example, whose wife had been murdered by a serf in revenge for some fiendish torturing inflicted on his sister, caused twenty-two innocent but suspected peasants to be flogged to death without the semblance of a trial. Fortunately the position of the Crown serfs was better than that of the lords' serfs. Even the Crown serfs, however, were heavily taxed.

Alexander, in his liberal phase, seemed inclined to do great things for the peasantry. One law allowed landowners to

Conditions in Russia

Serfdom

Savage punishments

Alexander's reforms

release serfs if they wished—but during half a century less than four hundred landowners did wish. Serfdom was, it is true, abolished in one or two of the non-Russian provinces, such as Esthonia and Livonia, and in Russia a proposal to buy out all the private serfs by the Crown was considered. It remained a proposal. Apart from this, two or three of the worse features of serfdom were indeed abolished—families might not be broken up by the sale of individuals (though they could still be sold *en bloc* with the lands), and punishment with the knout was (theoretically) limited to fifteen strokes.

In regard to other reforms in Russia, Alexander contemplated much and achieved little. The finances and the currency of Russia remained in a chaotic state, perhaps the best indication of the nature of Czarist rule being the fact that one-third of the annual expenditure went on the army and one-third of the annual income came from the sale of vodka. Drunkenness and corruption were everywhere prevalent, and nothing was done to discourage them. A new army system, 'Military that of 'military colonies' was introduced, with the benevolent colonies' idea of settling soldiers on the land, and thus allowing them to be with their families and to spend part of their time on their customary agriculture. The other idea behind the colonies was that this would be a cheap way of maintaining a large army. The system, however, only ended up by enslaving the local populations in the colonies, for the peasants' sons had to become soldiers and their daughters soldiers' wives.

A codifica- A proposed codification of the law was no more successful, tion pro- the work being abandoned after 1815. In this connection a posed story is told of Jeremy Bentham, the famous English reformer, whose life gospel was the principle of 'utility' and the 'greatest happiness of the greatest number.' Bentham, an expert on the subject, whose works had already been printed in St. Petersburg by command of the 'liberal' Czar, wrote to Alexander offering to undertake the codification without payment on condition that he should have a completely free hand. Alexander replied thanking him for his offer, enclosing a ring as a token of gratitude, accepting his 'advice,' but somewhat naturally declining to entrust Bentham with complete authority over the subject. Bentham thereupon returned the ring with the stinging remark that he had desired nothing except "to be of some utility"—he had realized the exact height of reform to which a Czar could rise, and preferred not to be associated in a "comedy of weakness and hypocrisy."

Finally, the promised Russian constitution was never forthcoming, and for actual reform the country had to be content with the foundation of several schools and three universities, including that of St. Petersburg, a great public library in the capital (stolen, incidentally, from Warsaw), the improvements in serfdom mentioned above, an increase in religious liberty, and a few details such as abolition of flogging as a punishment for parish priests, and even, some years later, for their wives. In general, however, greatly though Alexander's projects exceeded his accomplishments, the first period of his reign was one of hope. At least someone was interested in promoting improvements, and under the stimulus of Alexander's ideas and free contact with Western thought some of the Russian nobility began to take on a reforming hue. In the international sphere we have already seen the idealism which prompted the Holy Alliance of 1815. The insignificant nature of Alexander's reforms

Alexander's change from half-hearted liberalism to downright reaction in international affairs has already been noted in connection with the career of Metternich. Events such as the Wartburg Festival, the murder of Kotzebue, the assassination of the Duc de Berri, the revolutionary movements in Spain, Naples, and Portugal, and finally two mutinies in his own imperial guards, together with the incessant prompting of Metternich, swung him round. He became convinced that to encourage the liberal spirit further would be to lose all his authority and to invite the fate of his own father, Paul. So the Holy Alliance and the Congress System, planned with such good intentions of keeping the peace, became merely instruments to suppress rebellion, however justified. Intervention by Austria in Italy and by France in Spain met with the Czar's approval, and only the work of Canning prevented an attempted restoration to the Spanish monarchy of the revolted South American colonies. Even in the Greek War of Independence Alexander was persuaded by Metternich that the Greeks, akin as they were to the Russians in religion, were Alexander abandons 'liberalism'
The reasons
The Congress System used for repression merely one more set of rebels against their legitimate masters, the Turks.

Alexander's religious beliefs

This change of front has sometimes been ascribed to religion. This would seem to be unjust. Alexander first felt deeply the impulses of religion after the delivery from the French during the Moscow Campaign. As he himself put it : "Through the fire of Moscow my soul has been enlightened, and God's judgments on the ice-fields have filled my heart with a warm glow such as I have never before experienced. . . . I resolved to consecrate myself and my government to God." An extremely religious Swedish baroness, under whose influence he fell in 1815, also confirmed this purpose. The direct effect, however, does not seem to have been repressive, for from this period date the Holy Alliance, which in theory was all love and kindness, the new constitution for Poland, the liberal treatment of the Finns, the proposed Russian constitution, and so on. Nevertheless his religious feelings now prompted him to take more notice of the Russian upper clergy, whose influence was all against freedom of thought. By the end of his reign a persecution of all except the Orthodox was commencing.

A stricter régime in Russia

Just as in foreign affairs Alexander changed to support of Metternich round about 1819, so his home policy veered correspondingly. Russians were no longer allowed to study abroad ; a strict censorship was imposed ; controversial subjects like economics were withdrawn from the university curriculum. Above all, the Polish constitution, which had promised so fair in 1818, was violated in several respects. A censorship was introduced in Poland, and the Czar deliberately neglected to call the Diet for five years—in any case its debates were to be no longer public. Secret societies were now rigorously suppressed there as in Russia. In Finland similar steps were taken—Russian officials were introduced, the Diet suspended, and a censorship imposed. On all sides the cloudy liberalism of the Czar was giving way to the clearest reaction.

Alexander's character.

Thus, in violation of his earlier promises, the Czar's reign closed. In 1825 he died suddenly, at the early age of forty-eight. Undoubtedly his mind had been brilliant and versatile, but it had lacked stability. Either he entertained contradictory notions at one and the same time, or else he succumbed to intense enthusiasms during which he could see only one side of a picture. His fervent Christianity was in flagrant contradiction to his immoral private life and his enormous wars of conquest. His liberal ideas did not accord with his keenly autocratic instincts : he could never harmonize his theories as a man with his interests as a ruler. At one period he could speak of "the absurd pretensions of absolute power" ; at another he could entertain them all. Even in his younger days there was his contradictory foreign policy—first the foe of Napoleon, then his friend, then again his foe. Napoleon, a shrewd judge of men, early remarked that the Czar's mind "could not pursue one line of thought" ; while Metternich was aware of a brilliant but incomplete personality—"I never know what part of his mind is missing," he once remarked. An interesting study for the psychologist and a depressing one for the reformer, Alexander has been not inaptly summed up as 'the Russian Hamlet.' *A bundle of contradictions*

2. *From Nicholas I to the Accession of Nicholas II, 1825–1894*

The reign of Alexander's brother and successor, Nicholas I (1825–1855), presents a more consistent picture. A dispute between himself and another brother over the succession gave the opportunity for a number of army officers and Liberals, including some of the finest minds in Russia, to attempt a revolution. The idea was not to abolish the Czardom, but simply to insist on a national parliament and a certain number of reforms, notably reduction of army service, abolition of military colonies, and emancipation of the serfs. About three thousand troops accordingly mutinied in favour of 'Constantine and a Constitution'—Constantine being the rival claimant and a Constitution being (in the opinion of some of the soldiers) Constantine's wife ! But they were entirely unsuccessful, and retribution swiftly followed. Apart from three hundred or so shot during the rebellion, a hundred or more were exiled to Siberia and the five ringleaders were hanged. As they were about to die the ropes broke and three of the victims fell to the ground. "Nothing's well done in Russia, not even hanging," murmured one of them as the noose was readjusted about his neck—a magnificent jest in the face of death. *Nicholas I, 1825–1855* *The December conspiracy*

The effect of this rising of the Decembrists (so called from the revolt having taken place in December) was naturally to determine Nicholas on a strictly anti-liberal policy. A **Strict repression** ruthless suppression of all liberal views was organized by the police—a special secret police, previously solemnly abolished by Alexander, being re-established. A chance remark, the possession of a banned book, and a life term in Siberia might be the result. Yet through all this we must remember that Nicholas himself was as sincere and high-minded a man as many of those so bitterly opposed to him. He honestly strove to do his best for his country and for civilization by maintaining an unquestionable authority. Agitation, disorder, liberalism, these were to him the foes most damaging to peace and good government. He was not blind to the need for reform, **A few mild reforms** and even introduced some measures, such as abolition of punishment by the knout, which would have proved admirable had they only been observed. A summary of Russian law was at last compiled. Technical institutes were founded. The currency was reformed. The first Russian factory acts were passed—though not enforced. Above all, the emancipation of the serfs, who numbered 44 per cent. of the Russian population, was . . . contemplated.

In spite of the above considerations and the personal uprightness of Nicholas, however, the government of Russia was in fact an intellectual and social tyranny. The annual expenditure on the army now increased to 40 per cent. of the budget. Serfdom was maintained, with the concession of a few small privileges, though there were on the average something like twenty revolts by groups of peasants every single **Factory conditions** year of Nicholas's reign. Moreover, serfdom in factories—both state and private—was on the increase. Here again the most brutal conditions often prevailed—serfs regularly working sixteen or seventeen hours a day, even at the tender age of eight or nine, serfs banished to Siberia, serfs flogged to death, so that even the horrors of the English factory system before 1833 were outdone. Serfs, too, were paid only half the wages of freemen. No wonder that the result was a tremendous growth of strikes, which were soon classed by the government as a serious crime. Serfs even began to commit offences with **Siberia** the deliberate hope of being exiled to Siberia, though that involved a terrible march on which many perished and possibly unspeakable conditions in the Siberian mines. Altogether in the reign of Nicholas I about a hundred and fifty thousand of all classes were ordered to Siberia as exiles.

The foreign policy of Nicholas has already been examined. It was based on two considerations—Russian expansion and the suppression of liberalism. In her Asiatic programme Russia acquired another million square miles of territory. In Europe Nicholas rapidly intervened to help the Greeks against the Turks and won privileges from the Ottoman Empire by the treaties of Adrianople (1829) and Unkiar-Skelessi (1833) (see pp. 190–192). We have seen how he proposed to split up the Turkish Empire, even offering England Egypt as a bribe for her compliance in the scheme. At another period (1833–1841) he seems to have been keener on the advance in Asia than the dismemberment of European Turkey. This question of Russian influence in the Balkan Peninsula led on, as we have seen, from a Russo-Turkish conflict to the disastrous Crimean War of 1854 to 1856. In the middle of this Nicholas died, though not before he had seen his military and governmental system shown up in all its hideous inefficiency.

Nicholas's foreign policy
(a) Russian expansion

In the Balkans

In Asia

The Crimean War

The maintenance of autocracy in Europe was an object almost equally important to Nicholas. Of this possibly the outstanding example was his despatch of Russian troops to help the Austrians against the Hungarian rebels in 1849. Again he more or less forbade Frederick William IV of Prussia to accept the crown of a united and liberal Germany from the Frankfort Assembly. These instances, being outside his own dominions, show the enormous importance he attached to the suppression of liberalism in whatever place it might break out. He regarded England (where the middle classes had been admitted to power by the Reform Bill of 1832) and France (where Napoleon III, the man of plebiscites, held sway) as traitors to the cause of European order.

(b) Maintenance of autocracy in Europe

In the Austrian Empire

In Germany

To complete the picture of Nicholas's autocratic policy, something must be said of the Polish revolt of 1830. When Nicholas succeeded to the throne in 1825, being hard pressed through the Decembrist Conspiracy, he had endeavoured to maintain the loyalty of his outer dominions by certain promises.

His suppression of Polish liberty

He had sworn, for example, to uphold the constitutions of Finland and Poland—"I promise and swear before God to maintain the Act of Constitution." Nevertheless a censorship was applied in both countries, contrary to the constitution, and Nicholas rapidly became extremely unpopular. The Poles especially disliked him because he showed no signs of redeeming Alexander's promise of including Lithuania in their kingdom. Instead he withdrew Polish officials from Lithuania and substituted Russians. The trial and condemnation of a number of leading Poles for complicity in the Decembrist Conspiracy gave offence too. Finally, when the French Revolution of 1830 broke out and was rapidly followed by the Belgian revolt against Holland, Nicholas prepared for war against France and proposed to use the Polish army for the purpose. The result was a revolution in Poland itself.

The Polish Revolt, 1830

Beginning at the close of 1830, the revolt lasted from first to last for about ten months. The Russian governor, the Grand Duke Constantine, was sent packing with some regiments of Lithuanian troops (who ought to have been retained for military purposes). In January 1831 Nicholas was declared dethroned by the Polish Diet, and the Russian invasion of the kingdom promptly began. To divide the Poles asunder, Nicholas, who knew the Polish Diet was considering reform of peasant conditions, lightened the burdens of the peasants on all estates captured by the advancing Russian armies. A number of fights took place, the Poles even at one time trying a desperate advance into Lithuania, but in the end there could be but one result. Outside Warsaw, in September 1831, a force of nearly 80,000 Russians beat a Polish army less than half that size, and the Polish capital was compelled to surrender. The remaining Polish forces in the countryside were rounded up or driven into Prussia, where they were disarmed. Nicholas had now only to make the enemy pay for their boldness in rebelling—a business which was performed with complete thoroughness.

The Polish Constitution withdrawn

The old constitution was officially withdrawn ; any privileges contained in a new one, granted in 1832, were never carried out. All the elections and the Polish Diet were abolished. All the leading positions were given to Russians. The Russian language was made compulsory for governmental purposes. The Polish army disappeared as an independent unit, being merged into the Russian one. For the rest of Nicholas's reign the process of repression and Russianization continued with extraordinary severity. Triumphant in maintaining Czardom intact in Russia, triumphant in crushing the Poles and the Hungarians, triumphant in helping to defeat German liberalism, Nicholas indeed deserved to be regarded, in the words of one historian, as "the cornerstone of despotism in the world."

It not infrequently happens that children react violently against the views of their parents. Heirs to autocratic thrones are more often than not Liberals—while they are still heirs. Nicholas's son Alexander II (1855–1881) was not a Liberal, but he was credited with certain reforming intentions. Naturally the mere prospect of a Czar who was not an iron autocrat aroused a mass of hope and enthusiasm which could never be fulfilled. From one great piece of reform Alexander has gone down to history as the 'Czar Liberator,' a name which might perhaps serve for the first few years of his reign. It does not tell the whole story, however, which was another tragedy of conflicting ideals. Alexander II, 1855–1881 "The Liberator"

The reign started promisingly by the granting of pardon to those still undergoing punishment for the December conspiracy of 1825 and the Polish revolt of 1830. The Crimean War was brought to a conclusion—though not before it had given a terrible blow to Czardom—and the country could breathe again. But the great work of Alexander's early years was the liberation of the serfs, an event which, as he very sensibly said, was "better to come from above than from below." By the terms of the edict of emancipation, issued in 1861 after some years' preparation, the peasants were not only freed but granted a certain proportion of the nobles' estates. Unfortunately the details of this arrangement proved less generous on closer investigation—personal serfs who were granted no land had still to do two years' service, while serfs who received land had to pay for it within forty-nine years. The effects of this measure were naturally very great. A desirable reform was indeed accomplished, but with cash and competition rather than service and custom becoming the basis of everything, many of the peasants got hopelessly into debt and lost Alexander's early reforms

(a) The liberation of the serfs

The results

THE YOUNG CZAR COMING INTO HIS PROPERTY.

Alexander II succeeded to his throne in the middle of the Crimean War.

their all.   A drift to the towns ensued, and this, together with the natural development of industry as the century went on, led to a whole range of new problems.   Peasant discontent was thus by no means eradicated, while urban discontent was actually increased.

Next in importance in the reforms of Alexander II was the granting of local self-government.   By an edict of 1864 special district and provincial assemblies (Zemstvos) were set up. *(b)* The Zemstvos The provincial was elected from the district assembly, and that from local assemblies of nobles, of peasants, and of townsmen. The main duties of the Zemstvos were looking after local transport, crops, education, and sanitation.   Although Russia lacked a central parliament, these local councils gave her a certain experience in such matters and hastened the demand for a national body.   Other reforms introduced in these years included trial by jury (though martial law was still retained *(c)* Trial by jury for political offences), the extension of education, especially to women, the abolition of military colonies, and the replace- *(d)* Education ment of the long term of military service by conscription.   On *(e)* Abolition of military colonies the material side progress was made in the construction of railways, which had been almost completely neglected under *(f)* Railways Nicholas I.   Nevertheless the intellectual classes failed to rally to the support of Czardom.   Socialism, often in its extreme forms, began to spread in the towns.   A generation of brilliant novelists and dramatists painted remarkable pictures of Russian life which demonstrated the desperate necessity of rebuilding society from top to bottom if anything really great were to be done.   In face of the hopelessness of But these seem quite insufficient —hence revolution- ism tackling the enormous problems of Russia by the cautious and piecemeal reforms of the Czar, men began to adopt one of two attitudes.   Either, like many nobles, they drifted aimlessly, aware of an impending crash yet robbed of any will or power to avert it ; or else, like many workers, they became avowed revolutionaries.   It was the growth of this latter class which made Alexander from about 1866 abandon his early attitude of reform and institute a thoroughgoing repression.

To this decision Alexander was aided by a second revolt in The second Polish revolt, 1863 Poland.   In spite of certain concessions, such as reopening Warsaw university and reinstating Polish as the official language, Poland still bitterly resented the Russian connection.

When a Polish body, the Agricultural Society, founded to improve the lot of the peasants, was forcibly dissolved, Poland broke out into open discontent and demonstration. Firing on the Warsaw crowd produced a counter-crop of terrorism aimed against the Viceroy, and eventually in 1863 the revolt broke out. There was never a chance of victory—it was simply an act of national desperation. The suppression was ruthless, though the Polish peasants were rewarded with a gift of the freehold of half their land for their failure to support the revolution. The spirit of Poland seemed now to be broken ; but Polish exiles, particularly in friendly France, never lost sight of the woes of their country. They schemed for the great day when an independent Poland should arise again. Nicholas and Alexander had made enemies indeed.

Foreign policy

In the realm of foreign affairs Alexander II's reign witnessed a continuation of historic Russian policy. The advance into Asia was continued by the acquisition of all Turkestan and Samarcand. This caused England, so long hostile because of Russian ambitions in the Balkans, now to redouble her hostility because of Russian ambitions in Persia and Afghanistan. If

Advance towards India

the process continued, India itself might be threatened. Apart from Asiatic developments, Russia also prospered in Europe by the Franco-Prussian war, when Alexander took the opportunity to announce his intention of reconstructing a Black Sea fleet. Developments in the Eastern Question led,

The Russo-Turkish war, 1877

as we have seen, to the Russo-Turkish war in 1877, in which Russia was so successful, though she had to submit the terms of the treaty of San Stefano to drastic revision at the Congress of Berlin. For a time relations with Austria were very strained, since Austria refused to help Russia in the Crimean War in spite of the debt she owed Nicholas for his intervention against the Hungarians in 1849. By 1872 friendship seemed restored

'The League of the Three Emperors'

through the efforts of Bismarck, and the 'League of the Three Emperors' announced the common intention of Austria, Prussia, and Russia of maintaining the cause of monarchy in the world. Conflicting Balkan ambitions, however, as demonstrated at the Congress of Berlin, soon widened the

But Russia drifts from German friendship

gap once more. In spite of Bismarck's success in retaining Russian friendship even after the Dual Alliance of 1879, it was obvious that Russia and Austria could not much longer be yoked together.

In domestic events the turning point in the Czar's reign probably occurred in the year 1866, when there was an unsuccessful attempt on his life. Official sympathy with the Liberals had already largely disappeared during the Polish rebellion. Now fear and the deadly repression born of fear began to grip the Government. They had indeed reason to be afraid. While the Liberals and some of the Socialists were pacific enough, the party of revolutionary violence grew on all sides as education progressed. Everything that was done in the way of founding schools only supplied more of the working class with the means to agitate and plot against the Government. Terrorist societies sprang up. At first they consisted principally of pure Nihilists (literally 'Nothingists'). The Anarchist movement also spread, directed abroad by Bakunin, a romantic figure who had served in the Imperial Guard, taken part in the German revolutions of 1848, been arrested and handed over to the Russian government, and finally had escaped from Siberia back to Europe by way of Japan. Knowing Czardom to be so bad, the Nihilists and Anarchists aimed at the abolition of all forms of government, which they had come to consider as wicked in itself. It was not till later on, in the closing years of the century, that a more practical and scientific form of revolutionary violence in the shape of Marxism obtained a hold.

Alexander II adopts a repressive policy

The Nihilists The Anarchists

Later, the Marxists (in reign of Nicholas II)

In any case the Government was quick to react. The censorship was tightened up, universities were strictly supervised, the Zemstvos were robbed of some of their powers. Everywhere the secret police and the courts-martial were busy. Already in the first twenty years of Alexander's reign over a quarter of a million people had been exiled to Siberia. Still the tide of agitation rose. Generals and governors were murdered. In 1879 five shots failed to find their destined target, the Czar. Later in the year three attempts to mine the Czar's train all went wrong. In 1880 a mine planted two storeys beneath blew up the Czar's dining-room in the Winter Palace at St. Petersburg. By chance the Czar had been unexpectedly delayed, and was not in the room, but sixty-three unfortunate soldiers were either killed or wounded.

Violence meets violence

The assassination of Alexander II

His escape did not long profit him.   In 1881, ironically enough just as he had signed a paper promising to call a committee to consider the question of granting a constitution, the conspirators at last succeeded.   The attempt was thorough enough, for six bombs and two mines were ready to greet Alexander on one of his drives through the streets of the capital.   The first bomb, thrown by a youth of nineteen, missed its mark, though it killed several of the Czar's escort. "That one?" said Alexander, walking towards the arrested assassin after he had attended to the wounded.   "Why, he's quite nice looking."   A moment or two later the second bomb landed at his feet and blew his legs to pieces.   Before the afternoon was out the Czar was dead.

Alexander III, 1881–1894

Fierce repression

The immediate effect of the crime was to divert all general sympathy from the terrorists.   The new Czar, Alexander III (1881–1894), a man of upright but unbending character on the lines of Nicholas I, was able to launch a campaign of fierce repression with some success.   The societies failed in their avowed object of getting him too, and the police managed to break up the worst of them.   Five of the actual ringleaders in the death of Alexander II were executed.   No steps were taken to carry out the late Czar's last promise.   The press, the universities, the law courts, the Zemstvos were muzzled and dragooned by the Government.   But though resentment might be difficult of expression except in isolated outbreaks (such as the conspiracy against Alexander III in 1887, for which an elder brother of Lenin, the founder of Soviet Russia, was executed), it existed, nevertheless, ready to flare up at the first opportunity.

3. *Nicholas II, 1894–1917*

Nicholas II, 1894–1917

The long-impending crash came with the completely disastrous reign of Nicholas II (1894–1917).   An omen of the calamities of the reign occurred at the very coronation of the Czar, when the collapse of a grandstand led to three thousand people being crushed to death—an example of that age-old Russian inefficiency which explains why Soviet leaders make no bones of shooting railway officials responsible for serious accidents.   Preparatory to and after the conclusion of the Franco-Russian alliance (1891–1895), French gold poured

The alliance with France

into the country in the form of loans and Russian industry French Loans
developed at a previously unheard of pace.   In the last twelve
years of the 19th century, for example, there was a 600 per
cent. increase in the production of cast iron.   In the same Development of Russian industry and towns
period the town population increased by 33 per cent., and
great factories sprang up, often with over five thousand
workers.   The vilest conditions persisted in these and the
overcrowded towns generally—as late as 1885, in spite of
factory acts, people were still being found working eighteen
hours a day, while child labour down to three years of age in
some cases still persisted.   Thus Russia, though its proportion
of industrial workers was far smaller than that of England or
Germany, exhibited in the towns it did possess the very worst Terrible social conditions
features of a developed industrialism—overcrowding, slums,
appalling factory conditions.   The combination of this class
of urban worker with the penniless university student so common in Russia produced a formidable revolutionary movement,
lacking neither in intelligent leadership nor in popular support. The character of Nicholas II

Nicholas II himself was the last man who should have
inherited the task of solving the overwhelming problems of
Russia.   His intelligence was as little developed as that of his
father, while he had neither the powerful physique nor the
iron will which had carried Alexander III through.   Without
the brains or the determination to control a village, let alone
a state the size of Russia, he nevertheless decided to rule as a
complete autocrat.   Even the virtues he possessed, a religious
and loving nature, personal kindness to his family, and so on,
were those most unfitted to his job.   His extraordinarily
narrow outlook persisted in regarding everything in Russia
in terms of loyalty to himself.   Since he was aware of the
entire honesty of his own intentions, nothing could be good
which did not begin by complete devotion to the Czar.   Other
people, however, looked at the matter in a different light.   To
them nothing could be good unless it began by complete
devotion to the needs of Russia's downtrodden peasantry and
proletariat—a devotion expressing itself in scientific plans for
social improvement, not merely in kindly thought or words.
Between these two attitudes there was no compromise possible.
Czar and people inevitably misunderstood each other and
drifted farther apart.

To the demand for a parliament from those sections of the country, notably the Liberals of the Zemstvos, who still hoped for peaceful reform, Nicholas II consistently turned a deaf ear. Such ideas, he announced, were but 'senseless dreams.' In face of this unyielding attitude, the parties of revolutionary violence naturally attracted more members.

The Social Democrats (Bolsheviks and Mensheviks)

In 1898 the Russian Social Democrat party was founded. It consisted of many shades of left-wing opinion, for different elements in Marx's writings were emphasized by different people. At one notable party congress of the Social Democrats in 1903, held abroad of course, the party began to split up. The technical question which caused the split was whether the party should consist purely of completely devoted workers, or whether it should admit passive members, encourage subscriptions from vaguely interested persons, and so on. The difference, in other words, was between a party which would be a fighting organization, or one which would be a far looser body, more dependent on public opinion and unable to make great demands on its members. The advocates of the more aggressive policy, led by Lenin, won the day. Henceforward they were known as Bolsheviks ('Majority Men'), since they had secured a majority at the Congress. The advocates of the looser group were termed Mensheviks ('Minority Men'). By 1911 the two groups had formally separated, the Bolsheviks to promote the revolution as soon as possible, the Mensheviks first to attempt reform by gentler means.

Strikes

To the thorough-going Marxist the working-classes had two weapons. The final one was armed rebellion, but before that was necessary the strike might do much. Partly through spontaneous discontent, partly through deliberate Marxist propaganda, a wave of strikes now overwhelmed Russia. In 1896 a successful strike in the St. Petersburg cotton factories, led by Lenin, wrung from the Government a factory act limiting hours to eleven-and-a-half a day. One success now bred many. Though bloodshed and clashes with the police regularly occurred, the strike movement spread. In 1904, for example, a big strike among the Baku oilworkers led to troops discharging volleys into the crowd, and the workmen in revenge firing the oil-wells "as candles for their dead."

Lenin

As though the Government had not enough enemies, about 1903 a deliberate persecution of the Jews was embarked upon. Alexander III, a great Jew-hater, had issued severe laws restricting Jewish political and social rights, and certain pogroms, or massacres of Jews, had taken place by mobs jealous of their wealth or resentful of their activities. These pogroms were now deliberately encouraged by the Czarist police. The idea was twofold. So far as the highest authorities were concerned it was to provide in the Jews an enemy sufficiently weak to invite the fury of the poorer classes, thus diverting them from attacks on the Government itself. So far as the police were concerned, they profited by the whole system, for they regularly threatened to unleash pogroms in order to wring 'protection-money' from the unfortunate Jews in their districts. The result may perhaps be seen in the extraordinary percentage of Jews in the later membership not only of Russian revolutionary groups but of extreme left-wing parties in all countries. *Anti-Semitism*

Not content with having incurred the opposition of Liberals, Socialists, and Jews in Russia, the Government of Nicholas II now added to its already stupendous difficulties by running into complications with other forces. In the first place the Baltic provinces of Esthonia and Livonia had their local liberties suspended, and like Poland were subjected to a great campaign of Russianization. Finland, too, was gagged by the introduction of a strict censorship and a Russian police. In spite of the oaths of successive Czars, quite illegal changes were made in the Finnish constitution, and all protests by Finland, including a petition of half a million people, simply received no reply from the Government. But the crowning piece of folly came in 1904, when the Czar embarked on war with Japan. *Repression in the subject provinces*

Just as Russia's ambitions of expansion in the Balkans had led her into hostilities with Turkey, and even at one point with England and France, so her constant expansion across Asia now led to a clash with an Asiatic power. Perhaps the best index of Russian development in this direction may be seen in the construction between the years 1891–1901 of the great Trans-Siberian railway at a cost of over £100,000,000. This enormous system, over 5000 miles in length, inevitably *The Russo-Japanese war, 1904–1905*

Russia's
ambitions
in Man-
churia and
Korea
encouraged Russian ambitions in Manchuria and Korea,
where they came violently into collision with those of Japan,
also determined to batten on the decaying Chinese Empire.
Japan was but an infant among the powers, only recently
awakened from mediævalism and enforced isolation from the
rest of the world.   In the 1850's an American naval commander had compelled her under threat of gunfire to open her
The
develop-
ment of
Japan
ports to foreign trade, after which the Japanese, realizing that
artillery was a decisive argument, had set themselves to attain
an adequate level of Western 'civilization.'   From a land of
kimonos and lotus-blossom Japan rapidly became a land of
factories and machine guns—a development which might
have made the American commander pause had he foreseen
it.   Extending the flattery of her imitation of the West to the
pursuit of foreign ambitions, Japan by 1895 had successfully
challenged China for the control of Korea, a valuable peninsula
on the mainland opposite Japan, and just south of Manchuria.
The cessions made by China included Port Arthur, a warm-
water port west of the Korean peninsula.

Port Arthur
It was at this stage that Russia decided to put a stop to
further Japanese development.   Port Arthur had long been
coveted by Russia, for, unlike Vladivostock, her most southerly
port in Siberia, it was free from ice all the year round.   With
the idea of eventually acquiring it herself, she now in concert
with France and Germany forced Japan to restore it to China.
The Japanese, who were not strong enough to resist, meekly
obeyed—and increased their armaments.   To their fury a
Russia her-
self acquires
Port
Arthur after
making
Japan
restore it
to China
year or two later Russia herself acquired a lease of Port
Arthur from China.   War feeling now ran high in Japan, but
hostilities did not actually occur before Japan had strengthened
herself by the alliance with England, to ensure England's
neutrality if one power were at war with Japan or England's
active help if Japan had to face two powers.   In 1904, after
she had vainly endeavoured to secure the withdrawal from
Manchuria and Korea of Russian troops and influence (greatly
increased since the Boxer rising against foreigners in China),
Japan
declares
war
Japan deliberately challenged Russia by a declaration of war.
To Europe in general this seemed rather like David
challenging Goliath : the result, however, was the same as in
the famous Biblical episode.   The Russian Pacific fleet was

beaten by the Japanese under Admiral Togo, and the Russians dislodged from Port Arthur. Beaten on land at the great battle of Mukden, the Russians pinned their last hope to the arrival of their Baltic fleet in Chinese waters. It set out in October 1904, and immediately nearly caused war with England by firing on fishing-trawlers off the Dogger Bank in mistake for hostile torpedo-boats—though what those would be doing in that part of the world no one could gather. Slowly the colossal voyage round the world proceeded, by way of the Channel, Madagascar, Singapore, until, eight months afterwards, the Baltic fleet at length appeared off Korea. All the world had followed its progress. And the very day on which it met Togo, it disappeared from history, only four ships surviving to reach Vladivostock. The Russians had thus suffered one of the most humiliating naval defeats on record, and a treaty was soon made (Treaty of Portsmouth, 1905) by which they had to evacuate Manchuria, give up Port Arthur and the surrounding peninsula to Japan, and recognize Japanese influence as predominant in Korea.

    The effect of all this on Russian internal affairs was naturally profound. Once more, as in the Crimean campaign, war had exposed the complete inefficiency of Czardom. The demand for a parliament, backed everywhere by strikes, grew irresistible. One of the Czar's leading ministers was assassinated. During the war, two or three weeks after the capture of Port Arthur, an enormous procession of strikers and their families, led by a priest, marched into the Winter Palace Square to present a petition to the Czar. When they refused to disperse and knelt in the snow, the soldiers on the orders of their commanders poured ceaseless volleys into the passive mass, the first shots bringing down a line of children, like falling birds, from their vantage points in the trees. Then the cavalry got busy. This dreadful massacre raised the fury of the nation to fever-point. Peasants attacked local landlords, strikes broke out everywhere, including the Baltic provinces, soldiers and sailors mutinied, and finally, just after the conclusion of peace, came a General Strike. Industrial and agricultural workers, railway and telegraph operators, even the children in the elementary schools all struck. Faced with such a movement Nicholas II could only give in, though

Mukden

The Baltic fleet fiasco

Treaty of Portsmouth

The effects in Russia

Universal discontent and savage repression

A General Strike

with the greatest reluctance.   On the advice of Witte, one of his few intelligent ministers, who had succeeded in obtaining very favourable terms from the Japanese, he agreed to considerable concessions.   During the earlier days of the mass movements he had promised to summon a Duma, or parliament.   This had not yet met, nor would it have been of any service in establishing democracy, since the franchise was to be very limited and the functions of the new body purely consultative.   Now Nicholas agreed to widen the franchise, to entrust the Duma with real law-making activities, and to allow certain personal rights such as freedom of meeting and association.   The General Strike was called off, but the slackening of the censorship only meant an increase in the amount of revolutionary propaganda.   Outrages and strikes continued, and brutal repression was started once more.   In certain districts where peasants had got out of hand whole villages were shelled and ringleaders even deliberately buried alive.

Extra privileges accorded the proposed Duma

In 1906 the first Duma met.   Any hopes that a real reforming period was about to begin were soon dispelled. The Duma was not for the most part an extremist body—the Bolsheviks, for example, had boycotted it on the ground that it was merely a sham.   Every reform asked for by the Duma, however, was refused ;   all the previous concessions were hedged about with impossible restrictions ;   and within three months, after the Czar had dismissed Witte, it was dissolved. By now only the Liberals retained much faith in a constitution or a Duma granted by the Czar ;   the working-classes organized instead their own town, factory, or village councils, known as 'soviets,' and determined that sooner or later these soviets should develop into a really democratic government.   In this movement a name of great significance for the future soon emerged—Trotsky.   The temper of the Czar's government in these circumstances is shown by the fact that by now practically the whole country was under martial law, and that the death penalty was inflicted for a mere insult to an official. Between 1905 and 1908 some four thousand people were executed, while in 1906 alone over 40,000 were banished to Siberia without trial.

The first Duma, 1906

Dissolved by the Czar

The Soviets

Trotsky

Siberia and executions

In 1907 certain concessions were made to the desires of the

peasants for greater freedom in selling, dividing, and leaving their land. A second Duma, however, proved as little to the Government's taste as the first, in spite of enormous governmental pressure at the elections. The police withheld ballot papers, for example, or announced the date of the local election wrongly. All the same, over a quarter of the members returned had at some time been sentenced for revolutionary activity. It is not surprising that this body, too, was dissolved within three months—on the ground that the members were not really representative of the people! Before the third Duma met, the basis of voting was considerably altered by the Government, fewer representatives being given to Poland, and more power in voting being extended to the rich business man and the great landlord. In consequence the Duma was quieter in character, and survived rather impotently till 1912.

Finally, as on two or three occasions before, foreign war was to prove of decisive importance to the internal history of Russia. In 1907 the alliance with France had been extended into the Triple Entente with England, by means of an agreement about Persia. England, more sympathetic since the institution of the Duma experiments, poured loans into Russia. England, France, and Russia prepared to stand together against any undue claims by Germany and Austria. In 1908 war came one stage nearer, when Austria annexed Bosnia and Herzegovina, with their Serbian population. Russia was persuaded under threat of war from Germany not to help her fellow Slavs, but she stored the incident in her memory and bided her time. Like those of the other nations, her armaments now expanded fast and furiously. Her Foreign Secretary was determined to score a brilliant success in the Balkans at Austria's expense. The Czar, in spite of his initiative in summoning the Hague Conferences, secretly longed for a victorious war to restore the shattered confidence of the country in his government. In 1914 the great opportunity occurred. When Austria presented her impossible ultimatum to Serbia after the murder of her Crown Prince at Sarajevo, Russia was the first of the great powers to order a general mobilization of her troops. Germany promptly mobilized her own troops and declared war on Russia.

The struggle on which Nicholas entered with so little

The second Duma

Dissolved

The third Duma

The Triple Entente, 1907

Russia resents the Austrian annexation of Bosnia and Herzegovina, 1908

Russia supports Serbia, 1914

9+

forethought was destined to produce the profoundest results.

The end of Czardom

Ghastly inefficiency and overwhelming defeat again exposed all the shortcomings of the government. The already fast rotting fabric of Czardom fell to pieces. Five million Russian soldiers paid for their Government's follies with their lives.

Bolshevik Russia

Nicholas and his family perished in the general chaos. And from that chaos there at length emerged, forged by the Bolsheviks, a new factor in world politics--the first Communist state.

RUSSIA IN THE 19TH CENTURY.

CHAPTER XII

The German Empire and the Third French Republic, 1871–1907

1. *The Establishment and Internal History of the French Republic, 1871–1907*

The new Germany
The Franco-Prussian War gave a new shape to the situation in Europe. Thanks to Prussia's victory, the process of Italian unity was completed by the capture of the last of the Pope's dominions. The Empire of Napoleon III, which in 1860 had been the principal power on the Continent, crumbled away. The Republic which emerged from the ruins was for many years torn by faction and impotent. In place of the supremacy of France there arose that of the new German Empire, strong in the legions of Moltke and the wits of Bismarck. A new European power had been born, and with it a new European culture. Increasingly during the next forty years men thought of Germany not as a land of great musicians and ineffectual philosophers, but as a land of industrialists, scientists, and soldiers. A distinctive German spirit became observable— confident, thorough, efficient, patriotic, and ruthless. The old Prussian military tradition became the tradition of the new Germany, fostered by all the Bismarckian ideas on the use of force. The generation following the Franco-Prussian war belongs to Germany in the same sense that the generation of the Revolutionary and Napoleonic wars, though far more completely, belongs to France.

The new France
Against the powerful new giant in Central Europe the infant French Republic appeared at first of pigmy stature. To begin with, it had the greatest difficulty in establishing itself. In the interval between the proclamation of the German Empire at Versailles in January 1871 and the signing of the peace treaty at Frankfort in the following May—in fact, before the treaty could be signed at all—France suffered one of the most desperate tragedies of modern times.

"AU REVOIR!"

GERMANY. "FAREWELL, MADAME, AND IF——"
FRANCE. "HA! WE SHALL MEET AGAIN!"

Many Frenchmen dreamed of a war of revenge against Prussia, especially for the recovery of Alsace-Lorraine.

The episode of the Paris Commune throws a lurid light on the divisions, stupidity, and barbarity which may mark even a great and civilized nation like the French. When famished Paris had at last to surrender in January 1871, there was still a party which desired France to fight on in her unconquered provinces. It disapproved of the idea of an armistice with the Prussians, although Paris had already endured one hundred and thirty-five days of siege, and it showed its disapproval by rioting. When the armistice, in spite of this, was concluded, the emergency government formed during the war arranged for a National Assembly to be elected at Bordeaux. The main function of this body was to conclude the definite peace treaty. To the horror of Paris, which had a strong republican tradition, the overwhelming majority in the National Assembly proved to be royalist. (The fact arose not from the desire of the provinces for monarchy, but for peace, which was supported by the monarchists.) The direction of affairs was entrusted by this body to the veteran politician Thiers, who had all along been against the war and who wanted to terminate it as speedily as possible. He now supported a republic, but one of an extremely conservative kind. The ministry he chose was not notable for any strong working-class sympathies, and this, together with the fact that Thiers was compelled by Bismarck to agree to an official entry into Paris by the Prussian troops, put Paris immediately on bad terms with the new government. Two or three measures passed by the Assembly in March added fuel to the flames. In the first place all back rents owing to landlords, commercial sums due, and the like, which had been suspended during part of the war, were now to be paid up in full with interest—a demand which was quite impossible for the poorer and indeed many of the middle classes. Secondly, the Assembly decided to move to Versailles, which had an unpleasantly royalist sound to it. Thirdly, the Paris National Guard was to have its war-time pay stopped and to be disarmed, so that Paris could no longer argue with any effect. When Thiers ordered a detachment of French troops to carry out the disarmament, the National Guards in Paris resisted, a fight followed, and Paris was in revolt.

Paris
objects to
peace,
royalism,
and Thiers'
conservat-
ism

Before March was out, following the example of one or two

traditionally revolutionary cities of the south such as Lyons and Marseilles, Paris had set up a Commune, or separate town government. The idea behind it was that by this defiance both the conservative-republican ideas of Thiers and the monarchical ideas of the Assembly could be defeated. Instead of a single government for the whole country under Thiers or a restored Bourbon king, France would consist of independent Communes, attached to one another in a very loose form of federation—an arrangement which would allow Paris full liberty to carry out its own policy. The Paris Commune itself, when elected, proved a mixed body, its ninety-two members ranging from extreme revolutionaries to sober middle-class citizens. It was supported by most of Paris except the wealthy west-end suburbs.

The Paris Commune defies the Assembly at Versailles

The Assembly at Versailles, however, led by Thiers, determined on rigorous suppression. The other Communes rapidly collapsed, but for two months civil war raged round Paris under the eyes of the contemptuous Prussians, who thus had the pleasurable spectacle of watching their enemies destroy one another. Failing to take Paris by assault and the fiercest bombardment, Thiers had to ask Bismarck's leave to increase the French army from 80,000 to 150,000 men. Even when, after five weeks' continuous attack, the Assembly's troops at last broke into Paris, they had to fight their way street by street and house by house until they captured the entire city. As the Communards retreated they set fire to important positions, and this, together with the incendiary shells used by the Versailles troops, reduced half Paris to a blazing inferno. When, by May 26th, the last heroic resistance was crushed, the Hôtel de Ville, the Ministry of Finance, the Palais de Justice, the Tuileries, all were smouldering ruins, to say nothing of theatres, stations, barracks, and whole blocks of streets—even Notre-Dame was spared only because there was a hospital close by. But the vengeance taken by the victors was perhaps even more terrible than the actual fighting. Paris prisons ran blood, Paris cemeteries burst with the dead, who had their revenge on the living by creating foul pestilences. Altogether more than twice the number of victims claimed by the 1793 Terror in two years perished in Paris in one week, either in the assault or the subsequent

Thiers and the Assembly crush the Commune by force

The damage in Paris

executions. As a gross total it has been estimated that as a result of the Commune material damage to the extent of £20,000,000 was done, while about 100,000 Parisians suffered imprisonment, exile, transportation, or death.

The results

The results of these disasters appeared on the surface to be of very little permanent importance. Thiers had re-established 'order' and could go on to conclude the final peace treaty with the Prussians. The ruined buildings were mostly rebuilt in fairly faithful and entirely dull copies of the originals. There was no longer any point in Cook's running special tours to see the ruins—anyway, disappointed English tourists had, according to one historian of the Commune, complained that they were no longer smoking. The Commune seemed like a hideous nightmare, no sooner suffered than ended. In actual

(a) Middle classes support Thiers, industrial working-class becomes socialist

fact, however, it had two very important results. In the first place it threw the middle classes solidly behind the government of Thiers, while the new industrial working-classes, resentful and embittered, strengthened their allegiance to Socialism. Secondly the struggles of the Paris workers to organize themselves into a government were examined

(b) A lesson in revolution for Marx and Lenin

critically and historically by the Communist Karl Marx, who drew from their success and failure certain principles in the technique of revolution. Marx's conclusions were again studied and re-examined by the Russian Communist, Lenin, in the early years of the First World War. The history of the Commune thus provided practical lessons for the maker of the great Russian revolution of 1917—a distant result but nevertheless an important one. Thus it has come about that the original Communards have been sometimes confused with Communists—a mistake arising not only from the similarity of the name, but from later Communist admiration for the 'heroic days' of 1871.

The Liberation of French territory

The first step in the reorganization of France was obviously to get rid of the Germans. There was an immediate rush to lend money to the government to pay off the indemnity, and the middle classes enjoyed the pleasures of patriotism while receiving in addition an interest of 5 per cent. Within two years the indemnity had been completely paid off, and France was free from the army of occupation. The country as a whole certainly agreed with the Assembly in hailing Thiers as the 'Liberator of French Territory,' though possibly the Paris working-classes would have expressed the matter differently.

Next, after the army had been reorganized by the introduction of compulsory service for all, came the task of framing a permanent scheme of government for France. The Republic had been proclaimed on the fall of the Empire, and this Thiers, anxious to continue at the head of affairs, strove hard to preserve. Yet the majority of the Assembly, being royalist, was anxious to abolish the new republic and set up a monarchy. It thus began to quarrel with Thiers, who resigned from his presidency in the belief that, being indispensable, he would be rapidly invited back as master of the situation. For once, however, the usually shrewd veteran had miscalculated, and the Assembly appointed instead a Royalist, Marshal MacMahon. The main difficulty of the Royalists at first was that they could not agree on a candidate. When, however, agreement was secured and MacMahon strove to re-introduce the Bourbon monarchy in the person of the Comte de Chambord, the negotiations unexpectedly broke down on one detail. Chambord, an elderly aristocrat of completely aristocratic principles, refused to accept the tricolore and demanded the restoration of the old Bourbon white flag, with its fleur-de-lys. This would never have been accepted by army, middle, or lower classes, and MacMahon himself saw it was quite impossible. Chambord refused to sacrifice his principles, and MacMahon then resolved to wait for the death of Chambord, when the next candidate, the Orleanist Comte de Paris, would have no objection to the banner of the Revolution and Napoleon.

This manœuvre was defeated by a few determined Republicans like Gambetta, who did some tremendous electioneering in the provinces, and from 1873 to 1875 secured the return of twenty-six republican candidates in twenty-nine by-elections to the Assembly. Eventually in 1875 the Monarchists had sulkily to agree to the formation of a new constitution, the actual measure for a republic being passed by a majority of only one vote. France was given a parliamentary democracy, with a Chamber of Deputies elected for four years by the vote of all males, a Senate above this with a considerable degree of power, and a President chosen for seven years by Chamber and

Marginal notes: Difficulties in establishing the Republic on a permanent basis — Thiers resigns — The Royalist MacMahon — The Republican Constitution

9*

Senate together. Since the President could not dissolve the Chamber except with the consent of the Senate, and since the Cabinet was responsible to the Chamber and not to the President, the latter became a kind of figure-head, corresponding to an English constitutional monarch. When MacMahon, supported by a royalist Senate, dissolved a newly elected Chamber in 1877, largely because it was too Republican for his fancy, he was taught such a lesson by the return of an even bigger Republican majority that no French President has since dared to employ this privilege. He soon after resigned to make way for an undoubted, though conservative, Republican, Grévy.

The Third French Republic, founded in the hour of defeat over the blood of the Communards and against all the desires of the Monarchists, endured surprisingly well. In spite of frantic party divisions and the First World War, it lasted for sixty-five years—nearly four times as long as any other government since the downfall of the old monarchy in 1791—until it collapsed under the weight of defeat in 1940. It weathered, too, a number of severe internal crises, notably in the Boulanger affair, the Panama scandal, and the Dreyfus case.

Crises in the early history of the Republic (a) The Boulanger affair, 1886

In 1886 a certain General Boulanger, ex-military governor of Tunis and Minister of War, captured the imagination of the French people. His handsome appearance on his black horse, his fiery speeches, his prophecies of a successful war of revenge and the recovery of Alsace-Lorraine, his attacks on the new constitution, all powerfully affected certain sections of the populace. He developed the habit of putting his name forward as candidate in any constituency where there was a vacancy, and constituency after constituency showed its approval by electing him. Obviously the man was aiming at a *coup d'état* and a dictatorship, but in fact he feared to take the final step. At length the divided Republicans plucked up courage to do something about it, and determined to charge Boulanger with high treason. At this the gorgeous bubble collapsed—the General's flight to Brussels and subsequent suicide showed that he was not of the stuff of which real dictators are made. France breathed again.

(b) The 'Panama Scandal,' 1892

The 'Panama Scandal,' which occupied the year 1892, was only noteworthy in that it provided the enemies of the

MAJORITÉ

VIVE LA
REPUBLIQUE

MACMAHON

COSTUMIER

[Reproduced by permission of the Proprietors of 'Punch.'

A DECIDED PREFERENCE.

FRANCE (*surveying herself in a Looking-glass*). "AFTER ALL, THIS STILL SUITS
ME BEST, AND I MEAN TO WEAR IT."

France decides that she is definitely republican.

Republic with a powerful weapon. The success of the Suez Canal, planned by the Frenchman de Lesseps, encouraged the idea of a similar project through the Isthmus of Panama. The scheme, as we know, has proved of the greatest service to humanity, but as organized by de Lesseps it collapsed disastrously. De Lesseps himself, a cousin of the ex-Empress Eugénie, and since the opening of the Suez Canal decorated with many orders, notably a Grand Cross of the Legion of Honour and an English knighthood, was seriously involved in the affair. Not only were his calculations in some places incompetent—such as not allowing for the tropical floods of the Chagres River—but on investigation it was proved that an amazing amount of extravagance, fraud, bribery, and even blackmail had taken place. The worst feature was that many deputies and senators were proved to have accepted bribes to advance the project, and the enemies of the régime in France could talk of 'Republican corruption.' De Lesseps was sentenced to five years' imprisonment and thousands of French investors lost their money. It was a nasty blow, but the Republic survived.

(c) The Dreyfus case, 1894-1906

The Boulanger episode and the Panama scandal were peace and quiet itself in comparison with the famous 'Dreyfus case,' which distracted the French nation from 1894 to 1906. In 1894 Captain Dreyfus, a Jewish officer, was condemned by court-martial to a life sentence on Devil's Island for offering to sell military secrets to the Germans. The whole case rested on one-half of an undated and unsigned document, which experts could not agree to be in Dreyfus's writing. His race and unpopularity, however, told against him. The nature of the trial led half France to believe that a great injustice had been done ; equally the other half held that to say this was to attack the honour of the army, which was more important than the comfort of a Jew. The strong Republicans and the intellectuals were passionately pro-Dreyfus, while the Clericals, Monarchists, and army circles in return launched a furious anti-Jewish campaign in their newspapers. Life-long friendships were sundered over the question. The fact that leakages of information still went on, though Dreyfus was now on Devil's Island, proved suspicious. In 1898 another officer was accused, thanks to the work of

Colonel Picquart, head of the Intelligence Department, a high-minded officer who dared to risk the enmity of all his colleagues. But the court-martial acquitted him, Picquart was disgraced, and affairs were as before. At this point the great French novelist Zola was sentenced to a year's imprisonment for libel following a famous letter in a newspaper protesting the innocence of Dreyfus. Later in the year, however, Colonel Henry, who had displaced Picquart at the Intelligence Office, admitted forging documents for use against Dreyfus and committed suicide. The Minister for War, who had accepted the document, promptly had to resign, and a fresh trial was ordered. At this the military authorities, unable to see that the 'honour of the army' was best maintained by justice rather than blind loyalty, still behaved with incredible meanness, and Dreyfus, instead of being acquitted, was found guilty 'with extenuating circumstances' and was condemned to ten years' imprisonment. The President of the Republic, however, quashed the verdict and released the prisoner. Still the struggle for the honour of Dreyfus against that of the army went on, and at last in 1906 the discovery of fresh documents completely cleared the character of the Jew, 'whose only crime was his birth.' It had been a most unsavoury episode, arousing the deepest passions, yet the eventual result was to strengthen the Republic, by bringing **The final** closer together the Radicals and the Socialists, its firmest **results** friends, and discrediting the Clericals and the Monarchists, its bitterest enemies.

These were the high lights in the domestic concerns of the **Reforms** Third Republic from 1871 to 1914. There were, however, a number of less spectacular but equally important points in the way of new laws and new developments. Of the former the most important from 1881 to 1884 were the laws giving complete liberty of the press and public meeting, permission to those exiled and transported after the Commune to return, full liberty to form trade unions, and the right to free and compulsory education. These were the work of a ministry of convinced Republicans, either Moderates like Gambetta or Radicals like Clemenceau. In 1894 further laws were passed to regulate female and child labour and to provide 'cheap and sanitary dwellings' for working men. The other main measures were passed by the Waldeck-Rousseau ministry

The
Waldeck-
Rousseau
reforms

between 1899 and 1905. Waldeck-Rousseau was himself a Radical, but his cabinet included for the first time a Socialist in Millerand, who was made Minister of Commerce. Millerand was responsible for some important laws, notably a Public Health act and limitation of the working day to nine and a half hours. Apart from this the cabinet was determined first to see justice done in the Dreyfus affair and then to crush the political power of the Clericals. It saw in them, acting with the Militarists, the greatest danger to the Republic. Accordingly a series of laws was passed by which schools run by religious orders were closed unless by special favour of the government, and Napoleon's 1802 Concordat giving Catholicism an official state position was cancelled. This last measure was the work of Briand, another Socialist admitted to Waldeck-Rousseau's ministry.

Financial
and
industrial
develop-
ment

To complete the picture of the establishment of the Republic before the War it must be remembered that enormous financial and industrial development was all this time taking place in France. Railroads, harbours, canals, coal-mines, land improvement, steamship services all made great progress. The wealth of the country increased by leaps and bounds, aided by the new colonial policy which began in the 1880's, and which will be detailed later. Nevertheless, in spite of the laws mentioned above, social conditions remained bad— France remained up to 1914 a long way behind both England and Germany in measures to benefit the lower classes. Old-age pensions, for example, were frequently proposed by

Extreme
Socialists
dissatisfied

Millerand, but never granted. Facts like this led a certain section of the Socialists to disapprove of some of their leaders, like Millerand and Briand, working in harness with Radicals. Thus although the Republic was undoubtedly strengthened by the admission of the moderate Socialists to office, the problem of the extreme Socialists, Communists, and Syndicalists (see glossary) remained. These in despair held that nothing could be achieved except by violence, either in the form of strikes or civil war, and thus constituted a great danger to the democratic Republic.

The French
birthrate
declines

One other problem, too, in this period beset the statesmen of France. Unlike that of many other countries of Europe, her birthrate began to fall. Her population remained at a level of forty millions while the new German Empire crept up to sixty-five millions. Her leaders became uncomfortably aware that to every four Frenchmen there were six and a half Germans—which leads us to the sphere of military and foreign policy, now to be examined in connection with Germany.

2. *Bismarck's Policy in the German Empire, 1871–1890*

The German Empire of 1871, though not so beset by problems as the French Republic, nevertheless in the years that followed experienced certain difficulties. Against these, however, two powerful considerations told in favour of the new state—unlike France, it was founded in victory, not defeat, and above all it had in charge of its destinies a statesman of the quality of Bismarck. Moreover, since the institutions of the new Empire (Reichstag and Bundesrath) corresponded closely with those of the North German Confederation of 1867, the Imperial Chancellor could direct matters without undue control by anyone except the Emperor—whom he knew how to manage. Thus with a skilled pilot at the helm, Germany seemed likely to weather the storms better than her rival France. All the same, Bismarck ran into trouble in two or three directions. Leaving aside for the moment foreign problems, which always constituted his major interest, let us see how Bismarck tackled his two greatest difficulties at home— the Catholic Church and Socialism. *Bismarck's home problems after 1871*

The trouble with the Catholic Church started in 1870, when the Vatican, at grips with the new Italian state and anxious to safeguard its spiritual power even if it lost its temporal possessions, proclaimed the dogma of Papal Infallibility. By this it was declared that the Pope, when officially defining what doctrines concerning faith or morals should be held by the Church, was by divine assistance infallible, and that his decisions were therefore unalterable. As six years beforehand the Papacy had issued a statement known as the Syllabus in which it had condemned liberalism, socialism, universal suffrage, recent scientific developments and much else of modern civilization, this was important. Some leading Catholics in Germany refused to accept the decree of Infallibility. The question now arose—if the Vatican excommunicated those who resisted, *(a) The "Kultur- kampf" Papal Infallibility* for example university professors, was the government to support the Papacy by suspending the professors from their posts, or the professors by seeing that they were not dismissed? If the government supported the Vatican, German education would be controlled by the Church, since those who objected to any theory could be excommunicated and dismissed. Naturally Bismarck could not allow this, and therefore opposed the Papal claims strongly. This made him fall foul of the majority of the German Catholics, who supported the Pope in the matter, and formed a special clerical political party known as the Centre. The new party soon began to occupy an important position in the Reichstag, where it vigorously criticized Bismarck, who determined to crush the clericals. He secured the passage through the parliament of the 'May Laws,' dating from 1872 to 1876, by which Jesuits were expelled, priests were no longer allowed to inspect schools, and the education, appointment and activities of priests were completely controlled by the State. When the Catholics objected, thousands of them, including bishops and archbishops, were imprisoned. The issue broadened into a struggle of Catholic doctrine in all forms against the new doctrine of the complete power of the State—hence the title 'Kulturkampf' ('civilization-struggle') by which it is usually known. Slowly the Centre party gained in numbers, while all Bismarck's imprisonings and bullyings could not suppress the opposition of the Church. Ultimately Bismarck saw that he was hopelessly antagonizing a third of his Empire. By 1878 the foreign situation, too, was dangerous, and the Socialists were giving him food for thought. So the 'Iron Chancellor' for the first time bent a little, and began to call off the campaign against the Catholics. By 1889 a bill had been passed which gave back to the Church much of its old independence and its power over its own members. Even so, Bismarck yielded so cleverly that the Pope, besides himself sacrificing some points, actually instructed the Centre to vote with Bismarck against the Socialists. For once the Chancellor had strayed rather out of his depth ; but he had managed to get back to dry land and even to bring with him a valuable catch in the form of the Centre party's votes.

The Socialist problem was one which Bismarck never solved. With the rapid commercial development of Germany,

Marginal notes:

Bismarck opposes claims of Church

The 'Centre' party formed

The 'May Laws'

Persecution of Catholics

Bismarck relaxes the Kulturkampf to win support of Centre in foreign affairs and against Socialism

(b) Socialism

unhealthy factories and dwellings, long hours, low pay, and the other unpleasant features associated with the English Industrial Revolution had made their appearance. Already in 1848, as we have seen, the Germans Marx and Engels in their 'Communist Manifesto' had called on the 'Workers of the World' to unite in throwing off their chains. Socialism in France, too, had played an important part from about 1828 onwards. The central idea of the Socialists was that while individuals were allowed to own land, railways, banks, factories, and the like, the workers would always be poor. This was because the object of the owners or employers was *The Socialist programme* naturally to make as much profit as possible—which meant paying the employees the lowest possible wage and obtaining from them the greatest possible amount of work. If, on the other hand, Socialists argued, the private control of such important things were abolished and the ownership of the State substituted, then there would be no employer to take the profit except the State—of which the worker was a part. Thus the Socialist programme was first to see that the workers got their correct share in political power by securing the vote, and secondly to see that the State, now controlled by the workers, owned the land and ran the key industries for its own benefit. Some Socialists thought this could be done gradually and peacefully ; others, however, to whom we now give the name Communists, and of whom Marx was the *The Marxian Communists* founder, believed that the employers would never surrender their power through anything short of revolution. It thus became, according to the Communists, the duty of the workers to advance their cause at suitable moments by 'direct action' —*i.e.* strikes and civil war.

Against such ideas Bismarck was bound to set himself. Obviously he would oppose the extremer form of Socialism, the Communists—but even the milder brand was completely detestable to him. As an aristocrat, a conservative, and a great landowner, he had resented the claims of the educated middle classes to a share in government—how much more would he resent surrendering power to the often illiterate working-classes, and giving them control over the whole economic resources of the country ! When, after a period of organization, the Social Democrat party (chiefly believers in peaceful Socialism, though the two types were not yet rigidly distinct) obtained half a million votes at the Reichstag election of 1877, Bismarck became alarmed. In 1878 he accordingly began a fierce campaign against the Social Democrats with the express object of crushing the whole movement. "Now for the pigsticking," he is reported to have said. Socialist papers were suppressed, clubs broken up, meetings stopped, leaders banished. Two of the twelve Social Democrat members of the Reichstag who dared to attend a session were all but handed over to the police. Horrified by the vigour of the persecution, the greatest living German historian, himself not a Socialist but a Liberal, and a zealous worker for the union of Germany, said that his dreams were shattered and freedom lost for years to come. It sounds very like the disillusioned Mazzini after the success of Italian unification.

Yet in spite of all the power of the State, Bismarck failed to crush Socialism. Too intelligent to rely on purely negative means, he also tried something more positive to kill the desire of the working-classes for the forbidden fruit. His scheme was to introduce small doses of Socialism by the State, in the hope of warding off larger concessions—rather as a doctor in the process of vaccination injects a mild germ into the system to forestall something more violent. In pursuit of this policy he introduced between 1881 and 1889 three measures of great importance—employers' liability in case of factory accidents, compulsory insurance against ill-health, and old age pensions. The Socialists, however, were not appeased. They denied that there was any real Socialism in this 'State Socialism' of Bismarck's, and their efforts to secure other measures, such as limitation of hours, fixed minimum wages, increase in the powers of trade unions, were all frustrated by the Chancellor. But the attempt of Bismarck to drive Socialism completely underground failed. By 1890 the Socialists polled one and a half million votes, and with the relaxation of persecution following the retirement of the Chancellor in the same year, the figure rapidly mounted until 1914, when it was four and a quarter millions. By that time, too, the Socialists were the strongest single party in the Reichstag. The battle against the Socialists was far from being one of Bismarck's victories.

Bismarck persecutes the Social Democrat party

Bismarck's other weapon— "State Socialism"

Insurance and Pensions Schemes

But the Socialists survive

Bismarck's difficulty in subduing first the Catholics and then the Socialists did not, however, prevent substantial progress being made in the organization of the Empire. Within five or six years of the ceremony at Versailles, a common currency and banking system had been established, together with a postal system for the whole empire except Bavaria, which had its own. Railways, though not state owned, were constructed and co-ordinated in the state interest. New codes of commercial, civil, criminal, and military law were framed. And, above all, industry and trade flourished, so that Germany soon became, like England, one of the 'workshops of the world'—a development which again had its effect on foreign policy.

The development of Germany

Before we at last pass on to this sphere of foreign policy, one other important step taken by Bismarck must be noted. In 1879 he decided to abandon a free trade policy for the German Empire and to substitute protective tariffs. The step was taken, he maintained, purely in the interests of German industries, since free trade, an ideal "worthy of the honourable German capacity for dreaming," could never lead to prosperity in a world of competing nations. What he did not emphasize was that a new series of tariffs would assure the government a permanent and probably rising revenue from customs duties very little under the control of the Reichstag. Under free trade direct taxes were necessary, which gave the Reichstag an important weapon, as its consent to them was essential. Under protection, however, customs tariffs would be voted for a term of years and would render much direct taxation unnecessary, thereby robbing the Reichstag of the opportunity of exercising annually its financial power. Thus in changing the economic system of the country Bismarck was also dealing a shrewd blow to the power of parliament. Incidentally the move, too, put the last nail in the coffin of the old Liberal party, for parliamentary government and free trade were the main items in their programme. Bismarck was adept at killing two—or three—birds with one stone.

Abandonment of Free Trade

The last of German Liberalism

3. Bismarck's Foreign Policy and the Framing of the Alliances, 1871–1907

Greatly as Bismarck was concerned with the developments in Germany mentioned in the preceding pages, his real interest after 1871 still lay where it had been in the years before that eventful date—in foreign affairs. The German Empire had been built largely by his skill in diplomacy, and to that same skill he looked to preserve his creation.

The central problem was the attitude of France. It can be argued that Bismarck in 1871 made a fatal mistake in annexing Alsace and Lorraine and thereby making of France a permanent enemy. In fact, it was an injury that France could never forgive or forget—for instance, the statue representing the town of Strasbourg in the Place de la Concorde, Paris, was even draped in black as a perpetual reminder of the lost provinces. The mineral worth of the two territories in coal and iron, however, and their strategical importance meant so much to Germany that Bismarck decided to risk the undying hostility of France. In arriving at this decision he calculated on three things—first that France would take years to recover from her defeat in the Franco-Prussian War, secondly that he could use the bogey of a French war of revenge to compel the Reichstag to maintain German armaments, and thirdly that his diplomatic genius could keep France 'isolated' from any ally of importance.

Bismarck's calculations

The first calculation was soon upset by the rapidity of France's recovery. The £200,000,000 was paid off in two years, the army of occupation had to be withdrawn, the Republic was established, and France seemed to be pulling herself together again. Bismarck was furious at the speed of all this (though he supported the establishment of a Republic, which he thought would have more difficulty in finding allies than a monarchy). Accordingly in 1875, when France had begun to reorganize her army and increase her armaments, Bismarck deliberately threatened war. He was certainly not the man to shrink from hitting an opponent as yet imperfectly on his—or her—feet. Nevertheless his object was probably only to bully France into abandoning her armaments policy. In this, for once, he was quite unsuccessful, as both England

But France recovers rapidly

Bismarck unsuccessfully attempts to bully France, 1875

THE BARBER OF BERLIN.

BISMARCK (*as Figaro, sings* "*Largo al Factotum*") :—

"BIZZIMARCK HERE,
BIZZIMARCK THERE,
BIZZIMARCK, BIZZIMARCK EVERYWHERE!!"

The famous 'Factotum's Song' from Rossini's 'Barber of Seville' has the chorus "Figaro here, Figaro there, Figaro everywhere." Bismarck's constant finger in every diplomatic pie is amusingly symbolized here.

and Russia refused to allow the balance of power to be completely destroyed by the annihilation of France. A visit to Berlin by the Czar and a letter to the Emperor William from Queen Victoria clinched the matter. Bismarck found himself confronted by three powers, not one—and just as he knew the moment for attack, so he also knew the moment for retreat.

Bismarck's importance in European diplomacy was clearly shown in the next two or three years when the Eastern question entered one of its periodically acute phases. It will be remembered that in 1877 after the Russian defeat of Turkey, Disraeli by a threat of war compelled Russia to present the treaty of San Stefano to a Congress of European powers for revision. That Congress met, as we have seen, at Berlin in 1878, where Bismarck played the part of 'honest broker' between Russia and England. In actual fact, however, he was himself almost as much interested as England in stopping Russian penetration of the Balkans, and the restoration of part of the new Bulgaria to Turkey was his triumph as well as Disraeli's. At the Congress of Berlin Bismarck saw clearly that Russian and Austrian ambitions in the Balkans were incompatible, and that he would have to choose between his two friends. (A treaty of general friendship existed between the three countries, known as the Dreikaiserbund, or League of the Three Emperors.) If both Austria and Russia aimed at controlling the new Balkan States in their own interest, they could not long remain on good terms. But which of the two was Bismarck to support?

His choice fell on Austria. His motives were threefold, possibly the main one being that an alliance with Russia would direct against Germany all the enmity of England, which was profoundly anti-Russian. Secondly, he knew that he could control Austria and be the predominant partner in the alliance, whereas the position would be much more doubtful with Russia. Thirdly, the support of Austria would leave open the Danube, the main trade route to the Mediterranean, and allow Germany herself to have considerable influence in South-eastern Europe. These three considerations and the fear of seeing Russia entrenched at Constantinople more than outweighed the danger of a hostile power on the Eastern boundary—for although he was now choosing an Austrian

The Congress of Berlin, 1878

Germany helps to limit Russian expansion

Bismarck chooses Austria rather than Russia— but does not wish to quarrel with the latter

alliance, Bismarck had no intention of being involved in war with Russia if he could possibly help it. The result was that in 1879 Germany and Austria concluded the Dual Alliance, an arrangement by which each party undertook to help the other in the event of an attack by Russia, or to keep neutral in the

The Dual Alliance, 1879

[*Reproduced by permission of the Proprietors of 'Punch.'*]

THE GAME OF THE DAY.

BISMARCK. " COME, ANDRASSY, WE KNOW EACH OTHER'S ' FORM.' YOU AND I TOGETHER AGAINST THE LOT ! ! "
RUSSIA (*to* FRANCE). " I THINK, MADAME, *WE* MIGHT BE A MATCH FOR THEM ! "
FRANCE. " THANKS ! I PREFER TO SIT OUT AT PRESENT ! "
ENGLAND (*to* ITALY). " NOBODY ASKS *US ! !* "

The Dual Alliance of 1879—Germany and Austria join together, while Russia courts France, and England and Italy feel out of it.

event of an attack by France. This, though purely 'defensive' in name, gave Bismarck everything he wanted, for he knew how to make a German war of aggression appear the reverse, while if Austria tried one for her own ends he could disown her. So the Dual Alliance was concluded, and remained for the generation preceding the First World War the firmest feature in the diplomatic world.

Bismarck, however, was not content with merely one ally. The Dual Alliance had ensured that if war came again with France, Austria would be neutral once more, as in 1870. But there was another power in Europe now, and on France's borders—Italy. Accordingly Bismarck schemed to draw Italy into the Dual Alliance. His technique was again brilliant. He secretly encouraged French ambitions in North Africa, partly to 'divert' her from Alsace-Lorraine and partly to bring her into collision with Italy, who had ambitions there herself. Moreover it could not exactly improve French relations with Britain, also a leading figure in the 'scramble for Africa.' In 1881 the French occupied Tunis—and the following year Italy joined the Dual Alliance, thereby making it the Triple Alliance. The terms of the understanding were again defensive, Italy having no obligation to support an aggressive policy on the part of Germany and Austria. Altogether Bismarck scored an enormous success in securing the adhesion of Italy to his system, for though she was not very formidable in a military sense she had a valuable historic friendship with Great Britain. Thus Bismarck now had Austria and Italy as allies, and Great Britain not only friendly with Italy but on bad terms with France over the matter of North Africa. The only danger of a crack in the whole edifice of the Triple Alliance was if France, otherwise completely isolated, should come to an agreement with Russia. This, however, Bismarck had already skilfully avoided, partly by playing on the natural objections of the Czar to the most democratic country in Europe, and partly by persuading Russia and Austria to define the old Dreikaiserbund in a firm treaty. This was done in 1881, and the arrangement then concluded—that none of the three powers would help a fourth power (*i.e.* France) if war broke out between that power and any one of them—was renewed in 1884. So the possibility of a Franco-Russian alliance seemed to be banished, France had no friend in Europe, and Bismarck's work was complete. It only remained now to keep it so.

About this time Bismarck's whole conception of foreign policy began to be challenged by another movement in

Bismarck 'diverts' France from Alsace to North Africa

and thereby secures the Triple Alliance, 1882

The Drei-kaiserbund Treaty of 1881 guards against Russia supporting France

The Colonial Question

SNUBBED !

Mossoo (*aside*). "HA !—WITH MY HATED RIVAL ! WHY WAS I SO
RUDE TO HER ?"

Italy joins the Dual Alliance.

Germany, which advocated that Germany should herself enter the race for colonies. Bismarck's ideas were essentially of Germany as a European power dominating only the Continent ; the Colonial school of thought looked rather to a Germany which would be a world power. It stressed the importance of colonies as sources of raw materials, markets for manufactured goods, creators of valuable positions for young men and absorbers of surplus population. Bismarck rather thought of the dangers of a colonial policy—how it would necessitate a big navy, and how that would inevitably bring Germany into rivalry with Great Britain. And once Great Britain was on bad terms with Germany, France would be no longer 'isolated'—instead she would have as her ally the greatest and richest empire in the world.

Bismarck's fears

These considerations, however, did not weigh with Germany as much as Bismarck would have wished. Germans, conscious of their new strength, were resentful when they saw Britain, with her great white dominions, her Indian Empire, her innumerable islands, ports, and bases from Gibraltar to Hong Kong, adding to such already vast possessions most of Africa. The Zulu War, the acquisition of Bechuanaland and later Rhodesia, the obvious trend of hostility against the Boer republics, the military occupation of Egypt in 1882, all infuriated many Germans who longed for a similarly acquisitive policy on the part of their Fatherland. Even the despised France was quietly building up the second greatest colonial empire. To her Colony of Algeria (settled in the reign of Louis Philippe) and her protectorates in Indo-China (begun under the Second Empire and now developed), she added Tunis, whence she began to extend over the vast regions of the Sahara and the Western Sudan. Little Belgium, too, had its valuable source of tropical products in the Congo. So the German demand grew. Bismarck had trained his countrymen to be ardent nationalists, and now they were going one better and becoming aggressive imperialists. It was exactly the sort of thing most difficult for Bismarck to resist—a demand inspired not by liberalism but by patriotism. Reluctantly the old statesman, who had described himself as 'no colonial man,' had to shift his ground and set about the acquisition of sufficient empire at least to keep the Germans quiet. Accordingly in

England still expands

and so does France

and Belgium

Bismarck has to follow suit

THE THREE EMPERORS;

OR, THE VENTRILOQUIST OF VARZIN!

Bismarck's control over the Emperors of Austria, Germany, and Russia is here depicted. Varzin was Bismarck's estate.

1884 Germany entered, as a last-minute candidate, the scramble for Africa, and made off with the districts known as South-West Africa, the Cameroons, and Togoland. In 1885 Tanganyika, or German East Africa, was acquired, so that within 2 years millions of square miles of territory went to Germany, without her so much as fighting a battle to capture them. It was a good beginning, but she was still a long way behind.

The German colonies in Africa, 1884–1885

In thus entering the colonial sphere, with Bismarck's hand still at the helm, Germany at first experienced none of the bad results he had feared. Indeed, with France at loggerheads with Italy over Tunis, England at loggerheads with France over Egypt, and Russia at loggerheads with England over both the Balkans and the Far East, Germany seemed in a particularly favourable position. Her Triple Alliance gave her valuable friends, while her possible foes' objections to one another were greater than their common objection to Germany. Bismarck was like a clever juggler who could keep five very costly and breakable plates—Austria, Italy, Russia, France, and England—spinning through the air. The plates were always in some danger of being smashed and of injuring the juggler in the process, but Bismarck's skill was such that the disaster never occurred. Consequently he earned a great deal of applause and enriched the employer for whom he worked. But sooner or later that employer had to give way to another—and what if the new employer himself should fancy his powers as a juggler (though he was quite an amateur) and desire to try his own hand with the plates ?

Bismarck's success

The death of William I, 1888

This in fact was precisely what occurred. In 1888 the old Emperor William I at last died, at the ripe age of ninety. It was his support, since the power vested in the Emperor was so great, that had enabled Bismarck to overcome all opposition. Actually, with his limited intelligence and strong sense of honour, his first instincts had been against nearly all Bismarck's most brilliant strokes of policy—the defiance of the Liberals in 1862, the lenient peace with Austria in 1866, the assumption of the Imperial title in 1871, the Austrian alliance in 1879. But Bismarck had known how to manage him and bring him round to the necessary viewpoint ; a firm partnership had sprung up, and the old Emperor's attitude was best expressed in the single word with which he greeted one of Bismarck's

offers of resignation (a customary and powerful weapon)—
"Never." Now he was dead, and his successor, Frederick,
was in the grip of a mortal disease, a cancer of the throat,
which within three months brought him too to the grave.
History sometimes turns tremendously on the lives of a few
individuals. Frederick, though a great German patriot, had
as Crown Prince shown himself liberally inclined. Married
to one of Queen Victoria's daughters, he had imbibed a more
constitutional conception of kingship than his father. The
carrying out of his ideas must have spelled ruin to everything
that Bismarck had stood for. When death snatched him so
soon the last hopes of a liberal Germany disappeared and a
great load vanished from Bismarck's mind. He was in turn
succeeded by his son William II, a brilliantly versatile though
fundamentally unstable young man of twenty-eight.

The new monarch, who had been carefully trained in the
Bismarckian principles, announced his intention of following
the aged Chancellor's policy, and concentrating not on the
traditions of his father but on those of his grandfather.
Nothing could have been more welcome to Bismarck. He now
regarded himself as secure in the possession of his Chancellor-
ship to the end of his days—yet within two years, to the
amazement of Europe and the consternation of his own
countrymen, the young and inexperienced William had
parted with the statesman who had made the German
Empire. The differences had rapidly become acute. The
headstrong Emperor longed to carry out his own ideas, which
were baulked by the Chancellor. In home policy Bismarck
desired complete persecution of the Socialists, whereas the
Emperor wished to reconcile them. In Europe the Emperor
apparently preferred to assure Austria of Germany's friendship
in all circumstances and let Russia go hang—Bismarck's
tortuous policy of keeping a foot in both camps and strictly
limiting Germany's obligations to Austria was far too complicated for his successors. Austria and Germany must control
the Balkans between them, thought the Emperor, and that
left little room for friendship with Russia. Finally, on the
colonial question the Emperor insisted on immediate German
expansion and the construction of a fleet which could hold its
own against any other—a policy Bismarck had always

avoided, since it inevitably involved the hostility of England. Bismarck therefore reminded the Emperor of the rule that the Chancellor alone was entitled to present advice to the crown—whereupon William demanded that Bismarck should advise him to alter the rule ! The Chancellor, horrified at the idea of being reduced to the level of other ministers, replied that he "could never serve on his knees." Pressed to tender his resignation, he at last did so. The veteran pilot was dropped.

Bismarck resigns

Policy of William II

Within a few years the Emperor and successive Chancellors had brought about all the developments Bismarck feared. Already in his own period of office the difficulty of maintaining friendship with both Austria and Russia had proved enormous—he even had to conclude with Russia a treaty (the 'Reinsurance' Treaty of 1887) promising to be neutral in the event of war between Austria and Russia, which was in flat contradiction to his promise to Austria in the Dual Alliance. Now, the young German Emperor allowed the Reinsurance Treaty to lapse, and determined to see Germany, not Russia, dominant at Constantinople. William's favourite project of a railway from Berlin to Bagdad *via* Constantinople would have opened up the Eastern Balkans and the Near East generally to German trade and influence, aided and abetted by Austria, whose share of the feast was to be the Western Balkans. Such a development at once offended Russia, whose historic policy was to advance to Constantinople, and England, whose historic policy was to maintain the Turkish Empire. Moreover, the pursuit of colonial aims still further antagonized England, not merely because Germany now acquired territory in China, but because the threat of a German fleet became a reality. In 1895 the Kiel Canal connecting the Baltic and North Sea was opened—an essential if Germany were to be a naval power. In 1898 and 1900 Navy Bills laid the foundation of Germany's battle-fleet. It was not long before a race began with England in the construction of dreadnoughts. Bismarck's main aims had been thoroughly violated—Russia and England were now Germany's potential enemies, not her friends. The isolation of France was ended.

Rein-surance Treaty with Russia lapses

Berlin to Bagdad Railway—German influence in Balkans

Colonial claims and a big fleet

Russia and England become hostile to Germany

It did not take long for France and Russia to come together. Even before Bismarck's fall the publication of the alliance with Austria had made Russia suspect the value of Germany's

DROPPING THE PILOT.

Punch's most famous political cartoon. William II and Bismarck part
company. Both of them, strangely enough, liked this representation.

professions of friendship, and now in view of the new Emperor's policy she was certain of their worthlessness.   The renewal of the Triple Alliance left her, like France, 'isolated.'   So the two countries naturally combined forces, in spite of the world of difference between Russian Czardom and French democracy.   By two or three stages an agreement was arrived at, the main feature being that each would come to the other's assistance if attacked by Germany.   So the Dual Alliance of France and Russia, published in 1895, stood opposed to the Triple Alliance of Germany, Austria, and Italy.   Bismarck's haunting fear, 'the war on two fronts'—against France and Russia simultaneously—was one step nearer.

The Dual Alliance of France and Russia (formed 1891–1895)

It remained to bring England into the new alliance.   Here the main difficulties were the very bad relations persisting with France on African matters and with Russia on the Near and Far East.   For some years, in fact, the position between France and England grew worse rather than better.   France, mindful of the Napoleonic traditions, bitterly resented the English occupation of Egypt.   England objected to the French acquisition of Tunis and her designs on Morocco.   Then a crisis blazed up over the Sudan in the famous 'Fashoda Incident.'   A certain Major Marchand with a handful of Frenchmen won his way, in a brilliant exploring feat entailing three years of hardship, right across Africa.   He planted the tricolore at Fashoda, a small village on the Upper Nile.   The trouble began when the English General Kitchener arrived, following his defeat of the native Sudanese forces at Omdurman (1898), and found English control of the all-important Nile blocked by a few individuals and the French flag.   For some time it seemed that the two countries were on the verge of war, when France climbed down and the situation was saved.   Delcassé, the French Foreign Minister, shrewdly calculated that English friendship might be more valuable to France than Fashoda or half a million miles of the Sudan.

England and France still on bad terms

The 'Fashoda Incident,' 1898

France gives way to England

For England a long process of political education was necessary to convince her of the need for friendship with France. Indeed, for a time she seemed to be turning rather to Germany, who, however, jealous of English colonial power and contemptuous of English liberalism, rebuffed Joseph Chamber-

Germany rejects England's overtures

lain's friendly overtures. Gradually England's outlook began to change. The hostility of almost every other country in Europe during the Boer War was one factor—particularly that of Germany, whose Emperor had already in 1896 sent a telegram congratulating Kruger on repelling the Jameson Raid. Then there was the death of England's expert in foreign affairs, Lord Salisbury, the exponent of 'splendid isolation'—the splendour of which was becoming less and less visible with each increasing cloud on the horizon. The passing of the old Queen, too, and the accession of Edward VII had its importance. Victoria had been pro-German in sympathy, whereas Edward not only intensely disliked his nephew, the Emperor William, but had a passionate fondness, quite understandable in view of his upbringing, for France and the French. In 1902 England took her first step away from isolation by an unexpected alliance with Japan, whose rapid westernization was the wonder, and not yet the dismay, of the world. In 1904 the next step followed—the Entente with France. *The end of English 'isolation'* *The Anglo-Japanese alliance, 1902*

The Entente, also very largely the work of Delcassé, was not a definite military alliance. In actual detail it was an 'understanding' arrived at on the main source of Franco-British hostility—Africa. Its terms were the obvious ones— that England should have a 'free hand' in Egypt and the Sudan, while France should enjoy a similar privilege with regard to Morocco. Nevertheless, although so limited in its form, the Entente was succeeded by military and naval arrangements between the staffs of the French and English forces for dealing with Germany if that should be necessary. If it was not an alliance in name, it rapidly became something like it in fact. At any rate the German Emperor was furious at its conclusion, both because it seemed to shut Germany out of Morocco and because it announced the future partnership of France and England. Delcassé was promptly driven to resign by German threats which France could not at the moment resist, her military ally Russia being engaged in the disastrous Russo-Japanese war. *The Dual Entente, 1904* *Egypt for England, Morocco for France* *Germany secures Delcassé's dismissal*

With the Entente thus concluded, the next step was obviously to iron out the differences between France's two friends, England and Russia. The main trouble, the conflicting aims *English agreement with Russia on Persia* of the two countries in the East, was solved by an agreement about Persia. Russian penetration southward towards India had long worried England. The new arrangement was designed to remove England's fears by limiting the Russian 'sphere of influence' to the north of Persia. England's influence was declared to be predominant in the south, and a neutral 'buffer' zone was left between. This, incidentally, was called an arrangement to secure the 'independence of Persia'! With Russian expansion in the direction of India

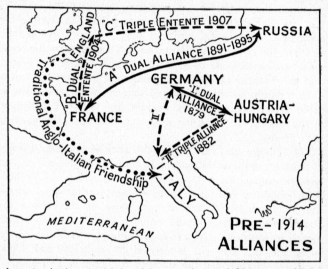

thus checked and with her Manchurian and Chinese ambitions thwarted by the Anglo-Japanese alliance, there remained only the historic question of the advance in the Balkans. To this, however, England had ceased to attach so much importance, for the Balkan nations had shown their independence of Russia. And, anyway, if Russia did get to Constantinople it would be no worse than having Germany in control there, the latest ambition of William II. So friendship at last came with Russia, and the Triple Entente was ranged against the Triple Alliance. Bismarck, dead in 1898 after eight years of bitter criticism of his successors, might well have turned in his grave at such fatal developments for Germany.

Triple
Entente
(1907) faces
Triple
Alliance

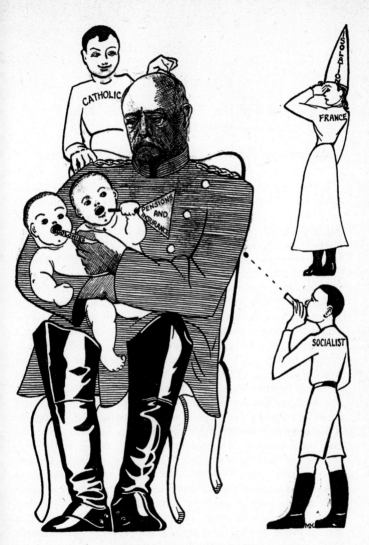

THE LATER BISMARCK.

CHAPTER XIII

The Balkans and the Approach to the First World War, 1900–1914

1. Increasing Tension. The North African Question and the Arms Race

Nationalism

By the end of the 19th century the great tide of nationalism —against which the breakwaters of the Vienna Treaties had operated so vainly—was everywhere in full flood. Two new major national powers, Germany and Italy, had been born. Belgium had asserted her independence of Holland, and Norway was on the point of severing the last ties with Sweden. The Ottoman Empire in Europe had largely dissolved into its component national fragments—Greece, Serbia, Roumania, Bulgaria. There still existed, however, certain districts of Europe where national feeling, strong as it was, had been unable to assert itself against a ruling race. Greeks and Bulgars in Macedonia, the district restored to the Ottoman Empire by Disraeli in 1878, dreamed of the day of liberation from the Turk. Poles, Finns, Letts consistently aimed at securing freedom from their Russian masters. Above all, in the Austrian Empire a hotch-potch of suppressed nationalities bitterly resented the supremacy of Austria and Hungary. They regarded the Dual Monarchy as an Austrian device to buy the friendship of the Magyars at the expense of the persecution of millions of Czechs, Poles, Ruthenes, Serbs, Croats, Roumanians, and Slovenes. From one or other of these dissatisfied regions trouble was sooner or later bound to arise.

Still unsatisfied in Macedonia, Poland, Baltic provinces, Austrian Empire

It may readily be seen that national feeling, when baulked of self-expression in the form of independence, has been a potent cause of war. An equally important point, however, is that even when nations have succeeded in winning their freedom wars are not less likely to occur. Desire for freedom for one's own nation does not necessarily imply recognition of

Nationalism as a cause of war

272

the rights of other nations. In fact, the historical tendency has been all the reverse. The easiest way for a Frenchman to prove himself patriotic, for example, has been for him to go out and kill a German (when once their respective countries have decided that for the time being Frenchmen and Germans may kill each other). The greatest age of national feeling in Europe proved to be also the greatest age of overseas colonization, or subjection of coloured races to European ones. So far from leading to respect for others, national feeling has actually led to the opposite ; strong nations, rigidly and patriotically pursuing their own national desires, have inevitably clashed with one another. The trouble has been that despite the beginnings of a code of international law, there has been no international authority strong enough to enforce it. In consequence, each nation has done what it pleased until some other nation whose ambitions or safety were threatened chose to object. If the objection was sustained to the limit, and the original party would not give way, the result was war. Thus in the state of world organization before 1914 wars were bound to occur, either because nations were not free enough or else because they were too free. Unfortunately, in spite of the attempts made after the two World Wars to improve matters by creation of international organizations, the same conditions persist to-day. National feeling, though probably declining, is still a highly potent factor in politics, and as long as national interest prevents effective surrender of the right to employ force to some international body, it is difficult to see how wars can be avoided.

International law, but no force to make it respected

The truth of the above considerations is amply demonstrated by the history of the years immediately preceding 1914. As we have seen, by 1907 the Triple Entente of Britain, France, and Russia was ranged against the Triple Alliance of Germany, Austria, and Italy. In the search for national security and in pursuit of their territorial ambitions the European powers had formed themselves into two groups, armed to the teeth and mutually antagonistic. The policies of these groups soon began to clash in many parts of the world's surface, and from 1906 a series of 'incidents' kept the international atmosphere in a state of chronic disturbance. Though conflicts might indeed occur anywhere, the two regions over which the

The main storm-centres— North Africa and Balkans

storm-clouds gathered heaviest were North Africa and the Balkans.

North Africa

The North African question was twice nearly responsible for war inside five years.   It will be remembered that in the course of the 19th century France had acquired Algeria and Tunis and had expanded southward over the Sahara.   Not many years after the construction of the Suez Canal, Britain and France had claimed control of Egyptian finance—a control soon extended by Britain into military occupation.   After Kitchener's victory over the Mahdi at Omdurman in 1898 the Sudan, too, was Britain's.   For a time relations had been strained between Britain and France, the two chief competing powers, notably over the Fashoda incident.   By 1904, however, with the Entente, France recognized Britain's position in Egypt in return for a British acceptance of her ambitions in Morocco.   This was where trouble with a third party began.   Germany, late in the race for colonial possessions, had earmarked Morocco as her own particular sphere of influence.   The German government, having secured the dismissal of Delcassé the statesman responsible for the Entente, now demanded that a conference should be called to settle the future of Morocco.   Kaiser William II even paid a surprise visit to Tangier and vowed to protect the independence of the Sultan of Morocco against France.   In 1906 a conference duly met at Algeçiras, but the German attempt to exclude the French from policing Morocco (a first step towards a French occupation) failed, owing to the fact that France was strongly supported by Russia and Britain.   The Entente, in its first trial, had held firm.

1904
France and
Britain
oppose
German
claims on
Morocco

The
'Tangier
Incident,'
1905
The
Algeçiras
Conference
1906

Germany, however, was not yet prepared to see Morocco swallowed up by France without a further protest.   When, in 1911, the French despatched an army into Morocco 'to help the Sultan keep order,' the Germans sent a gunboat, the *Panther*, and later a cruiser, the *Berlin*, to Agadir harbour to protect German interests.   This was a violation of the Algeçiras settlement, by which France and Spain were alone entitled to policing rights.   Britain took a very serious view of the situation, fearing that the Germans were seeking to acquire an Atlantic naval base.   Lloyd George, then the Chancellor of the Exchequer in Asquith's government, in a speech at

The 'Agadir
Crisis '
1911

"MOSÉ IN EGITTO!!!"

A notable coup in the struggle for colonial influence was Disraeli's acquisition of the Suez Canal Shares held by the Khedive of Egypt.

Here the title of a famous opera by Rossini is used to signify the presence of Disraeli and England in Egypt.

a Mansion House banquet practically threatened Germany with war if she persisted in her attitude. The result was that Germany, as yet not fully prepared, climbed down and agreed to the establishment of a French protectorate over Morocco. As 'compensation' she obtained some territory just north of the Cameroons, but this could not disguise the fact that the Entente had again scored a notable success.

The list of powers interested in the troubles of North Africa, however, did not stop at Britain, France, and Germany—or even Spain, who had her own section of Morocco. Italy was desperately anxious to fill her pockets and to illustrate her new claim to be a major power by the acquisition of colonies. We have seen how the French occupation in 1881 of Tunis, on which Italy had herself cast longing glances, had been partly responsible for the Italian adhesion to the Austro-German Dual Alliance. Frustrated over Tunis, the Italians had planned to absorb Abyssinia. They were successful in securing two coastal strips by the Red Sea (Eritrea in 1885 and Italian Somaliland in 1892), but their larger object came to grief when the Abyssinians, catching an invading Italian army in hopelessly inferior numbers, won a tremendous victory at Adowa (1896). The result of this battle was that Abyssinia continued to be ruled by Abyssinians—a state of affairs so outrageous to Italian dignity that revenge had eventually to be sought, and obtained, in 1935.

Having by 1900 thus been unsuccessful in acquiring anything worth mentioning, the Italians now developed ambitions in connection with Tripoli, the last remaining piece of the Ottoman Empire in North Africa. It was true that it consisted largely of desert and that anyway Italy had no quarrel with Turkey, but these were minor matters to a country out for colonies. In 1911, taking advantage of the general commotion caused by the Agadir crisis and of certain restrictions on foreign trade introduced by the new nationalist movement in the Ottoman Empire, Italy declared war on Turkey. As the Turkish navy was not strong enough to afford Tripoli any effective relief, the Italians were able to overrun the province in a year. This action, too, produced one effect of some importance in general European politics. The Triple Alliance was shaken, partly because Germany had

Germany
climbs
down

Italy also
interested
in Africa

Abyssinian
campaign
Eritrea

Adowa,
1896

Tripoli

Italo-
Turkish
War gives
Tripoli to
Italy, 1911–
1912

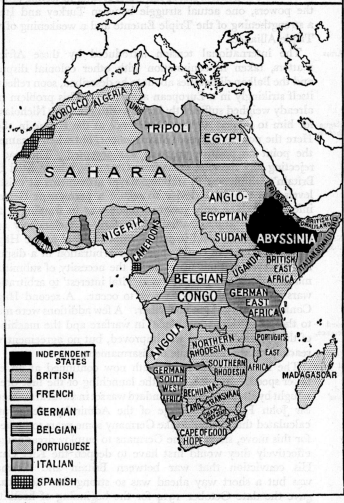

THE SCRAMBLE FOR AFRICA
1914

MOROCCO
ALGERIA
TUNIS
TRIPOLI
EGYPT
SAHARA
ANGLO-EGYPTIAN SUDAN
ABYSSINIA
BRITISH SOMALILAND
NIGERIA
NIGERIA
CAMEROONS
UGANDA
BRITISH EAST AFRICA
ITALIAN SOMALILAND
BELGIAN CONGO
GERMAN EAST AFRICA
ANGOLA
NORTHERN RHODESIA
PORTUGUESE EAST AFRICA
MADAGASCAR
GERMAN SOUTH WEST AFRICA
SOUTHERN RHODESIA
BECHUANA-
LAND
TRANSVAAL
ORANGE FREE STATE
NATAL
CAPE OF GOOD HOPE

	INDEPENDENT STATES
	BRITISH
	FRENCH
	GERMAN
	BELGIAN
	PORTUGUESE
	ITALIAN
	SPANISH

herself begun to regard Tripoli as a suitable acquisition and partly because Italy had attacked Turkey, now a centre of German patronage and commercial development.   Thus in the five years from 1906 to 1911 North African affairs caused two threats of general European wars, greater ill-feeling among the powers, one actual struggle between Turkey and Italy, a strengthening of the Triple Entente and a weakening of the Triple Alliance.

Italy drift-ing from Germany

The international tension introduced by these African matters, taken in conjunction with other colonial disputes and the Balkan difficulties about to be described, soon reflected itself strikingly in a European arms race.   This problem had already weighed sufficiently heavily with the Czar Nicholas II for him to suggest a great Conference at the Hague in 1899. Here the powers discussed disarmament, but when it came to the point no positive proposal was accepted.   The lead in rejecting any measure came from Germany, who insisted that Britain's willingness to stabilize naval armaments at existing levels was simply a device to secure a permanent German inferiority.   The only progress made was in framing a few rules for the 'humanization' of warfare—a melancholy con-fession of failure—and in setting up a tribunal at the Hague to which countries could appeal for arbitration in a dispute. As, however, nations were spared the necessity of submitting matters of 'national honour' and 'vital interest' to arbitration, wars were just as liable as ever to occur.   A second Hague Conference in 1907 got no further.   A few additions were made to the list of things 'not done' in warfare and the machinery of the Hague Tribunal was improved, but no agreement was reached on the main issue of disarmament.

The Arms Race

The Hague Conference, 1899

The Hague Tribunal

A second Conference, 1907

The European dance of death now continued at an ever faster speed.   In 1906, with the launching of the first dread-nought by England, a new standard was set in naval armaments. Sir John Fisher, in charge of the Admiralty, deliberately calculated that it would take Germany some years to make up for this move, since for the Germans to employ dreadnoughts effectively they would first have to deepen the Kiel Canal. His conviction that war between Britain and Germany was but a short way ahead was so strong that he actually gave the date October 1914 for the beginning of hostilities.

Naval competi-tion : 'Dread-noughts'

Further, he even suggested to King Edward that Britain should 'Copenhagen' the German fleet—*i.e.* demand that it should be handed over, and on refusal, annihilate it, in the same way as the Danish fleet had been destroyed in 1807! Since war was bound to come, he argued, it might as well come while England still held the superiority—why wait for the Germans to catch up? His cynical advice was not accepted, but there were large numbers of people both in Britain and Germany who thought on exactly the same lines, and who caused the possibilities of peace to become fainter and fainter. The fact that Fisher, too, was one of the British representatives at the Hague disarmament conference in 1899 helps to explain why disarmament conferences then, as now, were all conference and no disarmament. In any case, the Germans, following the policy of Tirpitz and the Kaiser, were not slow to take the next step. The Kiel Canal was deepened, dreadnoughts were constructed, new navy bills budgeted for frantic increases in the fleet. Between 1909 and 1911 Germany built nine dreadnoughts. Britain consequently built eighteen. The tremendous armour of the German vessels indicated that they were destined for use not far from home, rather than the distant preservation of colonial connections. The British countered by concentrating 80 per cent. of their fleet in the North Sea, and by arranging that France should look after the Mediterranean.

On the military side the arms contest proceeded with equal fury. The German army was enlarged and trained to the highest degree of efficiency, while the French and the Russians increased the length of conscript service with the colours. Even Britain, under her War Minister Lord Haldane, organized a small but strong Expeditionary Force for service on the Continent, coupled with a Territorial Army for home defence. Once started, it was almost impossible to slow down the arms race. On each side there was a complete absence of trust in the other's intentions; on each side national pride refused to budge from a position once taken up; and on each side an enormous vested interest in the war industry was being created in the form of groups of people, ranging from arms manufacturers and shareholders to newspaper proprietors, who profited financially from a state of international tension.

Military competition

German
'militar-
ism'

In Germany, a country always liable to be misled by the power of ideas, certain circles, taking their lead from the historian Treitschke or the army chiefs, preached not only the inevitability but the desirability of war. The great theories of Darwin on evolution and the 'survival of the fittest' were perverted to mean that war, the highest form of struggle, tones up the human race, and, by eliminating the unfittest nations and giving greater power to the fittest, advances the cause of civilization. The Germans from 1864 to 1871 had been so successful in warfare that they regarded future victory as certain. Then, with victory achieved, the German *Kultur* of science, strength, and state supremacy could displace in Europe the decadent civilization of France, based on liberty and literature, and that of England, based on comfort and cricket.

The public
largely
unaware of
develop-
ments

These ideas, and the full realization of the trend of international affairs, were, however, by no means universally recognized. German naval commanders might toast 'The Day,' German university professors might proclaim their absurd theories, the Kaiser might rattle his sabre in the scabbard, Fisher might strain at the leash, French and British generals might concert military arrangements, Austrian and Russian foreign ministers might plan diplomatic coups in the Balkans—but the great European public went on blind to the true state of affairs. Foreign policy, even in a democracy like England, was always shrouded in mystery—several members of Asquith's cabinet, even, were not aware until the last moment how far the Prime Minister and his Foreign Secretary, Sir Edward Grey, had committed Britain to France. The ordinary Englishman, though, and especially the sailor, resented the new German naval claims. The business man resented the loss of trade to German firms, which were undercutting British goods in many markets, notably in South America. Everyone resented the Kaiser's speeches. But very few people realized quite what combustible material surrounded them or quite what calamity would befall them were it to take fire. Even if a war did come, war was traditionally a matter for the army and navy, while the rest stayed at home and enjoyed the accounts in the newspapers over breakfast. Thus, in a curious mixture of unconsciousness and deliberateness, of blindness and awareness, Europe approached the disaster. In truth, it mattered little how much the masses were aware that all Europe was a powder magazine liable to explode at any moment. The fact of the powder magazine remained. It had nearly gone off over the North African incidents, though before 1911 the average man

Europe a powder magazine

[Reproduced by permission of the Proprietors of 'Punch.'

L'ENFANT TERRIBLE!

CHORUS IN THE STERN. "DON'T GO ON LIKE THAT—OR YOU'LL UPSET US ALL!"

Kaiser William II's indiscretions were notorious.

had never even heard of Agadir. And now in 1914, though the average man did not know Sarajevo from the Sahara, the catastrophe was to come all the same from the Balkans.

2. *The Balkans, 1878–1914. The Guns go off*

The fact that most of the subject races of the Turks had gradually gained independence during the course of the 19th century had not brought lasting peace to South-Eastern

Europe. As we have seen, by 1878 Greece, Serbia, Montenegro, Roumania, and Bulgaria had all been formed from the
Ottoman Empire. The end of the century, however, had not
seen the completion of the process, for the Greeks and Bulgars
of Macedonia and the Albanians were still under Turkish
rule. The districts of Bosnia and Herzegovina, too, containing
a million Serbs, while nominally still under Turkish sovereign-
ity, had been administered since 1878 by Austria. Trouble
might easily arise from these unliberated districts. Further,
the formation of four or five new states had simply quadrupled
the conflicting national policies in the Balkans. No state was
satisfied with its existing boundaries, while to most of them
revolution and fighting came almost as second nature.

The history of the Balkan Peninsula from the Congress of
Berlin to the First World War is neither simple nor edifying.
It would be fruitless to attempt to follow it in detail. Until
1908 the main incidents which affected Bulgaria were the
expulsion of Russian 'advisers,' the union with East Roumelia
(1885) in spite of the Treaty of Berlin, a war with Serbia
(1885), and the kidnapping and deposition of the first
Bulgarian prince (1886). In Serbia restless intrigue among
politicians and army led to the brutal crime of 1903, when
a number of conspirators broke into the royal palace, tracked
the Obrenović king and his queen in the dark to their hiding-
place in a cupboard, murdered them as they sheltered in
each other's arms, and threw their outraged bodies out of a
window. The 'coup' was completed by a 'purge' of other
opponents—after which a Karageorgović naturally ascended
the throne. Roumania, whose ruler proclaimed himself a
king in 1881, enjoyed a less violent history during the same
period, the main disturbances being either peasant revolts
against bad economic conditions or the traditional Roumanian
persecution of Jews. Greece, in 1897, went to war with
Turkey about the future of Crete and Macedonia, but was
badly beaten inside three weeks. In the Turkish Empire
itself the main excitement was caused by the hideous misgovernment of Abdul Hamid II, who, following unrest among
the Armenians in Asia Minor, organized extensive massacres
of that unfortunate Christian race. He rapidly became known
in England as 'The Great Assassin' and in France as 'The Red

Racial discontent in Balkans

1878-1908

Bulgaria

Serbia

Roumania

Greece

Turkey

Sultan.' In six weeks alone of the year 1895 over 30,000 Armenians were butchered. In the following year the order was given to attack the Armenian quarter in Constantinople, and 6000 souls were done to death during a two-day slaughter. The whole ghastly episode confirmed the truth of the jest that while Christianity provides martyrs, Mohammedanism creates them. The powers, of course, protested, but took no effective steps to see that their protests were heeded.

These events were by way of being standard Balkan activity—they had little effect on the main stream of European history. The year 1908, however, witnessed some momentous changes which led directly to general warfare. In that year a revolution, known as the 'Young Turk' movement, broke out in the Ottoman Empire. The conspirators aimed at imitating the methods and efficiency of the West in a fervently nationalist effort at checking the rapid decline of Turkish power. They demanded a parliament and a modern constitution, and to strengthen Turkey were prepared to allow Christian subjects equal privileges with Mohammedans. Fostered in Paris by exiles, the movement in 1908 transferred itself to Macedonia, where it was officially proclaimed. Sympathetic Turkish regiments prepared to advance and install the leaders in Constantinople. Finding himself without support, Abdul Hamid agreed to restore the constitution which had been momentarily in force in 1876. The censorship was relaxed, over 80,000 exiles returned, the different subject races seemed closer than brothers, and Liberals all over Europe wept tears of joy.

Within two or three months the picture began to look a little different. Taking instant advantage of the natural disorganization at Constantinople, Bulgaria proclaimed herself freed from the last shreds of her dependence, and elevated her prince into a czar, or king. Austria annexed unconditionally the Turkish provinces she was administering, Bosnia and Herzegovina. Crete proclaimed itself united with Greece. Serbia and Montenegro demanded a rectification of their frontiers. In face of these events the 'Young Turks' naturally began to lose their desire to improve the lot of Turkey's Christian subjects, more especially when the Christians began to demand not reform but independence.

When Abdul Hamid tried to restore autocracy he was deposed, but the Young Turks soon received an additional incentive to concentrate on their nationalist rather than on their democratic principles. In 1911 the problems of Turkey tempted the Italians to wrest Tripoli quite wantonly from her. And before this difficulty was over, Turkey in 1912 suddenly found herself confronted by a union of the Balkan powers, momentarily induced to forgo their mutual hatreds for the purpose of despoiling the Ottoman Empire.

This 'Balkan League' (largely the work of an astute Greek politician, Venizelos) found its opportunity to attack Turkey in the fact that the 'Young Turks' had now, like their older brethren, begun persecuting Christians in Macedonia. Disunited in home affairs and with the Italian attack barely over, the Turks could do nothing against the combined onslaught of Greece, Serbia, Bulgaria, and Montenegro. The allies soon overran different sections of Macedonia and made other conquests with equal ease. In 1913 a peace conference met at London, and by the treaty then concluded Greece acquired Crete, Salonika and South Macedonia, Serbia was rewarded with North and Central Macedonia, and the Bulgarians received Thrace and a section of the Ægean coast. Since much of Macedonia, which was inhabited largely by Bulgars, went to Serbia by this treaty, Bulgaria could not be satisfied with the division of the spoils. The Serbs, in fact, although they had actually conquered a large section of Macedonia, had intended most of it to go to Bulgaria, while they themselves took Albania, with its valuable sea-coast. Austria, however, had insisted on the erection of an independent Albania, partly to stop Serbia becoming too powerful and partly because Albania was inhabited not by Serbs but by Albanians. Thereupon Serbia, baulked of her desired coastland, had insisted on retaining the sections of Macedonia she had conquered.

The Bulgarians now in a fatal moment allowed themselves to be prompted by the wishes of Austria, and pressed their grievance to the point of attacking Serbia and Greece. Thus within a year a second Balkan war had broken out. Montenegro supported Serbia, and when matters began to go badly for Bulgaria, the Roumanians and the Turks joined in against

Side notes (left margin):

Italy takes Tripoli

The 'Balkan League'

Balkan wars, 1912–1913

The Turks defeated

The spoils shared

Bulgaria dissatisfied

The second Balkan war, 1913

Bulgaria beaten

her as well. Bulgaria was now fighting alone against five powers. In such circumstances she was naturally over-whelmed, and at the resulting Treaty of Bucharest (1913) much of what she had gained in the first war was lost. Turkey got back Adrianople, Serbia and Greece were confirmed in their possession of Macedonia, and Roumania gained some valuable territory.

The results of these two Balkan wars were profound, in spite of the fact that none of the great powers had been involved. In the first place Turkey was now at last reduced in Europe to regions racially Turkish. Secondly, all the Balkan powers obviously regarded the Treaty of Bucharest as something to be consigned to the wastepaper basket at the first opportune moment. None of them contemplated the settlement as permanent : all were ready for another war before long ; and in particular Bulgaria nursed her hatred against Serbia and Greece. Thirdly, the great gains made by Serbia filled her with confidence and inspired her with the object of uniting all remaining Serbs in the Balkans under her rule. In particular she was brought even more sharply into collision with Austria, partly because Austria had taken the lead in denying her Albania, partly because Austria ruled eight million Serbs and Croats, including the million Serbs of Bosnia and Herzegovina.

It was this last fact which led on to the First World War. In Serbia a great agitation for the acquisition of Bosnia and Herzegovina was launched. The Serbs within these two districts grew extremely troublesome. The temper of Austria ran short. She began to dream of a campaign which would annihilate this increasingly dangerous Balkan race, confirm her in her possession of the two Serbian provinces, and remove the barrier which stretched across her path to the Ægean Sea. Already in 1913 Austria sounded Italy on the possibility of a war with Serbia, only to receive the reply that Italy would not support such aggression. But if one member of the Triple Alliance was doubtful, there was no hesitation about the other. The Kaiser repeatedly assured Austrian statesmen that they would have Germany's backing if matters came to a conflict. Further, Austria might rely on Turkey, a natural enemy of Serbia, and now, since the beginning of the Berlin

Results of Balkan wars

(a) Turkey drastically reduced

(b) Increased tension and preparation for further war

(c) Serbia encouraged in aggression

and more hostile to Austria

The Serbs agitate for Bosnia and Herzegovina

Austria relies on German support

to Bagdad Railway and the appointment of Liman von Sanders to reorganize the Turkish army, increasingly under German commercial and military control. Austria waited for the opportunity which Serbian agitation was sure to present before long.

The opportunity duly occurred on June 28th, 1914. On that day the Austrian Crown Prince Franz Ferdinand and his wife were driving through the streets of Sarajevo, capital of Bosnia, when they were assassinated by a local Serb. The murderer had come straight from a meeting of an anti-Austrian society in the Serbian capital, Belgrade. There was actually no evidence to show that the Serbian government had any hand in the affair—indeed, there is some reason to believe that the Austrian government hoped such an incident might take place, for the Crown Prince's political views were unwelcome to them and they knew the danger of Sarajevo on a Serbian festival day. For nearly a month nothing much seemed to come of the crime—the Austrians made their investigations and public excitement cooled down. But behind the scenes preparations for war were progressing, as Austria received Germany's final 'blank cheque,' or permission to deal with Serbia as she pleased. Suddenly, on July 23rd, the Austrian government launched an ultimatum at Serbia, demanding acceptance within forty-eight hours. The terms were so framed that a refusal was bound to be the answer. Not only was Serbia to suppress all anti-Austrian activity and dismiss all Serbian officials to whom Austria objected, but Austrians were to enter Serbia to investigate Serbian guilt in the murder and to supervise the suppression of the anti-Austrian societies. Serbia's reply, in fact, was extremely conciliatory. She agreed to the first two demands, and offered to submit the third to arbitration by the Hague Tribunal. Had she accepted the last point it would have meant almost the loss of her independence. Even the Kaiser thought the reply was satisfactory, and urged moderation, but Austria was not to be baulked at the last moment. On July 28th Austria declared war on Serbia.

Within a week the whole of Europe was ablaze. Britain, France, and Russia had been warned by Germany not to interfere in what was to be an Austro-Serbian contest. But

Russia especially was not willing to see a fellow Slav country crushed by a vastly stronger opponent while Germany held the ring. Russia too had Balkan ambitions of her own, and here was an opportunity to pursue them. Accordingly on July 30th Nicholas II ordered general mobilization of the Russian armies. Russia mobilizes to support Serbia Germany now chose to regard this as a threat to her, resisted all the efforts of Grey to refer matters to a conference, and despatched two ultimatums. One German ultimatums to France and Russia demanded of Russia that she should stop her mobilization. The other insisted that France should give a clear and forth-right guarantee of her neutrality. When neither country heeded these threats, Germany declared war, first on Russia Germany declares war on Russia and France (August 1914) (August 1st) and then on France (August 3rd).

There remained one doubtful factor—Britain. Grey had made tremendous efforts in the final fortnight to avoid the catastrophe, but it had come. What was Britain to do? She had no military alliance with France, but she had an The position of Britain 'understanding,' had concerted plans in case of war, and had arranged that the French fleet should be predominantly in the Mediterranean. Could she now allow Germany to enter the Channel with her North Sea Fleet and attack the French coasts? The British Cabinet wavered, while French politicians indignantly demanded whether the word 'honour' should be expunged from the English vocabulary. Ultimately, on August 2nd, before Germany had actually declared war on our neighbours, but when it was obvious that war would come, a majority of the British cabinet decided to give at any rate a limited support to France.* But some of Limited support for France their own colleagues disagreed violently. How would the country as a whole react? Would the House of Commons toe the line obediently, or would the government be rejected as having committed Britain to war unnecessarily and collapse ignominiously? Fortunately for the future of the Allies, fortunately for the unity of Britain, fortunately for the peace of mind of the cabinet, fortunately in fact for everyone except the Belgians and their own cause, the Germans prepared to invade France by way of the shortest route, Belgium.

* By promising to protect French Channel ports and shipping if the German fleet entered the Channel.

NO THOROUGHFARE

F.H TOWNSEND Aug. 1914.

[*Reproduced by permission of the Proprietors of 'Punch.'*]

BRAVO, BELGIUM!

The typical British attitude in 1914. "Gallant little Belgium" defies the German bully.

By the treaty of 1839 both Britain and Prussia, as she then was, had promised to guarantee Belgian neutrality. If Germany violated it now she would put herself hopelessly in the wrong with every section of British opinion. When the British Ambassador in Berlin stated what Britain's attitude to such an action would be, the German Chancellor inquired whether Britain would plunge into war for the sake of 'a scrap of paper.'* But a Belgium under German control meant more than tearing up a 'scrap of paper' to England—it meant the danger of a great hostile naval power being within easy striking distance of her shores. For centuries England had made the freedom of Belgium from control by a major naval power the main point of her foreign policy. For that she had aided the Dutch against the Spaniards in Elizabeth's reign, had fought France in the war of the Spanish Succession, and later in the Revolutionary and Napoleonic wars, and had prevented a French prince ascending the Belgian throne after the revolution of 1830. For that Gladstone in 1870 had warned the Prussians against invading France through Belgium, and had seen that Prussia took the more difficult route through Alsace. Now, on August 4th, after the Belgians had appealed for assistance in repelling Germany, Britain sent her ultimatum demanding that Belgian neutrality be respected. On the afternoon of the same day she learnt that the Germans had penetrated farther into Belgium, and when midnight came with no satisfactory reply, Britain had in effect declared war against Germany. The Conservative opposition, the Irish party, the Socialists all lined up behind the British government. The militarists of Germany were violating the sanctity of treaties—it all put the Allies so magnificently in the right. As the statesmen made their decisions and European youth on both sides rushed unhesitatingly to sacrifice itself in the cause of patriotism and the right, few can have realized that before the hideous conflict could end forty million men would be killed or wounded.

And all from an assassination in an obscure town in the Balkans—or so it appeared! But, in fact, although we may

Belgian neutrality and its importance for Britain

British ultimatum to Germany

Britain declares war on Germany (August 4th, 1914)

* This translation caused much ill-feeling at the time. The actual German words used would have been more accurately rendered as 'a piece of paper'—which is less offensive, but means the same.

apportion 'war-guilt,' deciding that Austria was certainly the main criminal, Germany and then Russia perhaps next in degree of culpability, the more we study the origins of the war the more clearly the general truth emerges that no state was free from blame. All were part of the same vicious system. All had their national policies and ambitions which could not but clash fatally some day. All frankly recognized the fact by piling up arms and preparing alliances in readiness for the conflict. Few really wanted war; but none was prepared to abandon the objects which made war inevitable. The spark happened to come from Sarajevo, but it might have come from anywhere. The result would have been the same. The powder magazine was there all the time.

War inevitable in the European system of 1914

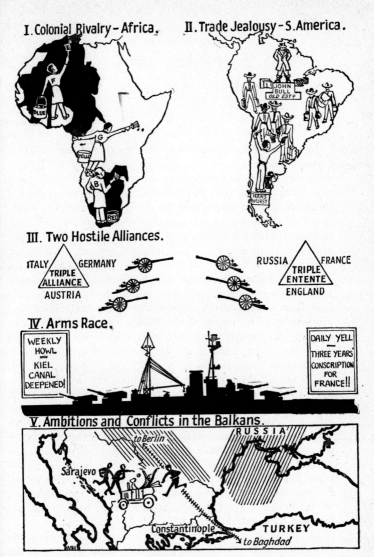

CAUSES OF THE FIRST WORLD WAR.

CHAPTER XIV

The First World War and its Aftermath, 1914–1939

1. *The First World War, 1914–1918*

The nature of the First World War

Just as the First World War was the inevitable result of certain tendencies before 1914, so the history of Europe since then has been very largely the result of that conflict. It was a struggle till then unparalleled in the forces involved— the number of warring states, the size of the armies, the deadliness of the weapons, the colossal expenditure of life and treasure. Other conflicts had lasted longer and by their savagery or prolongation had inflicted greater suffering on some given tract of the world's surface—notably Germany in the Thirty Years' War (1618–48)—but nothing can previously have caused so widespread a sum of human agony as the four years which followed the assassination of the Archduke Franz Ferdinand. The whole of the British Empire in India and Canada, for example, was acquired with a loss in men less than that reported in a single British advance of two miles on the Western Front in 1917. At the battle of Plassey in 1757, which settled the fate of much of India, the British lost less than a hundred men ; during the Somme offensive in 1916, which settled nothing, they lost (in killed, wounded, and missing) nearly half a million. The result of such a slaughter was to convince nearly everyone of something they had never previously believed—that war was an appalling catastrophe. It made the possibility of its recurrence a haunting nightmare to millions upon millions in countries all over the world. For one moment it almost seemed as though it had frightened the nations into good sense—but nations are harder material to teach than individuals.

The initial German advance

In this short space it is impossible to give more than the barest indication of the military events of the War. On the Western Front it began with a tremendous German attack through Belgium and Luxemburg which drove the Allies back at lightning speed. The idea of the Germans was to concentrate an overwhelming proportion of their forces on the west, knock out France, and then revert to the east to deal with Russia. " We can be at Paris within a fortnight," said the Kaiser. His words were almost true. German superiority in numbers, organization, training, and equipment carried all before it. The efficient and heroic little British Expeditionary Force under Sir John French was compelled to retreat from Mons (in Central Belgium) ; the French armies fared no better ; and by the beginning of September, a month after the outbreak of war, the Germans were less than fifty miles from Paris. The French Government fled to Bordeaux, on the Atlantic coast. At the critical moment, however, the situation was saved by a combination of skill, good luck, and German mistakes. The French commander Joffre turned in his retreat, reformed his armies, and, reinforced by troops rushed from Paris in every available vehicle (including taxicabs), defeated the Germans at the Battle of the Marne. It was one of the decisive fights of the war : the German attack was stemmed. After the French had recovered a little of their territory, the Germans dug themselves into their position by means of an elaborate trench system, protected against destruction by the inadequacy of the Allied artillery and against capture by barriers of barbed wire. The Allies followed suit, and enormous lines of opposing trenches soon stretched from the Alps to the Belgian coast. The war on the western front settled into a dreary struggle to pound the opposing forces and their entrenchments to pieces by gunfire, and then capture a few hundred yards by an infantry advance. To the bewilderment of many military minds, cavalry became completely useless and 'crack' regiments had to take their place beside the ordinary 'footsloggers' in the lines.

Stemmed at the Battle of the Marne

Trench warfare sets in

Meanwhile in the east the Russians, to relieve the pressure on France, had launched a premature invasion of Germany. In August, at Tannenberg in East Prussia, they were overwhelmingly defeated by Hindenburg, an old general recalled from retirement for his knowledge of local conditions, and Ludendorff, his chief of staff, one of the few generals in the war whose tactics might be termed brilliant. Another of the decisive battles of the war had been fought. Austria, however,

The other fronts : Russians stopped at Tannenberg, 1914

began to suffer defeat both by the Russians in Galicia and by the Serbs, whose territory she had invaded. Nevertheless Austria and Germany received a useful reinforcement when Turkey, for long under German influence, came in on their side in November ; the position of Serbia, between Austria and Turkey, might well soon be desperate.

Turkey
supports
Germany
and Austria

The state of deadlock on the Western Front and the danger of Serbia now resolved the British cabinet to extend its strategy. An 'Eastern school' grew up which maintained that the best way to win the war was first to knock out the Turks and then proceed to smash up the Austrian Empire. Germany would thus be exposed to attack from the south. This strategy was powerfully advanced by Lloyd George, the Chancellor of the Exchequer, and Winston Churchill, the First Lord of the Admiralty, who had so successfully seen that the Fleet was completely ready at the outbreak of war. Naturally, however, the French and the British generals on the western front bitterly opposed the diversion of valuable troops to objectives outside France, where the position was never too secure. The first attempt at such a plan was an effort by the British Fleet to force the Dardanelles (March 1915), and later there came an amazing landing by British and 'Anzac' forces at Gallipoli, in the face of deadly fire from the Turkish positions. Neither venture succeeded, however —the Dardanelles was too well mined (and the project too well advertised) and the Gallipoli peninsula had later to be evacuated. An important drawback to every 'Eastern' scheme was the administrative difficulty of supplying a large force in the Balkans.

The
"Eastern-
ers"

The
Dardanelles
and Galli-
poli, 1915

In 1915 the Germans, held up in the west, temporarily reversed their policy and drove eastwards against Russia. A series of brilliant successes not only carried the Germans through Poland and Lithuania but also brought Bulgaria into the war on their side (September 1915). The crafty Bulgarian king, Ferdinand, 'the Fox of the Balkans,' had long been waiting to see which way the cat would jump. Now the adhesion of Bulgaria meant that the Central powers could overrun Serbia without difficulty. The only crumb of comfort for the Allies was that they managed to induce Italy into the war on their side (May 1915) by an offer of the two Austrian

German
successes
against
Russia

Bulgaria
joins
Germany

districts of the Trentino (the Tyrol) and Trieste (on the Adriatic). The Italians (who had refused to support Germany and Austria in 1914 on the ground that the war was one of aggression and that they had no obligation to fight against Britain) had always considered these districts as 'unredeemed Italy.' In fact, however, many of the inhabitants of the Trentino were German, and the bargain to transfer them to Italy was an example of how far from their proclaimed ideals Britain and France were being driven by the necessities of war. The effect of Italian intervention was to occupy in combat a large Austrian army in the Alps which divide the two countries. *Italy joins the Allies, 1915*

The lack of success of the Allies thus far naturally brought about changes of command. In the field Joffre lost his position, and French was displaced by Haig. The British, like the French, began to forget their party politics and by 1915 formed a National Coalition, at the head of which the energetic Lloyd George was soon to take the place of the more cultured but less efficient Asquith. New armies, millions strong, were created—three million men volunteering from Britain alone before conscription was introduced in 1916. New weapons emerged—the Germans, for example, beginning the use of poison gas, contrary to international treaty. Aeroplanes, at first used merely for scouting, began bombing on a large scale not only military objectives but transport and industrial targets (and therefore civil populations)—a process originally commenced by the German Zeppelins, which had proved too bulky to defend themselves. In 1916, too, the tank (an invention which was cold-shouldered by the War Office for some time, and was developed largely through the foresight of Winston Churchill at the Admiralty !) was first employed. Little use, however, was made of it as yet, though when properly employed later it was to be the decisive instrument of the war. *Reorganization of Allied War effort* *New weapons: Gas* *Zeppelins and aeroplanes* *Tanks*

On the Western Front in 1916, the main features, apart from the new weapons, were some tremendous battles in which the French held the Germans at bay near Verdun and the British attacked by the River Somme. The dead of all nations as a result of the Somme campaign numbered over one million. In the east a revival by the Russians encouraged *Verdun and the Somme, 1916*

The Rou-
manians
join the
Allies, but
are soon
overrun the Roumanians to enter the war on the Allied side in the
hope of wresting Transylvania from Austria-Hungary. The
Russian recovery was purely momentary, however, and
Roumania was soon captured, for its oil and wheat to be
placed at the disposal of the Central powers.

Naval
warfare The year 1916 also saw the one naval battle of any great
importance in the war. There had been an earlier roundup
of the German Pacific fleet off the Falkland Isles (1914),
but so far there had been no encounter with the Grand Fleet,
Mines in harbour at Kiel. Mines off the German coast had greatly
hampered British activity. In May 1916, however, the Ger-
Jutland,
1916 man fleet emerged and fought a 'hit-and-run' battle at Jutland
before the British could bring up their full resources. The
result is claimed as a victory on both sides—by the Germans
because they inflicted twice as much loss in men and ships
as they themselves suffered, and by the British because the
German Fleet steamed off home and never again emerged
during the rest of the war. Whatever the damage, the fact is
Britain
keeps
command
of seas indisputable that the British remained in command of the
seas, with all the enormous consequences that this entailed—
blockade of enemy coasts, capture of enemy colonies, maintenance of communication with Allied armies, preservation
of the vital British food supply.

The inability of Germany to challenge the British Fleet in
open contest led to one other result of enormous importance.
The
unrestricted
submarine
campaign The Germans determined to employ their submarines in an
unrestricted campaign against merchant vessels trading with
Britain, in the hope of starving the obstinate island into submission. In doing this Germany knew that the United States
would certainly show her resentment at the sinking of her
vessels by entering the war on the side of the Allies—in fact,
some circles in the U.S.A. had wanted to enter the war *against*
the Allies because of the British turning back ships trading
with Germany. Sinking vessels, however, was far worse than
turning them back. The Germans knew the result of their
decision, but calculated on putting Britain and France out
of action before American intervention could become effective.
U.S.A.
join the
Allies, 1917 So the submarine campaign reached its height, and the United
States duly declared war on Germany (March 1917). For a
time things were extremely awkward for Britain, where

food-cards and rationing were introduced, but ultimately the menace was defeated by technical devices such as the depth charge, the hydrophone, and above all by employing destroyers to convoy groups of merchant vessels. Certain Admiralty officials assured Lloyd George that the merchant captains would never possess sufficient skill to sail in the requisite groups, but fortunately the Prime Minister insisted on the adoption of the system.

The entry of the United States was at first offset by the departure of Russia from the Allied camp (November 1917). The Russian defeats had revealed the customary Czarist inefficiency : in some battles thousands of bewildered Russian peasants were even called to fight the latest forms of scientific death with no more effective weapons than pitchforks or scythes. The government could envisage nothing more effective than reliance on its inexhaustible resources of man-power, and send more and more millions to the slaughter. Soon an immense war-weariness became obvious in the masses : food riots and mutinies occurred, and in March 1917 a revolution in the capital disposed of Nicholas II with almost ridiculous ease. The government fell into the hands of moderate Socialists and parliamentarians, such as Kerensky, and a genuine constitution on British lines now seemed possible. But Kerensky, subsidized by Britain and France (who regarded the revolution not unfavourably, since it might make the Russian war effort more effective), was determined to keep Russia in the war. Consequently his provisional government never gained a hold on Russian popular opinion : the urban masses, organized in their local soviets, demanded both peace and a more revolutionary social policy. This was the programme of the Bolsheviks, whose determination to withdraw Russia from the war was obviously so good for Germany that the Germans allowed Lenin, the exiled Bolshevik leader, to travel across Germany from Switzerland to Russia. Once in the capital Lenin took charge, and with brilliant technique brought about the Bolshevik revolution and the fall of Kerensky. Peace was concluded with Germany, who showed her militarist temper by stripping Russia of enormous stretches of territory, including the Baltic provinces and Russian Poland. Russia dis-

The submarine menace defeated

Russia knocked out, 1917

The end of Czardom

The Kerensky Government

The Bolshevik Revolution November 1917

solved into the anarchy of opposing factions, whence after years of agony she was to emerge, still in the strong hands of Lenin and his commissar for war, Trotsky, as a thoroughgoing Bolshevik or Communist state. It is one of the ironies of history that this state, made possible in part by Germany's encouragement of Lenin, was soon to become the main threat to the security of Germany and her Nazi government.

Though the entry of the United States and the exit of Russia were the main events of 1917, fighting of great importance of course continued in the west. A disastrous failure in an effort to advance near the river Aisne caused so many casualties in the French armies that the morale of many of the troops broke. Mutinies occurred, and the commanders were in the greatest difficulties. To give France an opportunity for reorganization the British now diverted attention to themselves by a sustained offensive near Passchendaele (July–December 1917). It relieved the French and killed many Germans, but got nowhere. All attempt at surprise, one of the greatest factors in achieving victory, was abandoned in favour of forewarning the enemy by tremendous bombardments. Then, over ground broken by gunfire or later a sea of mire from autumn rains, the British troops were supposed to advance. Hundreds actually drowned in the mud. Altogether the British suffered some three hundred thousand casualties in this fiasco. The story of Allied disaster for the year was completed by a great Austrian advance at the expense of the Italians. The battle of Caporetto, in which an Italian force attempting to capture Trieste was repulsed and pursued, was the nearest thing to an absolute rout since 1914. The only crumb of comfort at the end of 1917 for the Allied cause was the striking success of Allenby in a Near Eastern 'side-show.' Here the open ground was more suitable for the use of cavalry, and the brilliant mind of T. E. Lawrence, scholar turned soldier, was responsible for raising a revolt among the Arabs of the desert against their Turkish masters. Palestine saw the beginning of the collapse of the Turkish dominions, and at Christmas 1917 Allenby entered Jerusalem.

While the Near Eastern campaign continued successfully and the Italians, stiffened by French and British reinforce-

[Marginal notes:]

Mutinies in the French Army, 1917

The Passchendaele failure, 1917

The Austrians rout the Italians at Caporetto, 1917

The Allies successful in the Near East

ments, no longer bent before the Austro-German attacks, things nevertheless went desperately against the British and French in the spring of 1918. With enormous numbers of troops released from the Russian front, Ludendorff now strained every nerve to deliver a knock-out blow in the west. A great German offensive began in March and carried all before it. The danger to the Allies was so great that at last they sank their mutual suspicions and jealousies and consented to the creation of a single Allied command under Foch. The Americans also rushed to send over their first levies to strengthen the bending lines. Brilliantly the German advance continued, until by June they were back to their farthest 1914 positions by the Marne and Paris was once more in danger. Then, as suddenly, the attack spent itself; the Allies held their ground; the Germans, worn out by four years of warfare against superior odds, lacked the reserves to push their effort home. The Americans arrived in increasing numbers. The hopelessness of continuing a struggle against an almost inexhaustible supply of American reinforcements, armaments, and wealth impressed itself on the Germans. The Allied counter-attack, Haig's best work, in August began to force back the German lines with such rapidity that people could hardly believe the news. By the end of September, when the British stormed the supposedly almost impregnable Hindenburg line, Germany was at the end of her tether—and Ludendorff knew it.

The German offensive, spring 1918

The unified Allied command

The Marne again

The Americans begin to tell

The Allied counter-attack, summer and autumn 1918

But it was not Germany who gave in first. An Anglo-French expedition long since landed at Salonika, in Greece (who had been practically forced by the Allies to enter the war on their side), at last justified itself. Bulgaria was knocked out of the war at the end of September and Serbia was recovered. Then in October Turkey collapsed before the further attacks of Allenby in Syria and the Allied successes in the Balkans. Next the Austrian Empire went under, following attacks by the Italians and brilliant propaganda work by the British, who bombed the Austrian lines with leaflets promising the Austrian subject nationalities their independence if they deserted the Empire. Czechs, Poles, Slovaks, Croats immediately responded to the offer, and under the combined influence of military defeat, the blockade and

The Salonika force knocks out Bulgaria, September 1918

Turkey gives in

Austria follows

disruptive propaganda the Austrian Empire fell to pieces. The British Department of Propaganda, under the skilled direction of Lord Northcliffe, whose experience as founder and owner of the *Daily Mail* well qualified him for the niceties of the art, thus at the expense of a few thousand pounds and with no loss of life helped to secure results of profound importance. With her friends all defeated and her own armies fast retreating, Germany had no alternative but to sue for peace on the basis of 'Fourteen Points' advanced by the American President, Woodrow Wilson. The German Navy, ordered out to certain destruction in a last desperate effort, mutinied ; the Kaiser and his family made a hurried and undignified exit to Holland and safety ; a republic was proclaimed ; and with inexpressible relief Europe soon learned that an armistice had been concluded between the Western powers. It came into effect at 11 a.m. on November 11th— a moment that will not soon be forgotten.

In considering the reasons for victory and defeat in the conflict we must remember what a task Germany had to face, in spite of her initial advantages and greater freedom from moral restraints. In the end the Central European powers, four in number, were at war with twenty-seven states, including the whole might of the British Empire, India, and the Dominions, France and her Empire, Japan, and the United States. With such forces behind them, including Russia in the first years of the war, it would have been a tremendous military disgrace had the Allies lost. Yet they nearly did lose, through their uninspired military leadership, their imperviousness to new ideas, their disastrous personal differences and lack of co-ordination. In the end the Allies 'muddled through.' The things which stood them in the greatest stead were their superiority in man-power (especially with the arrival of the American contingents), the almost inexhaustible wealth of the British Empire and the United States, and the control of the seas which the British Navy never for one moment lost. The last factor was tremendously important—as the years passed the Allied blockade slowly brought about the starvation of the Central Powers in both food and raw materials. On the other hand, the Allied fleets could and did ensure Britain's vital food

Margin notes:
Germany asks for peace

The Armistice, November 11th, 1918

Germany's amazing performance

The reasons for Allied victory :
(a) Men
(b) Money

(c) Command of seas

THE SANDS RUN OUT.

Mr. Punch, like most other people, thought of the defeat of Germany as the defeat of militarism for all time.   He seems to have been sadly out in his reckoning.

supply, the transport of troops to convenient centres of operation, the capture of enemy colonies.   There was no Trafalgar
in this war, but no more than the Napoleonic war could the
struggle have been won without the British Fleet.   On the
German side the greatest mistakes which cost them the war
were the invasion of Belgium and the unrestricted submarine
campaign.   Both were gambles which came very near to
success, but when once the immediate menace was checked
both decisions proved fatal to their authors.   The first
offended the moral conscience of the world and united Britain
in an unremitting opposition.   The second reinforced the
universal hatred of German militarism and brought about
the ultimately decisive intervention of the United States.

*The two
main Ger-
man mis-
takes :
(a) In-
vasion of
Belgium
(b) Sub-
marine
campaign*

2. *The Peace Treaties.   Europe after the War*

Though the carnage had now stopped, an official peace was
not at once drawn up.   It took months of bargaining and
doubtful diplomacy among the Allies before the treaties were
concluded.   At last in June 1919 the Versailles treaty, signed
in that Hall of Mirrors which had witnessed the foundation
of the German Empire half a century before, was given to
the world.   Other treaties, with Austria, Hungary, Turkey,
and Bulgaria, took even longer to frame, the final settlement
with Turkey (which began fighting again with Greece) not
being achieved till 1923.   The peace treaties as a whole
constituted a redrawing of the map of Europe comparable
with the settlement of 1815.   The work of those who framed
them was fantastically difficult.   They had to deal with
enormous problems, such as the racial complications of
Central Europe and the Near East, or the best financial
settlement obtainable, which they but very imperfectly
understood.   And they had to work in an atmosphere poisoned
by four years of desperate warfare, with its inevitable crop of
national hatred, not to be forgotten in a few weeks.   In
general the most liberal attitude to the conquered was taken
by Wilson, an idealist to whom detachment was possible in
view of his country's greater distance from Europe.   The
opposite attitude, of stripping Germany of all possible,
territorially and financially, was exemplified in the veteran

*The peace
treaties,
1919–1923
(Versailles,
1919)*

Clemenceau, 'the Tiger,' who could never forget what France Wilson, Clemenceau, Lloyd George had suffered not only in 1914 but in 1870. Lloyd George represented something of a middle term between the other two, not illiberal himself, but with a constant eye on the fury of British opinion, then expressed in the twin cries of 'make Germany pay' and 'hang the Kaiser.'

The settlement produced by compromises between these three men naturally bore marks of all of them. On the one side there was the application of the 'principle of self-determination'—the release of subject races all over Europe. Subject races released From the ruins of the Austrian Empire emerged the free republics of Czecho-Slovakia (including the old Bohemia) and Yugo-Slavia (Serbia enlarged by Montenegro and the Croats The new states and Slovenes of the Austrian Empire). Hungary was stripped of its subject races all round, Roumania being the chief gainer. Austria was limited to the strictly German section, a drastic alteration from the days when Vienna lorded it over thirteen races. The Baltic republics of Finland, Lithuania, Esthonia, Latvia appeared, and Poland was reassembled as an independent state. New Arab states, freed from Turkish control, were set up in the Near East. Alsace and Lorraine were restored to France. All these arrangements in general conformed to national limits, and in this respect the great principle of nationality, so constantly enunciated in the 19th century, at last received full recognition. Nevertheless in some respects it was violated by the incorporation of foreign minorities in the new states. Three million Hungarians, for A few racial minorities still example, were placed under alien rule, and three million Germans were included in Czecho-Slovakia, besides others in Poland. These decisions made future trouble inevitable. All the same, the subjections to foreign rule, sometimes necessary in the interests of military frontiers, were insignificant compared with those that existed before the war—and, furthermore, guarantees on the fair treatment of minorities were required from the ruling powers. A more vital defect was that the creation of so many small states multiplied economic boundaries, caused new tariffs, and made trade infinitely more difficult in South-eastern Europe.

Though the territorial conditions of the treaties were, if by no means perfect, rather fairer than nearly all previous

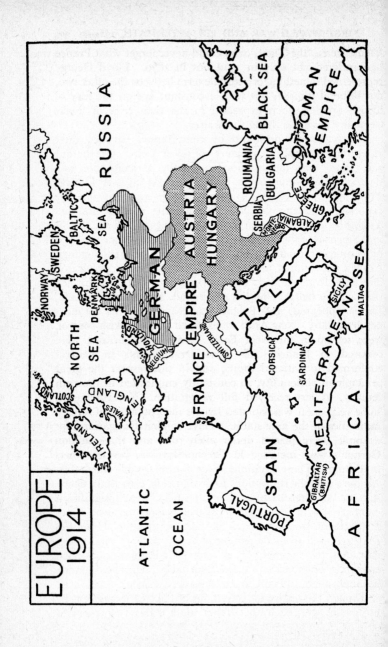

EUROPE
1914

ATLANTIC
OCEAN

NORTH
SEA

BALTIC
SEA

NORWAY
SWEDEN
DENMARK

RUSSIA

SCOTLAND
IRELAND
ENGLAND
WALES

HOLLAND
BELGIUM

GERMAN
EMPIRE

AUSTRIA
HUNGARY

SWITZERLAND

FRANCE

ITALY

SPAIN
PORTUGAL

GIBRALTAR
(BRITISH)

CORSICA

SARDINIA

SICILY
MALTA

MEDITERRANEAN
SEA

AFRICA

ROUMANIA

BULGARIA

SERBIA

MONTENEGRO

ALBANIA

GREECE

BLACK SEA

OTTOMAN
EMPIRE

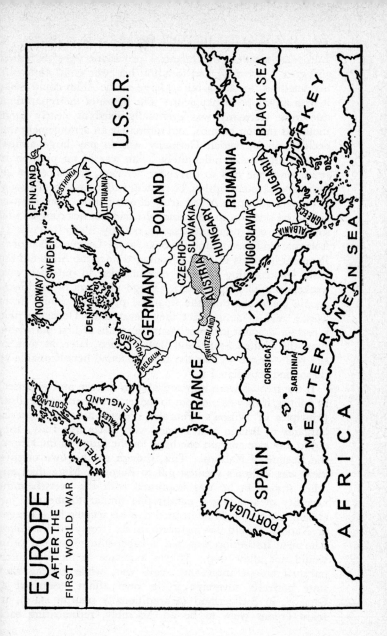

EUROPE
AFTER THE
FIRST WORLD WAR

The financial terms

European treaties, the financial provisions were extremely stringent. Germany had to admit her 'war guilt' and, with her satellites, to face a bill as large as the Allies could make it with any hope of payment. The figure of the reparations due from Germany was eventually fixed at nearly seven thousand million pounds, and ultimately an arrangement was decided on by which Germany was to pay large annual instalments almost indefinitely. She was in no position to resist, since she had to surrender her fleet, renounce her air force, abolish conscription, be content with a small professional force, and admit an Allied army of occupation. But she was also in no position to pay, since she had lost her colonies and some of her best industrial districts, notably Silesia (to Poland), Lorraine (to France), and the Saar (to the League of Nations).

Impossibility of carrying them out

Payment in goods was not encouraged since the Allies did not wish, by accepting German commodities, to put their own workers out of employment. Large numbers of intelligent people could see that the financial provisions would never work ; and in actual fact they never did. Germany paid a certain amount for some years by means of first borrowing from the United States and Britain; then, later, as soon as she really began to foot the bill, she found herself unable to do so, and repudiated it.

The League of Nations

If the treaties were impracticable in finance and imperfect in politics, if they carried out to the letter neither the idealistic principles of Wilson's 'Fourteen Points' nor the material bargains of Britain and France with states like Italy, they did at any rate contain one hope for the future in the form of the League of Nations. This, though not his own original idea, was Wilson's greatest gift to Europe. More than any other statesman he was impressed with the overwhelming necessity of avoiding a catastrophe similar to the war just ended. Accordingly he insisted that his scheme for a League of Nations should be included in the treaty of Versailles. The new institution was not a super-state—national pride would not allow that. It was a device to increase international co-operation and avoid war, while leaving each state perfectly sovereign in its own affairs. Situated at

Its organs

Geneva, in Switzerland (a traditionally neutral state), its main organs were to be an Assembly, representing each member, and a Council, representing the greater members plus some smaller powers in rotation. The International Court at the Hague was recognized as a valid authority for arbitration. Later an International Labour Organization was added, for co-operation on problems of health, social conditions, and so on.

The obligations of each member were enshrined in a The Covenant. The main promises undertaken in this remark-Covenant able document were that members would decrease their armaments to the lowest level compatible with safety, guarantee the integrity and independence of other members' territory, submit any international dispute to some form of arbitration or peaceful decision, and take instant action against an agreed aggressor by economic and possibly military means. (The last point was the famous 'Sanctions' clause—Article XVI.) Further, the members promised to publish their treaties, to exchange information on armament programmes, to use their best endeavours to obtain humane labour conditions in their own and other countries, to entrust the League with control of measures against disease, slavery, and the opium trade. It will readily be understood why this Covenant, with its aims of peace and a better life, appealed to many thoughtful people as the one thing which made some of the appalling sacrifice of the war years worth while. But unfortunately a terrible blow was dealt to the League at its very birth by the refusal of America to ratify Wilson's work, and without the United States the League was to prove only the shadow of the institution Wilson intended.

One other innovation was included in the Covenant—the 'Mandates' idea of 'mandated territories.' These were districts which had been captured by the Allies, such as the German colonies in Africa or parts of the Turkish Empire in the Near East, but which it was difficult with justice for the conquerors to retain. The war had officially been fought on the Allied side 'to break militarism' and 'to protect the rights of small nations'—even, according to Wilson, "to make the World safe for democracy." Clearly, it would not look well to indulge in wholesale annexations in the good old imperialist fashion—more especially since it was by a promise of future independence that the Arabs had been induced to revolt against the Turks. Equally,

South Africa and Australia, for example, after having conquered German colonies, did not want to see them restored to Germany to constitute once more a menace to their security. Yet the territories were too backward to govern themselves in accordance with standards acceptable to Western nations and were too important to forgo lightly. The solution arrived at was the 'Mandate' system, first suggested by the South African General Smuts, who was also one of the fathers of the League itself. By this system the territories were entrusted to a mandatory power, whose duty was to rule with the benefit and the ultimate independence of the natives in mind. The mandatory power had to give an account of its stewardship to the League of Nations. On the whole the system scarcely succeeded. The French encountered enormous opposition in Syria and British rule over Palestine completely failed to reconcile the Arabs to the establishment of a Jewish 'National Home' there. Germany of course regarded the mandatory system as a mere device by which annexation was cloaked in 'morality,' though Britain very soon surrendered her mandate over Iraq. The most important—or least troublesome—mandates were those over the old German colonies in Africa, which were virtually absorbed by Britain, France, and South Africa.

Events after 1919 gave little satisfaction to those who dreamed of a new era of peace after 'the war to end war.' Till about 1923 fighting continued in various parts of Europe. Civil war convulsed Russia—a civil war in which Britain, France, and Poland by active intervention on the side of the 'Whites' strove to destroy the 'Red' Bolshevik government. The Roumanians, encouraged by the Allies, took advantage of a Communist revolution in Hungary to plunder the Hungarians. The Turks, in a wonderful national revival at the very moment of defeat, found a saviour in the soldier Mustapha Kemal, who had earlier been the decisive factor in frustrating the Allied Gallipoli campaign. Kemal led the Turks against the Greeks, who were first encouraged by the Allies to occupy part of Asia Minor and then deserted at the critical moment. The previous settlement with Turkey now had to be revised very greatly in her favour. Most of the new states, including the German Republic, had the very greatest difficulty in establishing themselves, and much blood

Europe after the war

Chaos till 1923

War in Russia—

—in Hungary

—and between Turkey and Greece

Mustapha Kemal

The German Republic

was shed before order could be established and government generally accepted. In Italy a wave of unrest, strengthened by dissatisfaction at Italy's small gains from the war and marked by strikes, the appearance of Communism, and the paralysis of parliamentary government, led to the virtual seizure of power by the Fascists. Their main aims were 'strong' government and flaming nationalism. Their leader was Benito Mussolini, son of a blacksmith, a notorious ex-Socialist who had been jailed and exiled by previous governments. In 1922 King Victor Emmanuel III had to accept him as Prime Minister after the Fascist 'March on Rome'—to which Mussolini himself came by train. The Fascists in Italy Mussolini

For some time the greatest factor in Western Europe in prolonging bitterness seemed to be France, who, perhaps understandably, took every step to humiliate Germany. Thus in 1923, for example, when Germany defaulted on reparation payments, the French Premier, Poincaré, ordered the French army to invade the Ruhr districts and seize the German coal-mines as a guarantee. Germany was already depreciating her currency to evade reparations ; the French move now sent the value of the mark plunging down completely out of control. It fell so rapidly that a man's wages paid overnight might be quite valueless by the time he went out to spend them in the morning. People in the streets of London bought ten-million-mark notes for twopence as souvenirs. Ultimately, of course, an entirely new start had to be made in German currency, bolstered up by loans, but meanwhile all savings in banks and the like had disappeared. It was a terrible experience for Germany, ruining her thrifty middle class and peasantry. The French invade the Ruhr, 1923 Collapse of the mark

Round about 1924 a new phase of greater hope for Europe began. The unimaginable confusion of the Eastern and Central European states had sorted itself out into some semblance of order. Industry began to adjust itself to a peace-time footing. A milder reparations agreement was made with Germany ('the Dawes Plan'). In 1925 a step of the first importance for European appeasement was taken in the conclusion of the Locarno Treaty by the work of Briand, Austen Chamberlain, and Stresemann, all of whom had the interests of Europe as well as of their own countries at heart. Better days, 1924 The Locarno Treaty, 1925

By this treaty Germany agreed never again to raise the question of Alsace and Lorraine, while Britain and Italy promised to defend France against German aggression and Germany against French aggression. The logical sequel came when Germany in 1926 sought and was granted admission to the League of Nations.

Germany
joins the
League,
1926

PEACE (SADLY): "THIS LOOKS VERY LIKE THE POINT WE STARTED FROM."

Disarmament, 1929. In Low's own words :—

"Peace is depicted here after ten weary years' journey upon her pathetic but holy mount, faced with the milestone of her starting-point. The only appreciable difference in the desolate scene is the presence of an empty champagne bottle and a stray top hat—evidence that some politicians have been holding another banquet to abolish war."

Unfortunately this line of policy was not carried far enough. The French, in their desperate distrust of Germany, had sought for security by concluding two important European alliances. One was with Poland and the other with a group which became known as 'The Little Entente'—Czecho-Slovakia, Roumania, Yugo-Slavia. Since all these states ruled former lands of the defeated powers, their interest was to oppose all revision of the treaties, and they were thus the natural enemies of Germany, Austria, Hungary, and Bulgaria. Germany thus felt herself once more 'encircled' by alliances, and this time she had not even arms to protect herself.

French pre-
dominance
in Europe

The Germans repeatedly called on the victors to reduce their arms, but—save in Britain and America—once the initial return to a peacetime establishment was carried out, little further disarmament was achieved, except in the naval sphere. For many years the subject was debated, while preparations were made for an international conference to settle the matter. When a Disarmament Conference did at last meet in 1932 the Russian proposal to abolish all arms was naturally treated as the cynical joke it was, the American proposal for a cut of one-third all round was rejected, and the 'experts' were left to squabble about technical points.   No agreement at all was reached and nothing was done. *The Disarmament Conference (1932) does nothing*

Meanwhile in 1929 an 'economic blizzard' had begun to hit Europe.   Trade tends to run in periodic waves of boom and slump, and now, following a sensational collapse on Wall Street, values of stocks and commodity prices everywhere fell rapidly.   Unemployment figures leapt up.   Countries, including Germany, found themselves deprived of loans from America, in low financial water generally, and completely unable to pay their debts.   Everywhere the governments in power, though it was not specially their fault, found themselves unpopular.   In Britain the socialists in 1931 had to give way to a National Government, which was nevertheless soon forced off the gold standard and compelled to abandon Britain's historic policy of free trade.   The unemployment figures reached three million.   In the United States the next election saw the triumph of the opposition under Franklin Roosevelt.   In Germany the existence of six million unemployed provided a tremendous economic source of discontent to add to the already considerable political grievances.   Communism spread and began to scare the middle classes.   Playing on this discontent by the power of his oratory, the fanatical leader of the till then rather unimportant National Socialist Party, Adolf Hitler, was by 1933 swept into power.   An Austrian of peasant stock by birth, a house-painter by profession, he had already in 1923 once attempted rather a ridiculous *coup d'état*.   The lenient German republic, however, had only imprisoned him for a short time.   His ideas were crude in the extreme—race and nationality were the qualities which counted.   All Germany's troubles were caused by Jews, *The slump* *Governments tumble* *Hitler and the Nazis in Germany*

Communists, and the framers of the Treaty of Versailles—all
three classes being roughly the same people under different
names. He promised, if he should be returned to power, to
restore Germany's might, to stop her humiliations at the
hands of Britain and France, to suppress Jews and Communists, and to make wide-sweeping social reforms which
would cure unemployment.   Such a programme at such
a moment was irresistible. Aided at the last minute by the
burning of the Reichstag—said to have been done by Communists but possibly perpetrated by the Nazis themselves
to discredit their opponents — Hitler was overwhelmingly
triumphant at the 1933 elections.

His policy

The moment Hitler came into power the international
outlook blackened.   In Germany itself his régime until 1939
was a mixture of efficiency and persecution completely
satisfactory to most Germans, but bitterly resented by a
minority who were not given an opportunity for self-expression.
Not only Jews and Communists, but moderate Socialists,
Liberals, and even Conservatives were persecuted out of
existence.   The attentions of Nazi Brownshirts and the
possibility of a spell in the horrors of a 'concentration camp'
sufficed to limit opposition to only the boldest spirits.   A
movement of disaffection by some of the leaders of his own
party led in June 1934 to a savage 'purge,' when in a single
night seventy-seven men were arrested and shot without
trial. (The figure seventy-seven is the Nazi one—opponents
placed it at more than one thousand.) But all this was offset in
German eyes by three achievements of Hitler—that he 'saved'
Germany from Communism, that he genuinely did a great
deal towards solving the unemployment problem (though
mainly by the fatal methods of Labour Camps and huge
armament programmes), and above all that he restored
Germany as a great power.   He successively announced himself as tired of the Allies' broken promises of disarmament,
marched Germany out of the League of Nations (1933), re-
introduced conscription (1935), ordered the German army
into the demilitarized Rhineland zone (March 1936), armed
his country to the teeth, and set up a vigorous campaign for the
restoration of German colonies. Britain and France watched
him tear up articles of the Versailles Treaty one by one, un-

His
achieve-
ments in
Germany

Persecution

Employ-
ment

Restoration
of Ger-
many's
might

Germany
leaves the
League

willing to intervene for fear of provoking a general war and at The end of
the Ver-
sailles
restrictions heart unable to deny the logic of many of his actions. It should be noted, too, that Hitler cleverly timed the remilitarization of the Rhineland for a moment when Britain and France were on the brink of war with Italy.

The advent to power of Hitler was followed by a series of major events which made the international outlook increasingly blacker and blacker. Against the conscience of the whole world Japan wrested Manchuria (already invaded by 1931) from China and set up the puppet-state of Manchukuo. Japan leaves
the League
after the
Manchuria
episode The unanimous condemnation of the League of Nations was flouted, and Japan set the example of leaving Geneva. In face of the difficulty of operating in the Far East against a major power, the powers took no steps to restrain the aggressor. Encouraged by this example Mussolini's Italy, which had long marked out as a sphere for Italian expansion the only large tract of Africa still ruled by Africans, invaded Abyssinia (October 1935). This time the powers resolved to do something more than protest. The League invoked Article XVI and sanctions were applied against Italy (November 1935– Italy leaves
the League
after the
application
of 'sanc-
tions' in
the Abys-
sinia crisis July 1936). But the policy was not wholeheartedly pressed; some influential quarters in Britain and France disagreed with it entirely, and the vital oil sanction was never applied, nor was the Suez Canal closed. Mussolini let it be known that he would regard both actions as tantamount to a declaration of war. The question became one of bluff, and Mussolini, relying on the divisions in his opponents' councils, their growing pre-occupation with Hitler and their greater reluctance to cause a general conflict, easily outbluffed Britain and France. The result was that the half-hearted sanctions failed to do anything except infuriate Italy, who regarded the whole campaign against her as selfish hypocrisy, since Britain herself had already acquired so large a share of the world's surface in roughly the same manner. The hostile atmosphere engendered by this episode persisted, and Italy too left the League.

From 1936 to 1939 a source of perpetual crisis hung over The
Spanish
Civil War
1936–1939 Europe in the form of the Spanish Civil War. In opposition to the left-wing and anti-clerical policy of the Spanish Republican government, General Franco attempted a *coup*

d'état.   It failed to achieve immediate success, and led to a
bitter struggle in which the forces of Franco, the Army, the
Church, and 'Big Business' were ranged against the legitimate
government, the Basques, liberals, socialists, and communists
generally.   Britain and France tried to maintain a policy of
Non-Intervention from outside, but this was flagrantly broken
by Italy and Germany on behalf of Franco, and Russia on
behalf of the government.   These three powers were not only
manœuvring for position, but were also using the occasion as
a dress rehearsal for a European war by trying out tactics and
equipment.   Russia abandoned intervention first, and Franco
was at length successful—a very dangerous result for Britain
and France, since he was likely to remain in the German and
Italian camp.   Throughout Britain's position was extremely
delicate, for she had no wish to intervene, but also no desire to
see German and Italian influence permeate Spain.   She was,
moreover, by now fully alive to the danger of the German
air force which Hitler had so swiftly called into being (and for
which officers were being trained in secrecy even before
the Nazis came on the scene).   Throughout these troubled
years, and particularly in the Czecho-Slovak crisis of 1938,
the inferiority of British and French air power to a Luftwaffe
expanding at an unparalleled rate was to be a governing
thought in many minds, and to determine Anglo-French
policy along lines of caution.

The worsening trend of international events was vividly
illustrated in the year 1938.   In the spring, Hitler, after a
brutal ultimatum to the Austrian Chancellor, Schuschnigg,
marched his newly formed legions into Austria, took over
complete possession, and merged it into the Reich.   Modern
Europe had seen nothing parallel to this overnight disappearance of an independent state with nearly a thousand
years of history behind it.   Hitler's plea, in so far as he
offered one, was that the Austrians had always desired the
'Anschluss' ('Union'), and that Schuschnigg (whom he
promptly imprisoned) was endeavouring to avert this by a
'faked' plebiscite.   After Hitler's entry, together with that of
his troops and secret police, a 'genuine' plebiscite was to be
held—and was held, with the customary totalitarian results.
Italy had prevented the Anschluss in 1934—when the Nazis

*The
disappear-
ance of
Austria—
the
'Anschluss,'
March,
1938*

made their first attempt, murdering the Austrian Chancellor Dollfuss in the process—by threatening to make the Brenner 'bristle with bayonets'; but she was now far too offended with Britain and France since the 'sanctions' episode to work together with them.   The result was that a startled Europe did nothing but protest, while Hitler duly planned his next coup.

A few months later in the year it became apparent that this was to be directed against Czecho-Slovakia, on the score of the oppression of the Sudeten German minority by the Czechs.   Actually important strategic motives lay behind the move, the command of the mountain range and mineral wealth of Bohemia, together with the destruction both of an outpost of the French 'security system' and the main obstacle to German expansion eastward.   In face of the rising German press campaign against Czech terrorism, Britain and France had to decide what their attitude would be at the decisive moment.   Both tried hints and threats to no avail, while at the same time they put very strong pressure on the Czechs to come to terms with Hitler, for since the German occupation of Austria the Czech frontiers were impossible to defend. Ultimately France, finding no support from Britain for a stronger policy, deserted her Czech ally, and allowed Germany to make off with the Sudeten areas and a bit beyond.   At one critical moment indeed, though the British Prime Minister, Neville Chamberlain, was pursuing a policy of 'appeasement,' Hitler's demands were so outrageous that Britain and France almost put their foot down.   The events of a never-to-be-forgotten fortnight included three hectic flights to Germany by Chamberlain, the digging of hastily improvised (and soon to be waterlogged) trenches in many of the parks, and the mobilization of the British Fleet.   Eventually, however, the intervention of Mussolini moderated one or two of Hitler's demands, and in any case the German people, in blissful ignorance of all but the specially selected fare of totalitarian newspapers, had no idea that war might be imminent.   The relief from the threats of war, following Chamberlain's flights—and concessions—brought the British Prime Minister an unparalleled popularity, though discordant voices were not wanting in the general shout of praise.   According to Mr. Churchill, the final agreement at Munich (September

Czecho-Slovakia: the 'September Crisis,' 1938

German occupation of the Sudeten areas

1938) meant only that "Herr Hitler had consented to be served with his courses one at a time in an orderly fashion instead of snatching his victuals all at once from the table."

Incorpora-
tion of
Czecho-
Slovakia
in the
German
Reich,
March,
1939

Up to this point it was still possible, if optimistic, to believe that Hitler's policy, brutal though it was, would stop short at the incorporation of those of German race in the Reich. To those who still clung to this theory the next move, in the spring of 1939, proved a rude shock. Not content with having stripped Czecho-Slovakia of her fortified frontier and many of her industries, he invaded the Czech sections themselves, occupied Prague, and declared the whole state dissolved, with Bohemia and Moravia included in Germany, and Slovakia as a 'self-governing' district. Germany, previously so outraged at the existence of a German minority in Czecho-Slovakia, thus acquired a Czech minority three times as large, to say nothing of the complete Czech air force, military equipment, and the vital Skoda munitions works. At about

the same time, while the going was good, the Germans seized Memel, which was, however, truly German, from Lithuania.

The policy of appeasement now lay in ruins, and the question became one of stopping further German advance. Chamberlain was infuriated at Hitler's violation of pledges given personally to himself, and a revolution occurred in Britain's conduct of foreign affairs. The British government offered guarantees of help in case of attack to Poland, Roumania, and Greece (threatened by Italy since the Italian seizure of Albania on Good Friday 1939), concluded a treaty of mutual assistance with Turkey, and together with France strove to include Russia in a great block of states pledged to resist German aggression. The negotiations with Russia dragged on unsuccessfully, however, all the summer. Labour circles at the time tended to place the blame on the well-known anti-Bolshevik sentiments of the Conservative leaders, but in fact Russia was demanding, as a condition of her adherence, the right to send her troops into Poland, Finland, and the small Baltic States. This, though necessary for the efficient conduct of war against Germany, could never be accepted by the States concerned, for once they let the Red Army in they would probably never get it out again. Britain and France did not feel they could honourably put pressure on the states, and the chance of building up a firm Eastern front was lost. But the guarantees to Poland, Roumania, and Greece still held good, and to give reality to her new determination Britain took the epoch-making step (for her) of introducing conscription. Germany countered by making the Rome-Berlin 'axis' into a hard and fast military alliance, and by seeking to extend this system to Japan, Hungary, Yugo-Slavia, and Spain. Thus, with the League discredited for its failure to withstand Japan, Italy, and Germany, Europe was back to the bad old system of two armed groups. All the powers feverishly hurried on their colossal armament programmes, in which the 'axis' powers had snatched a valuable lead, and which made the preparations for 1914 seem like child's play in comparison. It was a method of seeking security which had been tried before, all too thoroughly, and which usually ended in war. It was to do so again.

As the summer of 1939 wore on, it became apparent that Germany was about to direct her next blow against Poland. *Germany threatens Poland.* Poles and Germans had long had no love for each other, but Hitler's government had actually concluded a non-aggression pact with Poland as one of its first steps in foreign policy. Germany, however, flushed with her recent successes and gambling on the kind of resistance from Britain and France which these powers had shown at Munich, determined not only to settle two long-standing grievances in her own favour, but also to win for herself a huge 'living-space' in the Polish and Russian Ukraine. Naturally it was the former which appeared as her public aim. She had never accepted willingly either the status of Danzig (populated largely by Germans) as a Free City, in which the Poles had certain guaranteed rights, or the existence of the Polish 'Corridor,' cutting off East Prussia from the main body of the Reich. Had Hitler not revealed his true objective by the occupation of Prague in the spring, some accommodation might have been attempted. As it was, the Poles and the whole of Europe knew every step in the well-worn Nazi technique by heart. A demand—an 'atrocity' campaign alleging ill-treatment of German minorities—an 'appeal' by the German minorities for Hitler's protection—more demands, every concession offered by the victim used to extort a further one, and finally the entry of the German army, with not only the disputed territory but the whole country at its mercy. In face of a shrieking German press campaign the Poles kept their temper and their determination, trusting to their own bravery and the help of their western friends—though this indeed, owing to Poland's geographical situation, could hardly be either direct or of immediately decisive effect. They announced their willingness to negotiate, but not under threat of force. Europe held its breath and trembled.

The Russo-German non-aggression pact, August 1939

On August 21st, the world knew the die was cast. The papers of that day contained the news of the Russo-German non-aggression pact, which was formally signed in Moscow two days later. Russia, while still negotiating with Britain and France, had 'sold out' to the Nazis in return for German recognition of a Russian interest in Eastern Poland, the Baltic States, and south-east Europe. Doubtless another Russian motive was to avoid trouble with Germany until the Red Army was better equipped and the disorganization following recent 'purges' had been righted. Russia probably also calculated on a lengthy war in which the great 'capitalist' powers of Germany, France, and Britain would exhaust one another.

This cynical volte-face on the part of German Fascists and Russian Communists, who had previously been at daggers drawn, astounded public opinion everywhere. But Ribbentrop, Hitler's sinister foreign minister, was sadly mistaken in his belief that it would frighten Britain and France into betraying Poland, or Poland into abject surrender. On August 24th, Britain signed the last formal stages of her alliance with Poland. Hitler and his advisers, however, refused to be swayed from their purpose by the certain prospect of a European war. The issue was clearly before them, but their new calculation was that, with the Poles irreparably beaten in a few weeks, Britain and France would be glad to withdraw before any further damage was done. In any case, Hitler knew that his policy would eventually lead to another European war, and he preferred to start it while he was still in his full powers. For another week the tension grew tauter and tauter. On August 31st, Germany suddenly announced a 16-Point Peace Plan, involving the return of Danzig to the Reich, plebiscites in the Corridor, German railways and roads through the Corridor before the plebiscites, and further concessions. Hitler announced that his 'patience was exhausted,' and that the German government, after two days' grace, were now tired of waiting for a reply or for the arrival of a Polish plenipotentiary. This announcement to the world was the first time the Poles had officially heard of the 16-Point Plan—a typical example of Nazi perfidy. On September 1st, without further ultimatum or declaration of war, Danzig was proclaimed reunited to the Reich and Germany invaded Poland. The invasion of Poland

At the last moment, once more, Mussolini came forward with a plan for a conference, but this time the Munich technique was not to be repeated. Britain and France demanded the slackening of the German pressure against Poland as an obvious prerequisite to peaceful discussions, and in face of the German refusal to do anything but go ruthlessly ahead, Italy's peace-move failed. For one day, indeed, Britain and France seemed to hesitate: in fact, their decision to help Poland was already made, but they could not agree on the best time for opening hostilities. Public opinion on all sides clearly indicated that this time there could be no escape— German aggression and our plain commitments had gone too far. The opposition parties in Britain and France—except, of course, a few Fascists and Communists—were at one with the governments, and the governments at one with the people. On Sunday, September 3rd, Britain and France despatched brief ultimatums to Germany, threatening her with war unless she withdrew from Poland. No reply was received, and by European war again 11.15 a.m. Chamberlain was broadcasting to the British people the news of the tragic breakdown of all his and their hopes and ideals. But if gloom was the prevalent mood, if an overwhelming despondency at a second sacrifice within twenty-five years was in the minds of all, there was lacking no determination to see the thing through to its bitter end. With no beating of drums or jingoist parade, but in a sad, sober, and steadfast resolution Britain and France prepared to fight, and overthrow the 'evil things' of which Chamberlain had spoken—'brute force, bad faith, injustice, oppression, and persecution.' It was war again; but never had the British and French peoples fought in a clearer cause, never against a more dangerous or malignant foe.

CHAPTER XV

The Second World War, 1939-1945

German invasion of Poland, September 1939

The Poles soon found that bravery was no substitute for tanks and aeroplanes. With their communications paralysed by overwhelming German superiority in the air, they were simply brushed aside by the onrush of the Nazi armoured divisions. On September 17th the Russians, as secretly arranged in the Nazi–Soviet pact a few weeks before, entered Eastern Poland ; on September 27th the Germans captured Warsaw ; and by the end of the month the swastika floated over one half of Poland and the hammer and sickle over the other.

Russian occupation of East Poland

Anglo-French policy

Only by launching an immediate all-out offensive against the strong Siegfried Line, in the west of Germany, could Britain and France have brought relief to the Poles. But the concentration of the French troops, most of whom were not mechanized, was a slow business; the small British Expeditionary Force was in the process of moving across to the Continent; and, except at sea, both Allies were determined to postpone the major clash for as long as possible, in the hope of reducing Germany's advantage in armaments. So the brief chance of forcing Hitler to fight on two fronts was lost, and by October the Germans were building up for an attack in the west.

The 'Phoney' War, October 1939–April 1940

For the next six months matters were surprisingly quiet—so quiet that impatient American journalists dismissed the whole contest as "phoney." In point of fact, Hitler, after giving the Allies a chance to recognize his conquest of Poland and meeting with a firm refusal, was preparing to strike in the following spring ; and the Allies were simply doing what they could—rounding up enemy ships, enforcing a blockade, countering Hitler's magnetic mine, showering German cities with leaflets—to damage Germany without provoking her to violent action. Meanwhile the Russians, anxious to secure the approaches to Leningrad against all comers, set upon the Finns, and after an inglorious start got what they wanted—

The Russo-Finnish War, November 1939–March 1940

RENDEZ-VOUS.

Hitler and Stalin, their long-standing and fundamental antagonism momentarily ended by the Nazi-Soviet pact of August 1939, meet across the dead body of Poland and exchange courtesies. (September 1939.)

fortunately before Britain and France, who were naturally indignant at the Russian action, became embroiled in the conflict.

German invasion of Denmark and Norway, April 1940

The strange calm was sharply broken in April 1940. Determined to safeguard his supplies of Scandinavian iron-ore from interruption by the British, Hitler struck without warning at Denmark and Norway—both unoffending neutrals. Denmark was occupied almost bloodlessly and Norway in a campaign which lasted only two months. With seaborne or airborne troops treacherously descending on all the key Norwegian ports and airfields at the outset, the Germans were able to gain a stranglehold which the Norwegians—who were none the stronger for a century's uninterrupted peace—could do little to loosen. Hopelessly handicapped by the lack of any major Norwegian port or airfield, Britain and France could bring no effective help to bear; and in any case they were bound to preserve their main forces for the forthcoming clash in the West.

Churchill's Coalition in Britain May 1940

German invasion of Holland, Belgium, and France, May 1940

Norway was an unexpected and bitter blow to the Allies— so bitter that it brought down the Chamberlain government in Britain and led to an all-party Coalition under Winston Churchill. But it was nothing to the almost mortal shock which followed. On May 10th, 1940, the German armies at last moved in the West. To by-pass the strongly fortified Maginot Line, covering the Franco-German frontier, the Germans struck at France, as in 1914, through neutral Belgium ; and this time their plan included the invasion of Holland. Overwhelmed by superior forces and a skilful use of paratroops, Holland succumbed within five days, the unopposed bombing of Rotterdam clinching the matter. The German right flank was secure.

The breakthrough in the Ardennes

Meanwhile the enemy's most powerful punch had been packed into the centre. Employing a big concentration of tanks and dive-bombers, Hitler's forces struck heavily in the Ardennes—a hilly region where a major offensive had seemed out of the question and where the French had therefore stationed the worst equipped and worst officered of all their armies. Quickly forcing the Meuse near Dinant and Sedan, the Germans cut through the French lines with absurd ease. Within a few days, with practically nothing in their path to stop them, they were motoring across France towards the Channel coast.   During this time vast French forces remained only slightly engaged in the Maginot Line, while to the north of the German break-through the B.E.F. and the French 1st Army, which had dashed forward into Belgium, were compelled to retire with almost equal speed.

By May 21st the German penetration had reached the Channel coast near Abbeville and completely severed the Allied armies in the North—the B.E.F., the French 1st Army, and the Belgians—from those in the south.   On these northern armies the Germans now concentrated, pressing them back from the east while the panzer forces which had carried out the break-through wheeled round along the Channel coast and drove at them from the west.   Soon there was only one port open to the northern armies—Dunkirk—and no choice but evacuation or surrender.   Exhausted, the Belgians laid down their arms (with remarkably brief notice from King Leopold to his allies), but thanks to a heroic rearguard action before Dunkirk and the most strenuous and devoted efforts by the Royal Navy, the Royal Air Force, and large numbers of merchant seamen and amateur yachtsmen, the B.E.F. and most of the French 1st Army were plucked from disaster. Only a hair's-breadth had separated the British army from a debacle unparalleled in its history.

The Dunkirk Evacuation, May 26th–June 4th, 1940

After Dunkirk the Germans turned against the French armies to the south—and the few British with them.   Sweeping across the Somme and the Seine, they occupied Paris (which was not defended) and split the French forces into helplessly isolated groups.   Meanwhile Mussolini's Italy, tempted by the prospect of loot, if not glory, on the cheap, entered the fray against the reeling Allies.   Appalled by the utter impotence of her armies against the German tanks and bombers, France now lost all heart for the struggle ; Marshal Pétain, the victor of Verdun in 1916, but now old and defeatist, became Premier to make peace ; and by June 25th—less than seven weeks from the opening blow—the whole campaign was over.   It was fairly typical of Hitler that he forced the French to receive his armistice terms in the old railway coach at Compiègne where the Germans had had to sign on the dotted line in 1918.

The entry of Italy, June 1940

The collapse of France

[*By permission of Low*]

ON TO GLORY—AND WHATEVER WE CAN GRAB.

Mussolini enters the fray against the reeling Allies. (June 1940.)

The governments of Poland, Norway, and Holland, and a 'provisional' Czech government recognized by the British, were now carrying on the fight from exile ; Pétain's government, on the other hand, refused to fight on from the French colonies, and preferred to knuckle under completely to the Germans. Pétain reasoned that France had been offered good terms (the Germans would occupy only Northern France and the Atlantic coast, leaving the centre and south 'free,' with a capital at Vichy), and that if the great French army could not stop the Germans, a handful of British divisions would certainly meet with no better success. Some at least of his countrymen disagreed, and a Free French (later called Fighting French) movement was formed in London under General de Gaulle. But as the French government was now ill-disposed towards Britain—it saved French self-respect to blame the disaster on insufficient help from her ally —the British government could afford to take no chances about the French fleet, which was lying intact in North African harbours. When the French refused to hand it over to Britain's safe keeping, the Royal Navy opened fire on the major vessels at Oran and Mers-el-Kebir and put most of them out of action. Naturally this did not improve relations between the former friends.

Supported by the Commonwealth (though Eire remained obstinately neutral), Britain had now to face the combined might of Germany and Italy. A second 'peace-offer' from Hitler, confirming him in his ill-gotten gains, was as resolutely refused as the first. Then the Nazi dictator was forced to contemplate a task outside the experience even of the German army—the invasion of England. But the German navy had no relish for the job while the Royal Navy remained in being, and insisted that the power of the British fleet should be 'neutralized' by the German Air Force. The Luftwaffe could not be sure of doing this, however, or of 'covering' the German vessels and landings until it had gained air superiority over the Channel and Southern England. In other words, before England could be invaded, the Germans had first to dispose of the Royal Air Force.

So began the Battle of Britain—an epic struggle in the air which lasted from early August till late September. In an

Pétain's Vichy government

de Gaulle's Free French

British action v. French fleet, July 1940

Projected invasion of England

The Battle of Britain, August– September 1940

effort to paralyse the carefully devised British system of air defence, the German bombers, more and more heavily escorted, shifted from one series of targets to another—first the South Coast ports, radar stations, and airfields, then the inland airfields, then London itself—but all attacks broke down before the superb equipment, valour, and skill of the British fighter pilots. At the same time British bombers played havoc with the hostile concentrations of shipping in the French and Belgian Channel ports. By the end of September, Göring—one of Hitler's main henchmen and the Luftwaffe's Commander-in-Chief—was no nearer his objective, and the weather ruled out an invasion later in the year. There was thus nothing for Hitler to do but to postpone the venture until the following spring. Fortunately by then he had embraced another project from which he was never to shake free.

Though preserved from immediate invasion, Britain was not unthreatened in other ways. Unable to sustain her heavy losses by day, Germany had begun to use her bombers against Britain by night—against the ports, the arms towns, and above all London. The Royal Air Force had already been attacking Germany by night since May, though in a smaller way than was possible to the enemy. From September 1940 to May 1941 the Luftwaffe visited London almost nightly, and dozens of other British towns were also badly knocked about. The science of night defence was then in its infancy and German losses were small ; but the science of night attack was also undeveloped and the bombing was more of an ordeal for the town-dweller than a mortal blow to the British war effort. Exposed to apparently indiscriminate attack, the British retaliated by going for German 'industrial areas' (which were easier to hit than the individual factories on which they had previously concentrated), and thenceforth the civilians of both countries were inescapably in the 'front line.'

To the bombing of British towns Hitler added a determined effort to cut Britain's life-line across the Atlantic. Franklin D. Roosevelt, the great President of the United States of America, had early resolved that his country should act as the 'arsenal of democracy,' and under his skilful guidance and the pressure of events the United States became increasingly will-

The 'Night Blitz' against Britain, September 1940–May 1941

British retaliation

American supplies and the U-boat war

Roosevelt

ing not only to supply the goods, but, by the Lease-Lend Act The Lease-
Lend Act,
of March 1941, to supply them virtually free of charge. March 1941
Obviously if this went unchecked British resistance could be
sustained far beyond what would otherwise be possible.
Installed by mid-1940 all round the coast of Europe from
Narvik to the Bay of Biscay, German aircraft and U-boats
were magnificently placed to prey on the transatlantic traffic,
and throughout the winter of 1940-41 the sinkings of British—
and neutral—vessels mounted.

While Britain battled on alone against Germany in The war
Europe, British and Commonwealth forces in Africa were in Africa
winning fantastic victories against the Italians. Attacked
simultaneously from Libya and Italian East Africa, the
ludicrously outnumbered British had at first to give ground
in all directions—in Egypt, the Sudan, Kenya, and British
Somaliland. Then reinforcements began to arrive from
South Africa, Australia, and India, while by a bold decision
an armoured brigade was sent out to Egypt from England at
the very height of the German invasion threat. The result
was that General Wavell soon had the Italians on the run.
The surrendered outposts in the Sudan and Kenya were
recaptured ; Italian East Africa was invaded ; and in a
brilliant advance against an enemy five times as numerous,
Wavell's forces pushed the Italians out of Egypt and overran
the whole of Cyrenaica (the eastern province of Libya). In British
conquest of
this advance Italian casualties amounted to about 150,000— Cyrenaica,
nearly all prisoners. Those of the British were less than three December
1940–
thousand. February
1941

To defeat in Africa Mussolini had by this time added disgrace in Europe. In October 1940 Hitler occupied Roumania
—to safeguard one of his main sources of oil. Whereupon
Mussolini, reluctant to see his fellow dictator stealing all the
limelight (and much else besides) in the Balkans, decided to
strike at Greece. In view of the small size of the Greek forces, Italian
attack on
he looked forward to a virtual 'walk-over.' But the Italians, Greece,
operating from Albania, were held up as soon as their victims October
1940
had time to rally from the first surprise blow ; and within a
few weeks the Greeks, helped by the Royal Air Force, were
invading Albania. At the same time half of Italy's battleships
were crippled by a torpedo-attack (delivered by the British

Taranto,
November
1940
Fleet Air Arm) at Taranto. Disaster, utter and complete, had attended all Mussolini's nefarious schemes.

German
inter-
vention in
Africa
Obviously Hitler could not tolerate the defeat of his ally. At the end of 1940 he sent a strong detachment of the Luftwaffe to Sicily, where it improved considerably on the performance of the Italian air force against Malta ; and in the opening months of 1941 German land and air forces were shipped across to Libya. At the same time in the Balkans the Germans began to infiltrate into Bulgaria and prepared to strike at Greece. Seeing the danger, the British resolved to do what they could—though it was far from enough—to protect Greece, and forces were hastily withdrawn from Egypt and sent across the Mediterranean. They had hardly
German
invasion of
Yugo-
Slavia and
Greece,
April 1941
taken up their positions when the Germans struck. Brushing aside the resistance of Yugo-Slavia (which at the last moment gallantly overthrew a government prepared to collaborate with Hitler), the Germans poured into Greece and within three weeks had driven the tiny British force from Greek soil. Fortunately it was nearly all rescued, as at Dunkirk, by the Royal Navy.

Meanwhile though the Italian fleet had taken another beating at the Battle of Cape Matapan, the Axis had recovered in North Africa. Deprived of the troops despatched to Greece and now called on to face the German Africa Corps under Rommel as well as the Italians, the British forces were driven
Loss of
Cyrenaica,
April 1941
back from Cyrenaica into Egypt, though Tobruk still held out as an isolated fortress. As though this double misfortune was
The Iraqi
revolt,
May 1941
not enough, Nazi sympathizers in Iraq overthrew the Regent and threatened British interests there—fortunately before the Germans were ready to take proper advantage of the move,
British and
Free
French
occupation
of Syria,
June–July
1941
which was soon dealt with. Shortly afterwards British and Free French forces entered and occupied the French mandated territory of Syria, where the Vichy-controlled government had given facilities to German and Italian aircraft en route for Iraq.
German
capture
of Crete,
May 1941
From Greece the Germans jumped to Crete, which they took—with stupendous losses—by airborne invasion. Once more the British force had to be extracted by the Royal Navy. The Navy also defeated a seaborne expedition aimed at the island, but the British ships suffered great damage in the process, and it became clear that naval vessels could no longer

operate effectively in narrow waters within range of a superior
air force.

The German occupation of Yugo-Slavia, Greece, and Crete, together with their 'peaceful' domination of Roumania and Bulgaria, cleared Hitler's right flank for his next, and ultimately fatal, venture. The Nazi–Soviet pact of August 1939 had never been more than an agreement of momentary tactical value to both sides—it had lessened neither Hitler's hatred of Communism nor his determination to expand in the East. With France knocked out in the West and Britain without a foothold on the Continent, the German dictator found the temptation irresistible to crush Russia while the going was good. The German General Staff reckoned it could all be done in eight weeks; the decision was taken in December 1940; and after some months of quiet preparation the blow was launched on June 22nd, 1941—a few weeks late on programme, probably owing to the British intervention in Greece. *German invasion of Russia, June 1941*

Moving forward with a great mass of tanks and using a large proportion of their air force in support—it had been transferred from the West, thereby ending the 'blitz' against Britain in any serious form—the Germans overran the Russian-occupied section of Poland and struck deep into Russia. In the north—aided by the Finns—they advanced almost to the suburbs of Leningrad ; in the centre they came within a hundred miles of Moscow ; in the south they broke right through to the Crimea. But though the casualties ran into millions on both sides, the Germans failed to destroy the Russian armies. Soon the summer and autumn wore away and the hard-baked plains lay beneath a deep covering of snow ; Generals January and February, Russia's traditional allies, were taking over.

While the German advance into Russia was being brought to a halt, fresh developments were occurring elsewhere. The campaign of the Commonwealth forces in Italian East Africa was brought to a victorious conclusion and a new offensive was mounted against the Axis forces in North Africa. For a second time the British overran Cyrenaica, but once more events in other theatres demanded the transfer of some of the British troops, and part of the captured ground had to be *Conquest of Italian East Africa (completed November 1941)* *Second British conquest of Cyrenaica, November 1941 January 1942*

given up. This time the diversion was no minor affair, as in Greece, but a major development as decisive for the future of the war as the German invasion of Russia.

The war with Japan

Since 1931 Japan had been carrying out an aggressive policy absorbing as much of the huge, weak, and disunited state of China as she could. Normally the big obstacles to her programme of dominating the Far East were Britain, France, and the U.S.A. All of these were now conveniently occupied elsewhere. Britain was fully engaged in Europe and Africa; France, under the spineless Vichy government, was not prepared to fight to retain her colony of Indo-China— a magnificent jumping-off ground for Malaya; and the U.S.A. was pouring her money, arms, and raw materials into Britain and Russia. Only the American Pacific Fleet stood between Japan and her dreams of conquest—a chance which might never occur again. On December 7th, 1941, without the slightest warning, Japan struck simultaneously in two opposite directions. To the west her troops, sailing from Indo-China, landed in north-east Malaya and Siam ; to the east, in the Hawaiian Islands, her carrier-borne aircraft by one swift, treacherous blow crippled the American Pacific Fleet at Pearl Harbour.

Japanese invasion of Malaya and attack on Pearl Harbour, December 7th, 1941

World War

The war was now world-wide with a vengeance. Germany and Italy hastened to support Japan by declaring war on the U.S.A. ; and soon the British Commonwealth, Russia, the U.S.A., China, and a host of smaller states, including many of the South American Republics, were in formal alliance against Germany, Italy, Japan, and the more willing of their 'satellites'—Roumania, Bulgaria, Hungary, and Finland. Deprived of the protection of the American fleet, the small British forces in the Far East were quite unable to resist the first Japanese onrush. Hong-Kong was an early victim ; Malaya was overrun within two months—the vaunted stronghold of Singapore falling with a huge loss in prisoners ; resistance in the Netherlands East Indies rapidly collapsed ; and by May 1942 the Japanese had penetrated right through Burma to the gates of India. To the East, the Americans were driven from the Philippines after a heroic struggle, and successive groups of Pacific islands rapidly fell to the enemy. In May 1942, however, a Japanese expedition aimed at Port

Japanese capture of Hong-Kong, Malaya, N.E.I., Burma, and Pacific Islands, December 1941–May 1942

Moresby, in New Guinea, was repulsed by the American fleet in the Battle of the Coral Sea, and the following month an invasion fleet intended for Midway Island, in the Central Pacific, was broken up with great losses by American naval aircraft. The period of unchecked Japanese success was at an end.

American victories of Coral Sea and Midway, May–June 1942

Until well on into 1942 the initiative remained in the hands of the Axis powers. At sea the U-boats, preying on vessels near the American coast, enjoyed a fresh wave of success ; in Africa Rommel attacked, and carried the Italo-German armies to within sixty miles of Alexandria ; in Russia the Germans, taking advantage of the summer conditions, swept forward on the southern front right into the Caucasus. But they could not take the town of Stalingrad, though the battle raged about, through, and over the city till every building was a ruin. Once more the Germans had shot their bolt ; and this time the inexhaustible Russians, succoured by Anglo-American supplies and drawing unexpected reserves of strength from arms factories built up or transferred beyond the Urals, were preparing to strike back with redoubled force.

Italo-German invasion of Egypt, summer 1942

Stalingrad, September–November 1942

Mid-1942 was thus the high-water mark of Axis success. There were many signs by then that, with good fortune, the Allies could stem the flood. The Japanese, struggling to secure the outposts of Australia, were being held in New Guinea and the Solomons ; and in the West an ever-increasing weight of bombs was falling on German soil. The R.A.F. had been steadily attacking since 1940 ; in May 1942 came the first 'thousand-bomber' raid, against Cologne ; and by the summer the United States Air Force was beginning to appear on the European scene. Unless Germany could finish off Russia and turn once more against England, she would find her foreign conquests mocked by the destruction of her homeland.

The mounting air offensive against Germany

The turn of the tide was clearly visible in the closing months of 1942. In October the British Eighth Army under Montgomery struck at Rommel's forces as they lay before El Alamein. After a sharp struggle the enemy cracked. Soon the Italians were being rounded up by the thousand, while the Germans, who had most of the transport, were being chased across the whole breadth of Libya into Tunisia. To seal off

Victory at El Alamein, October–November 1942

the enemy retreat and to re-establish control of the Mediterranean, on November 7th the first of the great Anglo-American expeditions under General Eisenhower landed in Morocco and Algeria ; French resistance soon collapsed, and aid was given to the Allies ; and by May 1943 the last of the Axis forces in Africa—over a quarter of a million men—had been helplessly cornered in the northern tip of Tunisia between the Allied armies advancing from either side of the Continent.   Meanwhile in November 1942 the Russians had begun their winter counter-offensive—at Stalingrad—and the Germans were being remorselessly pressed back .

Anglo-American landings in French North Africa, November 1942

The end in Africa, May 1943

By mid-1943 the Allies were definitely winning.   On the Russian front, a huge German army had capitulated at Stalingrad ; the siege of Leningrad had been raised ; the German summer offensive was halted almost at once.   At the same time the U-boats were being driven out of the Atlantic as Allied aircraft of increasing range, equipped with radar, reinforced the efforts of the Allied navies.   In the German homeland the great industrial centre of the Ruhr, attacked more accurately with the help of radar devices, was already a scene of devastation, and the main effort of R.A.F. Bomber Command was being switched to German ports.   In all the occupied countries of Europe the local 'resistance' movements, sustained by supplies secretly dropped from aircraft, were giving the German occupiers an increasingly uneasy time.

German failures in Russia

The turn of the U-boat war

The air bombardment of the Ruhr and the German ports, spring–summer, 1943

To crown these developments the Anglo-American forces in Africa moved across the Mediterranean to invade Sicily. Thanks to the overwhelming air superiority of the Allies, a foothold was easily obtained, and the local Italian forces once again preferred not to put up a serious fight.   The Germans, however, offered a stiff resistance, and held out for five weeks before they escaped across the Straits of Messina to the Italian mainland.   Meanwhile Mussolini, overwhelmed by incessant defeat, had been driven from power and imprisoned ;   and General Badoglio, working closely with the royal family, had taken over the Italian government.

Anglo-American invasion of Sicily, July 1943

The fall of Mussolini, July 1943

On September 3rd, 1943, the Anglo-American forces swept across from Sicily to the mainland.   Again it was only the Germans who fought—the new Italian government had secretly negotiated with the Allies to shake off the hated

Anglo-American invasion of Italian mainland, September 1943

alliance with Hitler, and shortly afterwards came in on the Italy accepts Allied terms, September 1943; and joins Allies, October 1943 Allied side.

A desperate coup by German parachutists soon rescued Mussolini, who set up a rival government in Northern Italy, but he was now only a shadow of his former self and a mere puppet in German hands. Rapidly the Allied armies advanced as far as Naples, but by then the German forces, at first disorganized by the Italian defection, had established a firm hold on Northern and Central Italy. Aided by the winter weather and the mountainous terrain, they fought with fanatical determination, and the Allied progress, at first so promising, settled down into a long 'slogging-match' up the Italian peninsula. The advance up Italy

Having knocked out their weakest opponent, the British and Americans then perfected their plan for the liberation of North-west Europe. The job was entrusted largely to the victorious team of commanders from the Mediterranean theatre, under Eisenhower ; preparations of the utmost thoroughness were made—including two artificial harbours to be towed across the Channel—and on 'D-Day' (June 6th, 1944) the Anglo-American forces touched down on the beaches of Normandy. By this time the sea-lanes of the Allies were reasonably secure against the U-boats and commerce-raiders ; and the Allied air forces, having reduced the north German ports and Berlin to the state of the Ruhr, besides bringing German production of bombers to a critically low level, had crippled the communications of Northern France. This latter achievement fatally handicapped the Germans' ability to concentrate their troops in the vital area, and gave the Allied armies a chance to make good their footing. Allied landings in Normandy, June 6th, 1944

After a few weeks tight struggle, during which the British and Canadians on the left attracted the bulk of the enemy to their sectors, the Americans on the right broke out from the lodgment area. Threatened by an encircling movement, thousands of Germans were destroyed in trying to get back over the Seine, and in rapid succession the Allies freed Northern and Western France and swept into Belgium and Holland. The break-out, August 1944

Meanwhile another Allied army, including the main Fighting French forces, landed in Southern France (which had

12+

Allied
landings in
Southern
France,
August
1944

been occupied by the Germans after the North African landings of November 1942), and moved up the Rhône valley towards the Upper Rhine. By September 1944 the Allied armies were across the German frontier in several places, but

The failure
at Arnhem,
September
1944

a bold attempt to leap the Rhine by a parachute operation at Arnhem, in Holland, failed, largely through bad weather. Soon it became clear that to bring up enough supplies the Allies must open the port of Antwerp—for on Hitler's orders the Germans, even after they had abandoned the rest of the country, clung desperately to the ports, and blew up all

Antwerp
in use,
November
1944

installations before surrendering. The island of Walcheren, which guards the Scheldt estuary, was cleared at the beginning of November, and before the end of the month Allied supplies were reaching the front through Antwerp.

The German cause was now obviously doomed. In July 1944 an attempt by a group of German anti-Nazis to blow up Hitler failed to achieve its very commendable object, but gave a clear sign that some of the enemy realized the madness of

The
Russian
advance

continuing the struggle. The Russians, who had advanced more or less continuously since Stalingrad, had by now eliminated Finland, Bulgaria, and Roumania, penetrated the Baltic States, Hungary, Czecho-Slovakia, and Yugo-Slavia (where Marshal Tito's resistance forces, aided by Allied aircraft, had for long kept a big German army pinned down),

The
German
V.1 and V.2
campaign,
June 1944–
March 1945

and had reached East Prussia. The German attempt to knock out London by one of Hitler's 'secret weapons'—the V.1, or flying bomb—had failed, and the V.2, or long-range rocket, promised little more success with the Allied armies

The effects
of Allied
air attack

overrunning the launching-sites on the Continent. To crown all, Germany's major cities were now masses of rubble, her oil resources (attacked from the air, and doubly weakened by the loss of Roumania) were down to a level which was crippling her whole war machine, and her railways and canals were just beginning to feel the full weight of Allied air power.

The
German
counter-
offensive
in the
Ardennes,
December
1944

In December 1944 the Germans in the West made their last effective stroke—a sudden counter-offensive through the Ardennes aimed at Antwerp. It failed, and the effort left the enemy still weaker than before.

In the spring months of 1945 the Russians completed their conquest of Hungary, liberated Lithuania, and reached the

KNELL

The knell of doom sounds for the German dictator, hammered between
the Anglo-American forces on the West and the Russians on the East.
(March 1945.)

[Express Newspapers

Oder. In March Eisenhower's forces launched their new
offensive, which quickly took them across the Rhine. Irre-
sistibly the Allied armies now converged on the heart of
Germany. In the west the Ruhr was encircled and captured
to yield an enormous bag of prisoners ; to the south the
Russians overran Vienna ; in the east the Russians reached
the suburbs of Berlin. On April 25th American and Russian
forces, approaching from opposite directions, met on the Elbe.
Three days later, with the German armies in Italy about to
lay down their arms, Mussolini attempted to flee across the
border into Switzerland. He was captured and shot by
Italian 'partisan' forces. Hitler did not long survive him, for
on April 30th the frenzied German leader, who had refused to
leave his bomb-proof underground headquarters in Berlin, in

The crossing of the Rhine, April 1945

The forces from East and West meet, April 1945

The end in Italy : the death of Mussolini

The suicide of Hitler

desperation committed suicide.* With him perished a number of companions, including Goebbels, the Nazi propaganda minister and one of the world's greatest liars. A few days later Hitler's appointed successor, Admiral Dönitz, accepted the Allied terms of unconditional surrender. On May 7th an armistice was signed at Eisenhower's headquarters at Reims, and on May 8th German resistance came to an end.

Germany surrenders

The end in Europe, May 8th, 1945

The Nazi Concentration Camps

As the Allied armies swept through a Germany where every large town was an appalling tribute to the work of the Allied airmen, they came across the Nazi concentration and extermination camps. The scenes of horror they there uncovered were ample proof, if any were needed, of the utter bestiality of the Nazi régime and the national selfishness of the German people, who for the most part had closed their eyes to its vices and crimes while it paid them to do so. Thousands upon thousands of men, women, and children imprisoned in the last stages of starvation, disease, filth, and every other human misery ; thousands subjected to hideous tortures, often for the sheer pleasure of their brutal guards (themselves recruited largely from the criminal classes) ; merciless floggings and 'beatings-up,' finger-nails torn out, lighted cigarettes held against the skin, lengthy exposure to extreme cold or repeated immersion in icy water ; millions—literally millions—of foreigners, Jews, and opponents of the régime worked to death ; millions more Jews and many thousands of elderly or mentally sick Germans exterminated in gas-chambers out of deference to Nazi racial theories—these were but a few of the practices which were revealed beyond any shadow of dispute, and which have made the names of camps like Auschwitz and Mauthausen a grisly and lasting memorial of "man's inhumanity to man."

The war with Japan

Allied successes, 1943–May 1945

With Germany prostrate and the Nazi leaders dead or awaiting trial as war criminals, the Allies proceeded to concentrate on Japan. By now the Americans, thanks largely to a generous use of aircraft carriers, had established a firm naval supremacy in Far Eastern waters. The Solomons had been recovered, New Guinea was being cleared up, the islands in the Central Pacific had been recaptured, and the Americans

* According to the story of those about him. His body was apparently burned.

were back in the Philippines.   Allied armies had also fought their way back from India to Rangoon.   Above all, islands within air striking range of Japan—first Iwo Jima, then Okinawa—were falling into Allied hands.   The Japanese homeland had already suffered severely from American long-range bombers based in China ;   now it was to feel the weight first of increasing bombardment by traditional means and then of a new and infinitely terrible weapon.   On August 6th an American Superfortress dropped an atomic bomb on the port of Hiroshima, devastating an area of four square miles and killing or injuring about 160,000 Japanese men, women, and children ;   on August 8th Russia, who had thus far remained neutral in the Far Eastern struggle, declared war on Japan and invaded Manchuria ;   on August 9th an atomic bomb was dropped on Nagasaki ;   and on August 14th the Japanese accepted the Allied terms of unconditional surrender.   The long nightmare was at last over, even if victory was clouded by the thought of what terrible powers of destruction now lay within the capacity of mankind.

American air attacks on Japan

The atom bombs, August 6th and 9th, 1945

The end in the Far East, August 14th, 1945

The main reasons for the initial success and later failure of the Axis powers are tolerably clear.   Germany won her early victories because she had a stronger and better equipped army and air force than the opposite combination of Britain, France, and Poland, and because of her greater freedom from moral scruples.   The same considerations apply to Japan's initial successes: the treacherous blow at the American fleet gained her the temporary command of Far Eastern waters and so enabled her to gather up weakly defended British and Dutch possessions at will.   Italy won no honours before her final co-operation with the Allies—her braggart dictator overlooked the fact that military virtues are not fostered in a non-militaristic people by setting them to fight at the side of a nation they detest against those who have always been their friends.

Reasons for early Axis successes

Many factors account for the turn of the tide after the early run of German successes.   Britain, protected by a small but highly efficient air force, her unfailing navy, and a twenty-mile stretch of water, gave a superb example of moral strength: a united people, supported by their cousins overseas, refused even to contemplate the possibility of defeat.   The Battle of

Reasons for later Axis failure

Britain—fought, in a sense, by the willing workers in the factories and the mines and the fields, as well as by the airmen in the skies—was the first great check to German ambitions. The prolonged and heroic resistance of Russia was the next ; unlike Western Europe, her vast territory offered room to absorb the first shock of the enemy's attack, and after their early victories the German armies became bogged down in a titanic struggle which wore out their heart and soul. Equally, the tremendous requirements of the German armies on the Eastern front made it impossible for Germany to maintain her early lead in the air, and so weakened her against the increasing power of the Royal Air Force. This, in turn, coupled with the ever-growing strength of the American air force— once Japan had brought the Americans fully into the struggle —tore the industrial heart out of Germany and made possible the continuation of Russian resistance and the Anglo-American invasion of Normandy. Nor must we overlook the effect of Allied sea superiority—obtained now by air forces as well as navies ; while it is obvious that the British Commonwealth, the U.S.A., and the U.S.S.R., once their forces were fully built up, represented a combination of man-power, wealth, raw materials, industrial capacity, and scientific skill infinitely more powerful than that of Germany, Italy, and Japan—even when Germany ruled nearly all Europe and Japan lorded it over most of the Far East.

After the opening phase, the Allies were also fortunate in
Hitler's their leaders. On the Axis side Hitler, rating his opponents
disastrous very low, at first scored by sheer boldness ; but his early
leadership successes, coupled with pre-war coups like the bloodless occupation of Austria and Czecho-Slovakia, most of which had been undertaken against the advice of his military commanders, gave him a fatal confidence and prestige. His mixture of ability, will-power, almost mesmeric influence, and utter ruthlessness imposed itself more and more even in purely military details. He brooked no argument, interfered in all directions, and strove to exercise not merely superior but detailed control over all his many armies. The needless attack on Russia was a frightful miscalculation which ruined the whole German cause ; and long before the end it became clear that he was ready to drag his country down into com-

plete and utter ruin rather than abandon the power he had so shamefully misused. At the last, even large elements among the German people could see him for what he was— a crazy fanatic with the moral code of a gangster.

By contrast, the influence of Churchill and Roosevelt was wholly beneficial to their causes. Churchill, though he was not infallible, applied the spur consistently in the right place and by his matchless eloquence and outstanding example inspired the people not only of Britain but of the occupied countries with his own dauntless spirit. Roosevelt, another great orator, picked his way with cat-like skill along the thorny paths of American politics, and brought into the war a nation united if not in admiration of their leader at least in its determination to settle the hash of Germany and Japan. The veil—or rather curtain—of deliberate obscurity surrounding Russia makes it impossible to speak in equally positive terms of Stalin, the third great Allied leader ; but at least it is clear that in steering Russia triumphantly through the ordeals of 1941 and 1942 he showed iron resolution and consummate skill. *The Allied leaders*

One other factor must be mentioned. Unlike Napoleon in his early days, Hitler owed none of his success to the enthusiastic welcome of the countries he overran. He was, indeed, aided in most of the occupied territories by local parties carefully fostered along Nazi or Fascist lines, but these represented only a small fraction of their country's population. The sentiment of the common people of Europe, throughout the war, was unquestionably on the Allied side. Hitler's "New European Order" was never popularly accepted for anything other than the sham it was. In the West the German soldiers on the whole behaved correctly, but the demands of the political authorities for forced labour and the constant fear of the 'knock on the door' from the German secret police made the Nazi régime detested beyond even the normal detestation of a foreign conqueror. In the East, where they came up against less civilized opponents, the German soldiers rapidly descended to the same savage brutality as the German political authorities. In both West and East they left, as a monument to all their tragically misdirected bravery, patriotism, and skill, only a general distrust and hatred of the German name. *Popular sentiment in Europe*

"A FINE TEAM—BUT COULD DO WITH A DASH OF UNITY...."

[*Express Newspapers*

Differences between the Allied leaders—Stalin, Churchill, Truman, and de Gaulle—became more pointed as soon as Germany was defeated. (June 1945.)

CONCLUSION

Nationalism, Dictatorship, Democracy

From the French Revolution to the Second World War the two conceptions dominating European politics were, as we have so frequently seen, the ideas of nationalism and democracy. How do they fare to-day?

Let us first consider nationalism. Obviously it still has a very strong hold on Europe. The peace treaties of 1919, by carving up the Austrian Empire and by establishing Poland and the Baltic republics, gave expression to the longing of peoples to be governed by men of their own nationality. It was on the rock of nationalism that the international experiment of the League of Nations came to grief. In countries like Germany and Italy, which emerged from the First World War with grievances, nationalism reached an unheard-of pitch, in part through the hysterical oratory of dictators ; and this unbridled nationalism was in turn directly responsible for the Second World War. It may seem strange, in view of all this, to hold that nationalism has probably attained its zenith and may henceforth decline. Those countries which have longest enjoyed national unity and freedom, while still deeply patriotic, are less fervent in their nationalism than before. Britain, for example, has voluntarily abandoned nearly all the legal ties which bound Ireland and the Dominions to her, has acquiesced in India becoming a republic and in Burma leaving the Commonwealth, and has long ceased to dream of acquiring further imperial territory. Nationalism is still one of the strongest forces in Europe to-day, with its armies, its foreign policies, its cut-throat tariff barriers; but the whole trend of modern civilization must ultimately militate against it. Education, ease of communication, the spread of common standards of culture, the sheer necessity of preserving the peace—all may be factors in speeding the decline of nationalism. The creation of the United Nations to replace the old League and the movement for some kind of 'Western Union' are indications of the increasing loss of faith in unadulterated national self-sufficiency.

Nationalism, one of the strongest forces in Europe, but somewhat on the decline

And what of the other conception, that of democracy? Here the high-water mark was reached immediately after the First World War, when Germany, Austria, Poland, Czecho-Slovakia, Yugo-Slavia, the new Baltic states all gave themselves democratic constitutions, with parliaments, written statements of citizens' rights, and the like.   From the French Revolution onwards the peoples of Europe had broadly assumed that the path of democracy was the path of progress. By 1914 different countries had attained different degrees of democracy—of the great powers in Europe, Britain and France were the most democratic, Russia the least, Germany and Austria-Hungary about mid-way, being autocracies with some important concessions to democracy.   The fact that Britain, France, and Belgium, and later Italy and the United States, all found themselves on the same side in the war of 1914–1918 cast a kind of democratic halo round the Allies. Even Czarist Russia, experimenting with a Duma, was supposed to be coming into line.   The sentiment of democracy as well as that of nationalism was deliberately appealed to by the Allies in their propaganda against Turkish rule over Arabs, Austrian rule over Czechs, Slovaks, Poles, Croats, and so on. When the Allies won, it was natural that new democracies should spring up all over Europe.   Even defeated states like Germany became democratic, anxious to repudiate the system which had led them to disaster.

Failure of democracy to work in many countries :

(a) Absence of experience and tradition

(b) Multiplication of parties

(c) Hence absence of clear majorities and resolute government

(d) The world economic crisis

Within a few years, however, the picture began to look different.   Most of these countries were lacking in parliamentary experience and tradition.   For many of them it did not seem to be a 'natural growth.'   Their party system worked badly, mainly because they adopted the idea of proportional representation, which by multiplying parties confused the electorate.   (In 1925 in Latvia, for instance, the electors were invited to choose between forty-three parties.)   It usually became impossible for one party to obtain a clear majority, and thus no resolute government was possible.   Then for most of the countries economic conditions were very difficult in the years after 1918, and became increasingly so in the slump of 1930.   Finally, the secure and established powers of the West did little to help some of these infant democracies— Germany, for example, was constantly kept aware of the fact that her Republic was founded in defeat by the way in which *(e) Unhelpful attitude of old-established democracies* moderate requests, such as a customs union with Austria, were refused. For Germany, at least, the idea of a democracy became associated with the idea of permanent inferiority to Britain and France—a mistake for which those two powers could have kicked themselves when it helped to produce Hitler.

So nearly everywhere in Europe democracy went down *The Dictators uppermost in Europe* before dictatorship. Hitler in Germany, Mussolini in Italy, Kemal in Turkey, Pilsudski in Poland, de Rivera and later Franco in Spain, King Alexander in Yugo-Slavia, King Carol in Roumania, Metaxas in Greece, Salazar in Portugal, Gömbös in Hungary, Dollfuss, then Schuschnigg in Austria— these were among the best known of those who between the two world wars exercised almost complete power in their respective countries.

To this formidable list of dictatorships we must also add that of the Union of Soviet Socialist Republics, in the person *U.S.S.R.* first of Lenin, then of Stalin. After the Bolsheviks, in the years following the revolution of 1917, had driven out their foreign enemies and crushed actual military resistance at home, they still had to 'liquidate' the opposition of most of the upper middle classes. This was done by the traditional means—a gigantic 'terror.' A full Socialist policy of state ownership was applied, the opposition of the peasants to having their holdings 'collectivized' being brutally suppressed. Under Stalin, 'Man of Steel,' who on Lenin's death gained *Stalin's 'Five Year Plans'* supreme power after a struggle with Trotsky, Russia concentrated on industrialism by means of the famous 'Five Year Plans.' The chief differences between Stalin and Trotsky *Stalin v. Trotsky* were that Stalin thought it better to go at a more steady pace than Trotsky, desiring to complete the revolution in Russia before starting trouble outside ; whereas Trotsky considered it essential to foment revolution all over the world from the start. The open, secret, and imaginary supporters of Trotsky were 'liquidated' by the victorious Stalin as ruthlessly as they themselves had 'liquidated' aristocrats and bourgeois capitalists. Officially the Union of Soviet Socialist Republics then advanced further along the path of democracy by a new con- *Soviet 'democracy'* stitution giving the secret ballot and greater guarantees of personal liberty.   But in fact the Communist either means by democracy something very different from what the non-Communist takes the word to mean or else he adopts it merely as a valuable catchword ; for while the Communist Party permits no opposition, looking for democracy in Russia would seem to be rather like looking for a needle in a whole collection of haystacks.

Causes of dictatorship   In considering the institution of dictatorship in Europe between the two world wars, two or three points should be remembered.   First, the dictatorships did not spring out of nothing.   They had historic causes—usually defeat in war or social chaos following parliamentary inefficiency and labour troubles, or economic collapse.   Communism, the dictatorship of the Left, also created, by reaction, Fascism or Nazism, the dictatorships of the Right and Middle.   Secondly, many dictatorships had the consent of the overwhelming majority of their people.   Plebiscites produced 99 per cent. in favour of the dictator, and so on—though naturally many of the figures were 'rigged.'   Thirdly, in many cases, the dictators brought, in the short run, considerable material benefits with them.   The only possible justification of the Russian dictatorship is that Lenin and Stalin succeeded in raising the standard of living in Russia, poor though it remained compared with that of Britain, to a height much above that of Czarist days.   Perhaps the most successful of all dictators was Mustapha Kemal Ataturk.   Not only did he rescue his country from real, not imaginary, peril and win back territory for it, but he successfully directed the progress of Turkey on European lines.   He even sent old men back to school to learn a new alphabet, and abolished the fez, the veil, and the institution of polygamy with hardly a murmur from his hypnotized people.

Material improvements

Responsibility of the dictators for the Second World War   The drift of Europe to dictatorship and the unrestrained behaviour of the dictators led directly to the Second World War.   Far and away the prime cause of the war was Hitler, a nationalist fanatic who determined to create a Greater Germany, irrespective of the rights or feelings of Poles, Czechs, or any of the other people unfortunate enough to live on the German borders.   Mussolini, for what he would get out of it for Italy, aided and abetted Hitler.   Stalin, who might perhaps have prevented the whole ghastly tragedy by closer co-operation with Britain and France, chose instead to purchase temporary immunity and advantage by giving Hitler the green light to go ahead against Poland.

Allied victory in the Second World War overthrew the Nazi and Fascist régimes, and has restored, for the time being at least, democratic government in Western Europe, in Italy, and—initially under Allied control—to a large degree in Western Germany. Britain, her great Dominions, and the United States of America, maintaining intact their liberties and their democratic way of life, by a supreme effort passed back to Western Europe the torch of freedom. To that extent democracy has once more come out on top. But Russia, by the circumstances of the German attack in 1941, also became involved in the war, contributed greatly to the final victory, and has finished up in control of the whole of Eastern Europe. And the Russian system is, like the menace against which Britain and America were fighting, a dictatorship—if a dictatorship of a different kind. *Re-establishment of democracy by the Allied victory* *Eastern Europe under Russian control*

Liberal, parliamentary democracy, then—the democracy for which Europe strove throughout the 19th century—is still a leading concept in the world. But it has now to face its greatest challenge. For the appeal of Communism, with its policy of despoiling the upper and middle classes in the interests of the masses (as determined by the Communist Party leaders), is very great, despite the restrictions on personal freedom and the right of opposition which it entails ; and among the poverty-stricken and land-hungry peasantry of Asia it may well prove irresistible.

The stage appears set, then, for a drama on an old theme with a new twist. It is still the struggle for freedom which is being played out, just as it was in the 19th century. But this time the protagonists are not autocratic kingship and liberal democracy, but liberal democracy and totalitarian Communism. Both concepts attract the ardent devotion of their supporters ; both claim to be able to achieve the best life not for the privileged few but for mankind as a whole. In the clash between these two creeds, so dissimilar in means, if not in ultimate ends, will undoubtedly lie much of the history of the next twenty or thirty years. *The struggle to-day*

MATERIAL FOR FURTHER STUDY

I.   History and Memoirs

History of Modern Europe	C. A. Fyffe
A History of Europe (Book III)	H. A. L. Fisher
Voltaire	André Maurois
The French Revolution	Louis Madelin
The French Revolution	J. M. Thompson
The Revolutionaries	Louis Madelin
Leaders of the French Revolution	J. M. Thompson
Marie Antoinette	Hilaire Belloc
Robespierre	J. M. Thompson
Napoleon	H. A. L. Fisher
History of the Peninsular War (abridged, published by Nelson)	W. F. P. Napier
Nelson	G. Callender
Nelson	Carola Oman
Talleyrand	Duff Cooper
The Congress of Vienna	Harold Nicolson
Three Studies in European Conservatism	E. L. Woodward
The Duke	Philip Guedalla
Palmerston	Philip Guedalla
The Second Empire	Philip Guedalla
The Rise of Louis Napoleon	F. A. Simpson
Louis Napoleon and the Recovery of France	F. A. Simpson
The Revolutionary Idea in France	Godfrey Elton
Makers of Italy	J. A. R. Marriott
Garibaldi's Defence of the Roman Republic	G. M. Trevelyan
Garibaldi and the Thousand	G. M. Trevelyan
Garibaldi and the Making of Italy	G. M. Trevelyan
Florence Nightingale (in " Eminent Victorians ")	Lytton Strachey
Florence Nightingale	C. Woodham Smith
Bismarck	C. Grant Robertson
The Habsburg Monarchy	Wickham Steed
Fifty Years of Europe	J. A. Spender
Twenty-Five Years (abridged)	Viscount Grey
The World Crisis (abridged, published by Macmillan)	Winston Churchill
History of the Great War	C. R. Crutwell
British Foreign Secretaries	Algernon Cecil
Studies in Modern History	G. P. Gooch
From Bismarck to the World War	E. von Brandenburg
A History of Russia	Bernard Pares
The Second World War	Winston Churchill
Hitler : A Study in Tyranny	Alan Bullock

II. Imaginative Literature

The historical value of most " historical novels " is negligible. If anything, they tend to choke with the tares of romance the good seed of historical accuracy planted by careful teaching. The best historical novels are those not written as such, but written in description of contemporary or recent events, and then read by subsequent generations. Of this type, the novels of Balzac, for example, admirably describe the France of the early nineteenth century ; Maupassant and Daudet have short stories which give glimpses into the realities of the Franco-Prussian War ; the rottenness of Russian society in Czarist times is vividly depicted in the pages of many of the great Russian novelists ; and the poignant days of 1914–1918 exist imperishably in a number of excellent works of literature. It is as yet too early to speak with confidence of the works inspired by the Second World War—so far the field has been largely given over to the reporters, the writers of eye-witness accounts, and the compilers of memoirs.

The following may be recommended with confidence :

Honoré de Balzac	Les Chouans
Victor Hugo	Les Misérables
Victor Hugo	'93
C. S. Forester	The Gun
C. S. Forester	Death to the French
C. S. Forester	Captain Hornblower, R.N. (and others of the "Hornblower" Series)
R. C. Sheriff	Saint Helena (Play)
Seton Merriman	Barlasch of the Guard
Seton Merriman	The Sowers
George Borrow	The Bible in Spain
L. Tolstoi	War and Peace (too long for most readers)
L. Tolstoi	Sebastopol
C. E. Montague	Disenchantment
Siegfried Sassoon	Poems
Wilfrid Owen	Poems

The following are interesting, and possess greater merit than most of their kind :

Stanley Weyman	The Red Cockade
Alexandre Dumas	The Count of Monte Cristo
Conan Doyle	The Adventures of Brigadier Gerard
Warwick Deeping	The Lame Englishman

Youthful readers will not need to be introduced to the well-known " historical " tales of Baroness Orczy and G. A. Henty : they may be warned, however, against accepting such excellent story-telling as more than—story-telling.

III. Films

Most " historical " films, of course, are ludicrously and fantastically unhistorical. The following commercial ventures (which unfortunately may be no longer obtainable) have both cinematic merit and a conception, though not complete, of historical accuracy :

The House of Rothschild
Marie Walewska
The Story of Louis Pasteur
The Life of Emile Zola
The Patriot (silent)

The atmosphere of the First World War is admirably captured in :

Journey's End
All Quiet on the Western Front

Among the notable films dealing with some aspect of the Second World War are :

The Way to the Stars
The Way Ahead
In Which We Serve
School for Secrets
Desert Victory (documentary)
Target for To-night (documentary)
12 o'clock High

There are not many short educational diagrammatic films concerned with 19th-century European history. There is, however, (besides various ' film-strips ') :

The Expansion of Germany (G.B.I.)

IV. Painting

For those lucky few who have the opportunity to travel and the inclination to look at pictures, there is a very great deal of material in the art-galleries of Europe. Most full-dress historical pictures have about as little historical, and, for that matter, artistic value as most historical films. J. L. David and Gros, however, have painted the formal occasions of the Napoleonic period well, and Meissonier has specialized on the army life. Several examples of the latter's work may be seen in the Wallace Collection. Delacroix has some splendidly turbulent, romantic scenes. The most valuable material of this sort, however, is in the form of engravings and cartoons. Of these, the works of Rowlandson and Gillray on the French Revolutionary period and Goya on the horrors of the Peninsular War (accessible in the Phaidon Press edition, published by Allen and Unwin) are strong, vivid, and unforgettable. Daumier is superb for the ironies and sorrows of French town-life. The more formal English cartoonists, Leech, Tenniel and Low provide a wealth of material, some of which is reproduced in this book.

V.   Music

The musically inclined may learn much from comparisons of works of different periods. Consider, for instance, the well-regulated beauty and cheerfulness of an early 18th century piece like Handel's " Harmonious Blacksmith "—a perfect reflection of a secure and firmly established social order. Then take a mid-19th century piece like Chopin's " Revolutionary Study," and see how faithfully its martial ardour and surging currents of violence depict the spirit of mid-19th century Europe. The same idea may be expanded indefinitely—contrast an early Haydn or Mozart symphony with Berlioz's " Symphonie Fantastique," for instance, or see " the two Russias " in the ' native ' or Slavonic style of Borodin and Mussorgsky on the one hand, and the ' westernized ' style of Tchaikovsky on the other. For those who have ears to hear, such differences may illuminate the essential characteristics of a period more vividly than the patient explanation of a hundred historians.

GLOSSARY OF POLITICAL TERMS
EMPLOYED IN THE TEXT

ABDICATION. Surrender of his ruling position by a king, prince, etc. (Literally " renouncing.")

ABSOLUTE MONARCHY, ABSOLUTISM. A system of government in which the monarch or ruler is unchecked by any form of parliament, and in which his own wishes are law.

AMNESTY. An act granting forgiveness (literally " forgetfulness ") to political opponents or those who have committed some offence against the law.

ANARCHISM. The belief that *all* government is bad, and that the world would run more smoothly if all kings, parliaments, dictators, and the like were abolished. (Literally " no rule.")

ARBITRARY IMPRISONMENT. Imprisonment at the will of a ruler without reference to the law. (Literally " by personal choice.")

ARBITRATION. A system of settling disputes, not by fighting but by appointing somebody to arbitrate or " choose " between the two parties to the dispute.

ARISTOCRACY. Literally " government by the best "—usually employed in the sense of ' the best ' by birth. All those belonging to the ' noble ' class.

AUTOCRACY. Absolute rule by one man. (Literally " rule by one-self.")

BONAPARTISM. The support, after the overthrow of Napoleon in 1815, of the claim of some member of his family to rule France.

BOURGEOISIE. The middle classes. (Literally, the townsfolk or " burgesses.")

CENTRE. Occupying a position between extreme socialism and extreme conservatism. (See also ' left ' and ' right.') Name of Catholic party formed in Reichstag to resist Bismarck's ' May Laws ' against the Church.

CHARTISM. Movement in England in the early 19th century to demand the six points of " The People's Charter "—i.e. vote for all men, equal electoral districts, payment of M.P.s, abolition of property qualification for M.P.s, secret ballot and annual parliaments.

CLERICALS. Party in France in the later 19th century aiming at increased power for the Catholic Church, and showing a preference for monarchy over republicanism.

COMMUNISM. Belief that system of private ownership of land, factories, railways, banks, etc., should be replaced by public ownership. This to be done in two stages :

(a) The populace, by ' direct action ' (strikes or revolution) captures the ' machinery of the state ' (army, civil service, police) from the control of the employers, and uses it to dispossess the employers of their property. (The " dictatorship of the proletariat.")

(b) When the employing class has been eliminated, the machinery of state to be abolished, as the use of force will have become superfluous.

First propounded in systematic form by the Germans Marx and Engels in the ' Communist Manifesto ' of 1848.

CONGRESS SYSTEM. System of settling international disputes by meetings of the Great Powers, propounded by Metternich and Castlereagh after the Napoleonic wars. Operative, with little success, from 1815 to about 1823.

CONSCRIPTION. Liability of all men to serve in the army both in home and overseas campaigns. First introduced by the French revolutionaries, and since imitated by almost all states in Europe.

CONSERVATISM. Belief that existing benefits should be ' conserved ' rather than be endangered by innovations, ' reforms ' and the like.

CONSTITUTION. Document or documents giving a parliament, fixed laws, freedom of speech or similar privileges. Limitation of the power of a ruler.

CONSTITUTIONAL. Legal, according to the constitution.

CONSTITUTIONAL MONARCHY. Monarchy where the king has little power, but is bound by the terms of a constitution to accept parliament's advice, etc.

CONVENTION. Agreement in documentary form. (May also mean " meeting " or " custom.")

COUP D'ÉTAT. Seizure of power.

DEISM. 18th-century creed held by many of the philosophers, maintaining a belief in God without recognizing the truth of the claims of the Christian church.

DEMOCRACY. Literally, " rule by the people "—system of government in which the masses have some control of policy, usually in the form of electing their representatives to some kind of parliament.

DESPOTISM. Absolute rule.

DICTATORSHIP. System of government in which one man has complete power.

DIET. Assembly or Parliament.

ECONOMICS. Study of the production and distribution of wealth.

ESTATES. Divisions or classes. In mediæval parliaments the three estates were usually represented separately—first estate clergy, second estate nobility, third estate remainder.

FASCISM. System of government in which the executive power (the dictator) has control over the legislative power (the parliament). Creation of Mussolini's in post-1918 Italy, marked by intense nationalism and intolerance of all opposition. Literally from the 'fasces,' bundle of rods and axe carried before a Roman magistrate to denote his power of inflicting punishment.

FEDERATION. System whereby many states group together to form a bigger state to which they surrender some, but not all, of their power.

FRANCHISE. The right to vote.

FREE TRADE. Absence of tariffs or customs duties.

INFLATION. Printing of paper-money out of proportion to gold reserve, causing higher prices.

ISOLATION. Freedom from alliances or commitments.

LAISSEZ-FAIRE. Absence of government action—"leave things alone." Belief that trade will flourish best without customs duties, subsidies, factory acts, etc.

LEFT. Holding extreme 'reformist' views, usually socialism or communism. So called from position of seats in semi-circular French Chamber of Deputies, where the conservatives sit on the right, the moderates in the centre and the socialists on the left.

LEGISLATION. Law-making.

LIBERAL. Used with a capital L for a member of a definite party believing in freedom from government restrictions on trade and liberty, and holding with constitutional rule. With a small 'l' implying similar views, or of a broadly tolerant nature, but not necessarily a member of any Liberal party.

NATIONALISM. Enthusiasm for the right and might of the nation. Desire to see the nation organized powerfully and free from oppression by other nations.

NAZI (NATIONAL SOCIALIST). Member of Hitler's post-1918 party in Germany aiming at dictatorship, control of the wealthy, and persecution of Liberals, Socialists, Communists, and Jews. Intense nationalist, believing that 'racial purity' is of the utmost importance.

NIHILISM. Russian belief in later 19th century that *everything* was bad, and hence that the only attitude to take up was a completely destructive one. (Literally "nothingism.") N.B.—Difference from anarchism, which considered that *government* was responsible for all evil.

PLEBISCITE. Vote by all citizens on some important issue.

PROLETARIAT. The working masses.

RADICAL. Aiming at a large programme of reform. (Literally "from or to the root.")

REACTIONARY. Tending to "put the clock back": opposed to all reform.

REPUBLIC. A state not ruled by a king.

RIGHT.   Conservative : see ' left.'

' SANCTIONS.'   Penalties or forms of compulsion which could be inflicted by the League of Nations on a state violating the League Covenant.

SOCIALISM.   Belief that the state, not private persons, should control ' the means of production (land, big factories, etc.), distribution (railroads, etc.), and exchange ' (banks, etc.).

SOVEREIGNTY.   Rule, supreme power.

SUFFRAGE.   Right to vote.

SYNDICALISM.   Belief that the power and wealth of the country should be controlled, not by private persons, but by the working-classes organized in trade unions.   (French ' syndicat '= trade union.)

ULTRAS.   Extreme reactionary party in France in early 19th century.

ZOLLVEREIN.   A ' customs union ' of several German states, headed by Prussia, in the 19th century.

INDEX